Shelby County
Tennessee

WILL RECORDS
C-1, 1830–1847

WPA RECORDS

Heritage Books
2024

HERITAGE BOOKS
AN IMPRINT OF HERITAGE BOOKS, INC.

Books, CDs, and more—Worldwide

For our listing of thousands of titles see our website
at
www.HeritageBooks.com

A Facsimile Reprint
Published 2024 by
HERITAGE BOOKS, INC.
Publishing Division
5810 Ruatan Street
Berwyn Heights, MD 20740

Prepared by
The Tennessee Historical Records Survey
Division of Community Service Programs
Work Projects Administration
1941

International Standard Book Number
Paperbound: 978-0-7884-8777-4

SHELBY COUNTY

WILL RECORD I-C
PROBATE COURT OF SHELBY COUNTY
JAN. 1830 to MAY 1847

I William Lawrence of the county of Shelby and State of Tennessee, aware of the uncertainty of human life, do make and declare this instrument as my last will and Testament. I desire that my debts be paid with as little delay as possible. I desire that all monies owing to me, be collected as possible except a debt owing to me from Thomas Phoebus for a printing press which my Executor is authorized to give indulgence on I desire that my wife during her life time have entire control and possession of the tract of land on which I now live and all the appurtenances to said tract of Land I give to my wife in her own right forever, all my household & kitchen Furniture, farming utensils, provisions on hand, stock of every description and all chatels except my begroes, Two shot guns and such papers as should go into the possession of my Executor. I desire that my wife have the use and possession of my negroes while she remains a widow, and that she be well provided for, by my Executor, during her widowhood.

I desire that my son William have my small shot gun, as it belonged to his Grandfather Lawrence after whom he is named. I desire that my second son, Thomas, have my large Shot Gun. The balance of my little estate not yet enumerated together with such as is given to my wife either during her widowhood or life time be equally divided among my children. I desire that my children shall be well educated, and for that purpose my Executor is hereby authorized to sell land if necessary. Should any of my negroes become unruly, then my Executor with the consent of my wife, may sell such negroes and appropriate the proceeds in educating my children, or otherwise for their benefit. As many of my lands are held in partnership with (Editor's Note: Piece out of page) for the purpose of making divisions and adjusting my estate, I hereby confer on my Executor as full powers and discretion in making divisions exchanges sales &c as I now(P-2) possess. And in settlement of adjustment of any unsettled matters of mine, I confer on my Executor full power and discretion, only enjoining upon him to keep out of law, and settle all cases by compromise if possible. I desire that my wife act as Guardian to my daughter and that my Executor act as Guardian to my sons, in which capacity I confer on them full ~~power and~~ discretion and power, hereby confiding my children and their interests entirely & fully to the,.

I desire that my Brother Robert Lawrence undertake to execute my will. Should he decline or die I then desire James H. Lawrence to execute it. Should he decline or die ~~I~~ then I desire that my wife shall undertake it. I desire that neither of these individuals be ruled to give security as Executor or Executrix but only desire that they will do justice to my children and their interests, as I confide fully in them.

Witness my hand and Seal this 17th day of January Eighteen hundred and thirty.

Harvy W Moseley
Robert Lawrence

William Lawrence - (Seal)

(P-3) JOHN PERKISON'S WILL

I John Perkison of Prince Edward County, being of sound mind and memory do make constitute and ordain this my last will and testament in manner & form towit, My will and desire is that all my just debts be paid

Item 2nd. I lend to my ~~wife~~ beloved wife Sarah Perkison during her life or widowhood, the tract of land whereon I now live with the crop that may be on hand or growing at the time of my death. Also the plantation utensils stock of all kinds together with the household and Kitchen furniture and the following negroes towit, Tom Lott, Jim, Robin, Jenny, Armisted Moses & Aggy Dyner, Molly Anny and her increase, Delph and her child Jerry Cloe, Haily Sandy, Davie, Should my wife marry I lend three choices of the above named negroes and the balance of the above enumerated property.

Item 3rd All the slaves with their increase and all other property which I may have heretofore given to my children I do hereby confirm to them and their Heirs forever.

Item 4th. I give my daughter Polly Miller my new Desk and dressing table at the Death of my beloved wife.

Item 5th. I give to my son Edmond Perkison the tract of Land which he purchased of M Cross Greer adjoining the lands of Stephen D Rowlett & Wm. Fowlkes & others Also one Feather bed & furniture at my death to him and his Heirs forever.

Item 6th. I give to my daughter Elizabeth Betts Cloe's child Dicy, the money Towit. one Hundred and fifty pounds which I gave her before her intermarriage with Spencer Betts together with the sd Negro Dicy to be in full of her portion of my estate forever.

Item 7th. A negro man And land and other property which I have heretofore given my son Rowlett Perkison I do hereby confirm unto him and his heirs forever; and at my death I give unto him the sum of one hundred dollars, to be raised out (P-4) of my Estate at the discretion of my Executor, which is to be his full portion of my Estate forever.

Item 8th. I give to my Grand Daughter Elizabeth Wooten, the sum of Seventy pounds, to be raised out of my Estate at the death of my wife by my Executors

Item 9th My will and desire is, at the decease of my wife that Tom Lott Aggy & Dyner shall be at liberty to choose which of my children they will live with and that my Executor furnish them with sufficient support to be raised first out of my Estate before a distribution takes place.

Item 10. I lend to my daughter Eliza Bolling and her children One negro woman named Milly, with her present and future increase, Also a negro boy named George during her life Should my Daughter be deprived of a house and land then and in that privisor, after the death of my wife my desire is that the said Eliza Bolling should have One hundred and fifty acres of Land to be taken off of the land I now live on including the houses

(P-4 cont.) the boundary lines to run North Eastwardly & South westwardly as my Executor may see cause, which land I lend her during her marriage with her present Husband Stith Bolling or widowhood but should she marry the second time, then in that Case She Shall relinquish her claim, and in case of her second marriage or death the said one hundred and fifty acres of Land is to be sold and Divided as the rest of my land, the above negroes lent to my daughter Eliza Bolling to be held in Trust by my Executors and by them to be appropriated in the way they may choose or think best calculated to promote her interest and her childrens' And - the death of Eliza Bolling I give to her children. And if my said Daughter should die leaving no issue nor their descendants and before her said husband, then in that case I give to my soninlaw Stith Bolling the whole of the property heretofore and hereafter lent in this my last will (P-5) except the one hundred and fifty acres of Land

Item 11th. I give my Grand Daughter Mary Giffriss One hundred dollars at my wife's death Also an equal portion with the rest of her Mother's children of my Estate

Item 12th. I give to my soninlaw Anderson Pellilten my Rattan Cane as a Mark of my respect.

Item 13 I give and bequeath to my Grand Son Sanuel D Burke my Silver Stock Buckle and the privilege of cutting and splitting twenty three thousand fence rails and the fire wood also from the same.

Item 14 I give to my Grand Soninlaw, William Dowell the sum of one hundred dollars to be raised out of my Estate at the death of my wife.

Item 15. Should my wife marry again It is my will that all my negroes lent her, except the three choices mentioned in Item 2nd be valued in current money by appointed by my Executors for that purpose - One Lot I give to my Daughter Polly Miller and her heirs, one Lot I give to my Son Edmond Perkison and his heirs and one Lot I give to my Daughter Sarah Morriss and her heirs and the other Lot I give to my Daughter Eliza Bolling and her children, to be held in trust by my Executors for their benefit nevertheless the legatees to each of the said four Lots of negroes shall pay to my Executors their proportion of the Seventh of the whole valuation of such negroes, one part of which I give to be equally divided between my Two Grandsons Samuel D Burke and Richard Burke. One other Lot to be equally divided between all the children of Nancy Hawkins, decd. One other Lot I give to be equally divided between the children of Patsy Miller decd. After the Death of my wife it is my will desire that what I have given in either case of negroes be divided in into four Lots as before described and the other remaining property and Land be sold on twelve month's credit and the money arising from such sale after paying off the Special Legacies Debts &c the balance to be (P-6) divided in the same manner as in the Four Lots of negroes mentioned in the foregoing part of this Item. My desire is that neither Lot ~~of negroes~~ of the four legatees shall sell or dispose of their respective Lots of negroes unless it be to the respective legatees so long as they, themselves may live

Item 16. My will and desire is that the land lent to my wife should be cultivated by her in such manner as no waste shall be committed,

(P-6 cont.) that is to say by renting of the said land out giving or selling timbers in any manner whatever, hereby authorizing my Executors with full power to suppress all kind of waste whatsoever.

Item 17th I give to my Grand daughter Nancy Hawkins one hundred dollars at the death of my wife and an equal [struck] portion with the rest of her Mother's children in my Estate. My desire is that she shall be supported at the expense of my Estate as long as she does live single or becomes of age.

Item 18th All legacies herein given, I give to each respective legatee to them and to their Heirs forever.

Item 19 Knowing that I have had previous to this period and for several years past, dealings and transactions with the most of all of them, and have to the best of my knowledge and recollection discharged every claim or claims, which either my son Rowlett or Edmond [struck] may have against me up to the date of this my will and should either of them justify or attempt so to do, any claims against me whatever or contend for such claim or claims, then in that case I revoke and make void all legacies given or intended to be given to claimant and his or their legacies shall be equally divided amongst the rest of the legatees.

Item 20th I give to my Grand daughters Parthena May & Susan Perkison, one hundred dollars each to be raised out of my Estate at the death of my wife.

(P-7) Item 21st And lastly, I do hereby nominate and appoint my friends Dabney Miller Dabney Morriss/McDowell and Anderson P Miller Executors to this my last will & testament revoking all other wills made by me whatsoever.

In testimony whereof, I have this 31st day of January, 1821, set my hand and affixed my Seal

Test. John Perkison (Seal)
Simeon Walton
William McGehee
Lucy Walton

At a court held for Prince Edward County December 17, 1821, this last will & Testament of John Perkison Decd. was presented in Court and proved by the oaths of Simeon Walter & William McGehee [struck] two witnesses thereto, ordered that the same be recorded On motion of Dabney Miller Executor herein named, he with Branch Wallhalt and Osborn Lockett, his securities, entered intend into and acknowledged their bond for the purpose in the penalty of twenty thousand dollars, conditioned according to law & took the oaths required by law. Certificate for obtaining a probate thereof in due form is Granted him.

Test B J Worsham D C

A copy Test B J Worsham C C 18 March 1821

Virginia Prince Edward County Towit:

(P-7 cont.) I, Branch J Worsham Clerk of the Court of the County aforesaid do hereby certify that the foregoing is a true copy from the Record of my office. Given under my hand as Clark of said County Court, with the Seal of my office annexed this 17 day of March 1821.

(L) B.J. Worsham Clk

Virginia Prince Edward County, towit.

I do hereby certify that Branch J Worsham is the acting clerk of the aforesaid County & that due fath and credit are paid to all his official acts. And also that I am the(P-8) eldest acting Justice of the aforesaid County. Given under my hand and Seal this 19th March 1827.

Robert Kilso (Seal)

The foregoing is a copy of the Will of John Perkison, Decd of Prince Edward County of the State of Virginia as appears by the Certificate of Probate in said county. Recorded in Shelby County Court office the 11th day of August 1830.

R Lawrence Clk

(P-9) C M. SMITH'S WILL

In the name of God, Amen. I Calvin M Smith of the County of Maury and State of Tennessee being in perfect health of body, of sound disposing mind memory and understanding considering the certainty of death and the uncertainty of the time thereof, and being desirous to settle my worldly affairs and thereby be the better prepared to leave this world when it shall please God to call me hence do therefore make and publish my last Will and testament in the manner and form following that is to say - First and Principally I commit my soul into the hands of the Almighty God and my body to the earth to be decently buried at the discretion of my Executrix hereinafter named and after my Debts and funeral charges are paid I devise and bequeath as follows:

Item I give and devise to my affectionate wife, Jane Eliza Smith, a tract of Land containing one hundred and Sixty eight acres be the same more or less it being the tract I purchased of Henry Gould, the deed for the same is now in the County Court Clerk's office to her the said Eliza Jane Smith her Heirs and assigns forever in fee simple

Item I give and devise unto my said wife all my bond, Bills, notes, and Book accounts together with all monies on hand and everything else in any wise belonging to me at my death. And lastly I do hereby constitute and appoint my Dear Wife Jane Eliza Smith and my friend Madison Carruthers, the present cashier (P-10) of the Bank(Editor's Note: part of page gone) of the State at Columbia, my Executrix and my Executor of this my last will and testament, revoking and annulling all former wills by me heretofore made, ratifying and confirming this and none other to be my last will and testament.

In testimony whereof I have hereunto set my hand and affixed my Seal this 9 ninth day of Feby in the Year of our Lord Eighteen Hundred and twenty seven.

Attest C M Smith (Seal)

Ben Reynolds

G M Egnew

(P-10 cont.) State of Tennessee)
January Session 1831
Shelby County Court)

The foregoing Last will and testament of C.M. Smith was produced in open Court and Established for record by the oath of W.C. Mitchell, who proved the handwriting of Benj. Reynolds a subscribing witness to said will and the said witness resides in the Chickasaw nation. And by the oath of W.C. Dunlap who proved the handwrite of G M Egnew another subscribing witness to said will and that he lives in the State of Louisiana. And ordered to be recorded

Robert Lawrence Ch.

Shelby County Court

A copy of the above Issued to Ro L 21st March 1833

(P-11) REUBEN BELL'S WILL

The Last will & testament of Reuben H Bell of the County of Shelby & State of Tennessee made this the 20th day of October 1830, as it has pleased God to protract my life to a fair age & knowing life to be uncertain being of sound mind & disposing mind and a will to give all my worldly goods as I may hereafter direct in this my last will & testament which I do hereby ordain and forever will and desire I first commit my soul to my God who giveth existence and through my life has always extended his bountiful providence to me his unworthy creature

Item the first my will is that my body be buried in a decent and plain manner in some suitable place

Item the 2nd I give and bequeath unto Hyram Bell Smith the son of Solomon Smith a fifty acre tract of Land lying and being in the State of Kentucky situated in the County of Caldwell joining Walden & Lafeedes' land agreeable to the platt made out by the Survey of said County by number of Warrant 13613 by platt 432 in number to him and his Heirs forever.

Item 3rd. I give and bequeath unto Alexander Oar the son of Wm. Oar of the State of Kentucky & County of Caldwell a fifty acre tract of Land lying and being in the aforesaid County situated adjoining the land of Waldon by Warrant number 13614 by number of plat 430 to him and his heirs forever.

Item 4th It is my will and desire that none of the monies due me out of the County of Shelby in the State of Tennessee or anywhere else should ever be collected by my executors or administrators except a note of hand against Wm. Cooke of Kentucky which note was given for twenty dollars which note I wish Reuben Robin ~~esquire~~ of Caldwell County Town of Prince to collect and put to his own use and I hereby give and bequeath the said (P-12) note to him and his heirs forever.

Item 5th I hereby nominate and appoint constitute and ordain James Warren of the County of Shelby and State of Tennessee Executor to this my last will & Testament and it is my will and desire that the said Warren my Executor collect all the money due me from any and all persons either

(P-12 cont.) by note or account in the county of Shelby and State of Tennessee and dispose of the whole amount in the following manner to wit

Item 6th It is my will and desire that in the first place my Executor fully satisfy himself for all the trouble and expense that he may be at in having me decently buried and for settling my Estate funeral charges to be paid and for taking care of me It is also my will & desire that all the balance of the money coming to my estate, not heretofore gaven away in this my last will & testament should be given by my Executor to the poor distressed strangers passing through the country. After the time of administration is out, and he the said Warren, my Executor gave all my clothing to said distressed strangers.

Item 7th. Its my will and desire that if Solomon Smith shall or ~~does~~ faithfully commit my saddle bags and the contents thereof and five bags of roots without ever opening or suffering them to be opened to the flames and burn them up that my Executor gave him my trunk and its contents my saddle and my spurs, if not it is my will and desire that my Executor sell them and gave the monies arising therefrom to the distressed poor.

As above witness my hand and seal on the day & date above written.

Reuben H Bell (Seal)

Attest

his
George X Deason
mark

James L Vaughan

(P-13) State of Tennessee)

January Court A.D. 1831

Shelby County Court)

Then this Last Will and testament of Reuben H Bell was produced in open Court and proved to be the act & deed of the said Bell and that he was of sound mind and disposing memory by the oath of George Deason and James L Vaughan and ordered to be certified.

Ro Lawrence Clk

A copy of the original now on file in my office this 8th day of Sept 1831

Ro Lawrence Clk

(P-14) (EDITOR'S NOTE: This page in Original MS is blank.)

(P-15) LAST WILL & TESTAMENT OF F EMMERY DECEASED

March the 3 day in the Year of our Lord 1829.

Be it remembered that this is my last will & testament in the name of God & these witnesses I am in my right mind and proper senses, that I do will all my the personal & real property that I have in the State of Tennessee & Shelby County to William Hadnot, consisting of nine negroes, namely Gracey Jim Pleasant Lizer, John, Henry Charles, Nancy Charlotte, Isaac, to 43 acres of land on which I now live to two horses to two Feather beds & furniture to one saddle one Handsaw one crosscut saw one gun one watch, one Big wheel one one Reel one Loom 8 chairs one chest 3 pails 1 churn, 1 Table, 2 Flat Irons, 2 ovens, 2 pots, 2 demijohns 2 chisels 1 auger, 1 coffee pot 3 Tin pans, 1 coffee mill 5 Axes 5 pans 2 pair of Harness, 2 of chains 3 chairs 2 singletrees 3 belts. 7 Hoes, 18 head of cattle 19 of Hogs, 1 round shave 1 cover, 1 Iron Wedge, 1 Tug 4 Books 19 of Geese. And also the Land that I have in Virginia 1,106 acres, and also the cattle to 6 feather beds, and furniture all to be sold and equally divided between my two sisters Fanny & Anna & 1 Brotherinlaw Thomas Elliphi and one of his sons William Hanly Elliph, At the death of my Mother and if she should come to this Country I will that she be maintained out of my estate in a decent & common way. I have wrote for my sister's child from time to time and you thought my house a disgrace to you and you would not let him come and Know I have give all away to a stranger to you and you shall not have one cent out of my will be done.

Frederick Emmery (Seal)

(P-16) State of Tennessee)
April Session A.D. 1820.
Shelby County Court)

On trial of the suit between Wm. Hadnot Plaintiff by his next friend Nancy Hadnot against Charles Bolton, administrator of Frederick Emmery, decd. to establish the will will of said Emmery. A jury of 12 good & lawful men on their oaths did say that the paper to which this is attached is the Last Will & Testament of Frederick Emmery deceased. Whereupon it is ordered by the Court that the same be admitted as having been fully proven and ordered to be certified.

Ro Lawrence Clk.

The foregoing is a correct copy of the original now on file in my office and recorded the 10th day of September A D 1821

Ro Lawrence Clk.

(P-17) WYLLY ALLEN'S LAST WILL & TESTAMENT

In the name of God Amen. I Willie Allen of the County of Shelby State of Tennessee in perfect mind but diseased in body do this day make this my last & true will, revoking all others.

(P-17 cont.) In Item 1 I wish all my just debts to be paid and the balance of my estate both personal and real I do bequeath to my wife Catherine Allen to be hers so long as she lives at her death I will it to my child Benjamin Franklin to be his to dispose of as he may think proper when of 21 years of age.

Item 2nd. I leave my wife Catherine Allen my Executor I do acknowledge this to be my last will to which I give my hand and seal ~~this~~ in the presence of these persons January 2nd 1831.

Witness   Willie Allen

Wyatte Christian

Harvy Bacon

State of Tennessee)
                                        July Session A D 1831
Shelby County Court)

Then was this paper writing purporting to be the last will & testament of Willie Allen produced in open Court and proved by the oath of Wyatte Christian and Harvy Bacon to be the act of the said Allen and that he was of sound mind And ordered to be certified.

Ro Lawrence Clk

A copy of the original now on file in my office 15 September 1831

Ro Lawrence Clk

(P-18) WILLIAM WILCOX LAST WILL & TESTAMENT

I William Wilcox of the County of Shelby & State of Tennessee, being of sound mind and disposing memory do make this my last will & Testament.

First I desire that my wife Susannah Wilcox have and hold all my real & personal property during her natural life time after paying all my just debts out of the same

Second After the death of my wife and the payment of my debts I desire that the property both real and personal descend to my nearest blood relation except a negro man named Archibald whom I wish after the death of my wife to be liberated set free and emancipated during his natural life time.

third I desire that my wife as the sole executor of & manager of my Estate be authorized to execute the same without being required by the County Court of said County to give security thereof or without the formalities of an administration

(P-18 cont.) Given under my hand and seal the eighth day of October Eighteen hundred & thirty

Signed Sealed and delivered in presence of Ro Lawrence
M B Winchester

William Wilcox (S)

State of Tennessee)
April Session A D 1831
Shelby County Court)

Then was this last will and testament of William Wilcox produced in open Court, and the execution thereof duly proven by the oath of R Lawrence & M B Winchester & that the said Wilcox was of sound mind and disposing memory. Ordered to be certified

Ro Lawrence Clk

A copy of the original now on file in my office 16 Sept. 1831

Ro Lawrence Clk.

(P-19) ABNER BOWEN'S LAST WILL & TESTAMENT.

The desire of Abner Bowen made known to the undersigned this 11th day of September 1828. Mrs. Bowen to have one Bay mare one waggon and the household and kitchen furniture the crop and the farming utensils stock of cattle & Hogs with the exception of one cow for each of the Girls and one bed that belongs to Elizabeth Bowen. Gideon B Bowen is to have one horse one gunn and whipsaw and al l the Hogs & cattle that is known by his claim.

NB One note that is in the hands of William Thompson G B Bowen is to collect for Mrs Bowen.

John M Carey
Isaac B Hickerson
Richard D Jameson

State of Tennessee)
Octo Term 18(Editor's Note: rest of the date or year gone with a nick out of page.)
Shelby County Court)

This writingis pronounced by Abner Bowen deceased as his last will & Testament, was produced in open Court and proven to be such by the oaths of John M Carey, Isaac B Hickerson and Richard D Jameson, Witnesses and ordered to be recorded.

Test Ro Lawrence, Clk S.C.C.

A copy of the original copied 14 Sept. 1831 and on file in my office.

Ro Lawrence Clk.

(P-20) WILLIAM BRICE HADNOTS LAST WILL & TESTAMENT

Be it known that I William Brice Hadnot being in sound mind do make this my last will & Testament To Wit: I bequeath unto my wife Nancy my negro boy Murlin I also give to my wife all the property of which I may be possessed of whatever kind making it her duty to maintain my children therewith

Signed on the 14 day of August 1828.

Witnessed by

his
Wm. BriceXHadnot
mark

William Bond Norman Bond.

State of Tennessee)
October Term 1828.
Shelby County Court)

Then was the execution of this the last will & of Wm. B. Hadnot proven in open Court by the oath of William Bond and Norman Bond, and ordered to be recorded.

Ro Lawrence Clk

A copy of the original now on file in my office this 15th Sept. 1831.

Ro Lawrence Clk

(P-21) LAST WILL & TESTAMENT OF WM. HARRIS

I William Harris of the county of Shelby & State of Tennessee being weak in body but of sound mind and memory do make this my last will & Testament in the words and figures following

First Will and desire is that all my just debts shall be paid out of this year's crop after paying Andrew Lynn his part of the crop and leaving a sufficiency to support the family. After taking out the above if there should not be enough to pay the debts, I want my Executor to sell such of my property as they may think proper to the amount of the debts The balance of property I want my wife to keep together during her life or widowhood and to raise and educate the children in the best manner she can after her death to be equally divided amongst her children And if my wife ~~and if my wife~~ should marry, my will is that the property be no longer hers but to go to the children. My wish is that my wife Lydia Harris and my friend Gideon Wallace to be executrix and executor to this my last will.

In testimony whereof I have hereunto set my hand and seal this 21 day of March, 1831.

his
Wm. X Harris
mark

(P-21 cont.) Signed Sealed and delivered in the presence of us.

Constant Scales
his
Andrew X Lymmerick
mark

State of Tennessee)
April Session A.D. 1831
Shelby County Court)

Then was this the Last Will & Testament of Wm. Harris proved by the oath of Constant Scales and Lymmerick and ordered to be recorded

Ro Lawrence CLK

The foregoing is a copy of the original now on file in my office Sept 21 1831

Ro Lawrence Clk

(P-22) WILLIAM ~~F~~ THOMPSON'S LAST WILL

In the name of God Amen

I William Thompson of the State of Tennessee & County of Shelby being weak and low in health but in perfect mind and memory. Calling to mind the mortality of my ~~soul~~ body and knowing that is appointed one for all mankind do make and ordain constitute and confirm this and no other as my last will and testament in manner and form as follows. VIZ It is my will and desire that my son Robert Thompson should have all my farming utensils, Carpenter's tools and Rifle gun and my ~~Land~~ Lying in the State of Virginia in Prince Edward County on the waters of Tandy Creek to him and his heirs forever. Also my part of the negroes that falls to me at the death of my Mother to be equally divided between my children to them and their Heirs forever. Also it is my desire that Naomi King my step daughter should have an equal portion of my property with my wife & children when she shall arrive at the years of maturity or marries to her & her Heirs forever.

Item Viz. Also it is my will and desire that my true and loving wife Bersheba Thompson should keep all my property together and raise and School my children and as they arrive to the years of maturity or marries to order an equal portion of my property to them and their Heirs forever. Furthermore - Viz I constitute and appoint my true and Loving wife Bersheba Thompson my whole & sole executrix to this my last will & testament

In witness whereof I the said Wm. Thompson have (P-23) hereunto set my hand and seal this 16 day of October 1825

Attest Off. Wm. Thompson (SEAL)
John Holloway

(P-23)cont.) State of Tennessee)
April Session A D 1829.
Shelby County Court)

The foregoing paper writing purporting to be the last Will & Testament of Wm. Thompson decd. was produced and proven by the oath of John Holloway a subscribing witness thereto and ordered to be recorded.

Ro Lawrence CLK

The foregoing is a copy of the original now on file in my office September 26 1831

Ro Lawrence Clk.

(P-24) THOMAS BLOUNT'S LAST WILL

~~I Thomas Blount~~

I Thomas Blount of the County of Edgecombe & State of No Carolina, being in a perfect state of health & of sound mind and memory, do in haste & to guard against the evil consequences that might result to my beloved wife from my sudden or unexpected death, in case I should die before my return from Warrenton whither I am about to go; intestate make & ordain this my last Will and Testament in manner & form following (viz.)

Item I give and bequeath to my beloved wife, Jacky S Blount all my land in the county of Halifax, all the negroes that she possessed at the time she married me including those since received by me from the estate of her deceased Brother McKinnie H Sumner with their increase, all my plate & household & kitchen furniture of every kind whatsoever (my books only excepted,) my Coach & the pare of Bay Hourses that I lately purchased at the City of Washington and my dwelling house with the Lots No. 56,57,67 & 68 in the town of Tarborough to her and her heirs and assigns forever.

Item I lend to my beloved wife Jacky S Blount during her natural life my Plantation called Hall Brook containing five hundred & eighty four acres with the stock and farming utensils thereunto belonging, and Lot No. 115 in the Town of Tarborough with its improvements, and I also lend to her during her widowhood all the rest of my negroes; but as soon as she marries or dies, in case she dies before she married the possession of these negroes ~~to pass~~ shall pass from her & be divided by my Executors hereinafter named among such of the children of my Brother, John G. Blount as shall be then living equally share & share alike and after her death my Executors are to sell the land as they are hereby authorized to do altogether or in parcels as they shall think best and divide among the children aforesaid equally share & share alike the nett proceeds of this sale -

Item I give and bequeath to my nephew John Gray Blount, son of John Gray Blount my tract of land containing (P-25) two hundred seventy six acres lying adjoining the Town of Tarborough on the North boundary thereof, also eight hundred & Fifty acres of Land in the State of Tennessee

(P-25 cont.) lying on Duck River at or near the mouth thereof, being the same conveyed to me by Deed from my Brother William Blount, to him and his heirs & assigns forever.

Item I give and bequeath to my nephew Thomas Harry Blount, son of John Gray Blount my tract of land lying in the fork ~~of~~ swamp Pitt County containing by estimation six ~~thousand~~ hundred & forty acres to him & his heirs and assigns forever..

Item I give and bequeath to the three sons of my brother John Gray Blount or the survivors or survivor of them at the time of my death my share of Shell Castle near Orcacock Hotel to be divided among them equally share & share alike to them & their heirs & assigns forever.

Item I give and bequeath to my two nieces Ann Blount Toole & Mary Blount Miller each a tract of land in the State of Tennessee containing six ~~thousand~~ hundred & forty acres to be set apart to them by my Executors hereinafter named out of my share of the land owned by John Gray & Thomas Blount to them & their heirs & assigns forever.

Item I give & bequeath to the three sons & two youngest daughters of my deceased Brother William Blount all the rest of my share of the lands in Tennessee owned by John G & Thomas Blount, to be divided among them or the survivors of them at the time of my death, equally share & share alike; but it is to be understood that out of those lands before a division is made such as is here directed, is to be raised by my Executors in such manner as they shall think best - a sum of money equal to all my just debts which they shall appropriate to the payment thereof.

Item The rest of my property I request & direct my Executors to sell & the money arising from the sale thereof, together with such sums of money as may be due to me (P-26) I give & bequeath to my beloved wife Jacky S Blount-

And lastly, I nominate, constitute, & appoint my Brothers John Gray Blount & Willie Blount & my nephew ~~John Gray Blount~~ Tho.H. Blount & William G Blount, Executors of this my last Will & Testament.

Signed with my hand & sealed with my seal this 23rd day of August 1808.

Tho. Blount (SEAL)

As my handwriting will be known by everybody acquainted with me & I have no fears or suspicion that any of my relations will be disposed to dispute it or contest the validity of this Will for the want of a subscribing witness to it - I have determined to have no witness to it.

Tho. Blount

Edgecombe County May Court 1812

The within Last Will and Testament of Thomas Blount decd. was exhibited into Court for probate & was proven in the following manner(to wit, Frances L Dancy Moses Mordecia & Robert Stuart appeared in open Court

(P-25 cont.) & upon their oaths did say that they are well acquainted with the handwriting of the deceased & that they believe the signature, as well as the whole of the writing contained in the said will to be the handwriting of Thomas Blount the said Deceased - And Thomas H Blount one of the Executors named in the said will was at the same time qualified thereto. Ordered that the same be certified & the will Recorded.

Test. Edward Hall C C

Edgecombe County, May Court 1816.

The will of the late Thomas Blount which was exhibited in this Court for probate at May Session 1812 was again produced for probate & its having been proved heretofore that the said will was altogether in the handwriting of the said Thomas Blount & it appearing (P-27) now to the satisfaction of this Court by evidence that the said Will was found among the valuable papers of said Thomas Blount - It is ordered that the Will be Recorded.

Test E Hall, C C

State of North Carolina)

Edgecome County)

I Micheal Hearn, Clerk of the Court of Pleas & Quarter Sessions of said County do hereby certify that the foregoing contains a true copy of the last Will & Testament of Thomas Blount filed & recorded in this office.

Given under my hand & seal of office at Tarborough this 24th day of March 1829.

Micheal Hearn, C.C.

State of North Carolina)
Edgecombe County)

I Richard Harrison presiding Justice of the Court of Pleas & Quarter Sessions County do certify that Micheal Hearn, who signs the above is Clerk of the said Court, that his above attestation is in due form & that full faith & credit may & ought to be given thereto-

Given under my hand & seal this 24th day of March 1829.

R G Harrison Chr. (Seal)

State of North Carolina)

Edgecombe County)

I Micheal Hearn Clerk of said County do hereby certify, that Richard Harison, whose name appears subscribed to the above certificate is the presiding Justice of said Court & is duly commissioned & qualified.

Given under my hand & seal office at Tarborough this 24 March 1829-

Micheal Hearn C.C.

(P-27 cont.) State of North Carolina

To all to whom these presents shall come, Greeting,

It is hereby certified & made known, that Micheal Hearn whose signature appears to the annexed certificate was, at the time of signing the same & now is Clerk of the Court of Pleas and Quarter Sessions for Edgecombe County; as such, he is an officer duly qualified and empowered to give said certificate, which has been done in the usual (P-28) and proper manner full faith and credit are due and ought to be given to all his official acts.

In testimony whereof, I John Owen, Governor &c have caused the great Seal of the State to be hereunto affixed and signed the same at our city of Raleigh, on the 25th day of March in the year of our Lord one thousand eight hundred and twenty nine, and of the Independence of the United States the fifty-third.

By the Governor Jno. Owen

Thos. B Moss private Secretary

State of Tennessee)
January Sessions A.D. 1832
Shelby County)

The foregoing paper writing purporting to be the office copy (issuing from the State of North Carolina, Edgecombe County) of Thomas Blount's last will & testament ~~&c~~. was produced in open Court regularly certified for registration and it is therefore ordered by the Court so to be ~~done~~ recorded.

Ro Lawrence Clk.

(P-29) THE WILL OF HENRY HAYNES

I Henry Haynes, through the great mercy & goodness of the all wise beneficient God, being of sound mind and ~~disposing~~ memory do constitute and appoint this instrument to be my last will & testament.

Item first. I do bequeath unto my affectionate spouse, Mary Haynes, during her natural life, my negro woman Levina about thirty one years old, & also Matilda about the age of sixteen years old.

Item 2nd It is my Will that my son Stephen shall have Levina after the death of my beloved wife.

Item 3rd. It is my will that my beloved daughter, Lucy McDuffee & heirs lawfully begotten of her body, shall have the negro girl Matilda on the death of my dear wife. But should she have no Heirs then and in that event the said negro Girl, and her increase to be divided between my son Stephen & my son George W L Haynes.

(P-29 cont.) Item 4th. It is my will that the balance of my property be sold to pay debts I may owe, and the expenses incident to the settlement of my Estate.

In testimony whereof I have hereunto subscribed my name to this instrument as my Last Will & Testament this the 10 day of May 1830.

his
Witnessed by Henry X Haynes
mark

John Stockton, Wm. Wilson
Thomas Wilson.

State of Tennessee)
October Sessions A.D. 1831
Shelby County)

This last will & testament of Henry Haynes deceased, was produced in open Court, and proven to be the act & deed of the said Henry Haynes by the oath of William Wilson and Thomas Wilson, witnesses thereto and ordered to be recorded.

Test Ro Lawrence Clk of C.C.
Recorded Feby 17 1832
R Lawrence Clk.

(P-30) LAST WILL & TESTAMENT OF JOHN CANNON

I John Cannon of the County of Shelby & State of Tennessee being this day the 26th September 1831, of sound mind and perfect memory to make and execute the following as my last will & testament.

I wish to authorize Arthur F Wooten, to sell so many of my negroes(not exceeding eight Hundred dollars) as will buy my wife Mary a comfortable home and also enough to pay my debts in this country.

The Ballance I leave to my wife during her Natural life, at her death to be equally divided between the Lawful heirs of my body.

CODICIL I wish to authorize and empower Wooten to sell the negroes at private sale.

Emanuel Baker (S) John Cannon (Seal)

Joseph Brooks

State of Tennessee Shelby County County Court Oct. Term 1831.

This the Last will & Testament of John Cannon decd. was produced in open Court and proven to the act & deed of the said John Cannon by the oaths of Emanuel Baker and Joseph Brooks witnesses thereto and ordered to be recorded.

Recorded 18 February 1832 Test Ro Lawrence Clk S.C.C
Ro Lawrence Clk.

(P-31) E YOUNG'S LAST WILL & TESTAMENT.

In the name of God, Amen.

I Emanuel Young of the Town of Memphis, Shelby County, and State of Tennessee being of infirm health but of perfect mind and memory, do make this my Last and only will & testament in the manner and form following to wit.

First. I direct that after my death my funeral expenses be paid without delay and out of my Estate before any division of the same be made.

Second. I require that all my just debts be paid and to this end, I direct the payment of them out of the merchandise I have now on hand, and out of the debts now due me, but in the event that in this way funds sufficient should not be had to pay them I require and direct that the balance still due be paid out of my real estate.

Third: I Give to my wife Ellena Young, at my decease, all my personal ~~estate~~ property not before disposed of of whatsoever description I may die possessed, including as well cash as every species of personal property remaining after the payment of my debts.

Fourth. I further give to my wife Ellana Young at my decease one fourth or a child's part in all the Real Estate I now have or of which I may die possessed.

Fifth. At my death I bequeath to my three sons, Thomas, William & Henry in equal and in just proportion the entire amount of three fourths of the real estate I now possess or of which I may die possessed or entitled to.

Sixth I direct that out of the real estate bequeathed my sons Thomas, William & Henry, as soon as the same shall come into their possession, they pay an equal proportion to my son Ferdinand Augustus the sum altogether of Five hundred dollars.

Seventh & Lastly: I appoint my wife Ellana Young at my death Executrix of my Estate, with provision for her (P-32) to choose if she should find it necessary after my death to aid her in the settlement of my Estate, two gentlemen executors of my estate in conjunction with her, provided she shall not choose either or any of my sons as such executors and that my executors executors if chosen by her shall not be required to give any security in the discharge of the duties hereby Imposed.

Eighth and additional. I hereby authorize my Execut~~ors~~ rix and executors if chosen by her at any time before both or either or my youngest sons shall arrive at lawful age to divide or sell my real estate or any part of it if my wife Ellana Young shall deem such division or sale advantageous to the interest of my wife and children.

Witness my hand and seal this the 4th day of May One thousand eight hundred & thirty one.

E Young (SEAL)

(P-32 cont.) Signed Sealed and acknowledged in the presence of us as the Last Will and Testament of the Testator.

Nathaniel Anderson

Isaac Rawlings

M B Winchester

State of Tennessee, Shelby County January Session 1832.

This the Last Will & Testament of E. Young, deceased was proven in open Court by the oath of N Anderson and Isaac Rawlings witnesses thereto, and ordered to be recorded.

Recorded 18 Feby, 1832 Ro Lawrence Clk

R Lawrence Clk.

(P-33) THE WILL OF THOMAS D CARR.

Know all men by these presents that I Thomas D Carr of the County of Shelby & State of Tennessee being of sound mind and disposing memory, but believing my dissolution to be near at hand doth make this my last will & testament.

In the first place it is my will, that my wife Peggy Carr, shall have as her own separate property, all the household furniture of every description which I now have on hand in addition to the provisions made for her by the Laws of the State.

Secondly: It is my desire & wish that all the property of whatever description which I own or possess in this world shall be kept together by my executors until the death of my wife Peggy Carr, As to my negroes they can be hired out or otherwise managed as my executors may think most desirable and beneficial for the estate.

Thirdly It is my desire that my grandchild Thomas Parran, son of my daughter Nancy Parran, Decd., shall be provided for in the following manner; I wish said child to have the same amount of property one thousand dollars which sum of one thousand dollars I consider I have already given to his Father Thomas O Parran in stock in my tan yard near Memphis, which he has and will receive out of said stock when worked out

I desire that my said grandchild remain with my wife Peggy Carr, and be raised and taken care of as my own children are, but if taken away from my wife said child shall not have any claim to a support from my estate, & should a division of my estate take place previous to my said grand child arriving to the age of twenty one years his interest in my said estate shall remain in the hands of my Executors and be managed by them for the benefit of said child and in the event of my said grandchild(P-34) dying before he arrives at the age of twenty one years, then, and in that

(P-34 cont.) event, I desire that the portion of my estate coming to said child shall revert to my legal heirs.

Fourthly It is my desire that my sons William and Dabney Carr, shall be the executors of this my Last Will and testament and act in accordance with the provisions thereof.

As witness my hand and seal this 23rd day of December 1831.

Witnesses: Thomas D Carr (LS)

Nathl Anderson
Tho. Wood
Wm. H Rose

State of Tennessee Shelby County, January Sessions 1832.

The execution of this the last will & testament of Thomas D Carr deceased was proven by the oath of Thomas Wood Nathl. Anderson and ordered to be recorded.

Recorded 22nd Feby 1832 Ro Lawrence Clk.
Ro Lawrence Clk.

(P-35) THE WILL OF Z T ROBERTSON

September 11th 1830

Shelby County State of Tennessee.

Know all men by these presents that I Zachariah T Robertson of good health and sound mind with a perfect memory do make this my Last will and testament.

I give and devise unto William H. Tate all and everything that belongs to me with the acception of three negro Girls namely Elizabeth Martha & Ann. I the said Robertson doth binde the said Tate to Keepe a negro man named Daniel as near his wife as possible.

I give unto Laura Jane Tate a certain negro girl named Martha to her & to her heirs to have and to hold from all other persons forever.

I also give unto Narcissa L Tate a certain negro girl named Elizabeth to her & to her heirs to have and to hold from all other persons forever.

I also give unto Masoura W Tate a certain negro girl name Ann to he_ and her heirs to have and to hold from all other persons forever.

I appoint James Jameson executor whereof I here unto set my hand and seal

Zachariah T Robertson (SEAL)

Test G W C Jameson R D Jameson

(P-35 cont.) State of Tennessee)
July Term 1832
Shelby County Court)

This writing purporting to be the last will & Testament of Zachariah Robertson deceased was produced in open Court by James Jameson the Executor therein named and was duly proven by the oaths of G.W. Jameson and R.D. Jameson two subscribing witnesses thereto and ordered to be Recorded.

Test. Ro Lawrence Clerk S C C

Recorded December 27th 1832
in Will Book A Page 35

Ro Lawrence Clerk S.C.C.

(P-36) THE WILL OF JOHN TURNER.

Be it remembered that I John Turner of the county of Shelby & State of Tennessee being weak of body but of sound and perfect mind & Memory, blessed be Almighty God for the same do make and publish this my last Will and testament in manner & form following to wit -

I give & bequeath to my wife, Elizabeth one negro womman named Nance with her son Called Sam also I give her all my household furniture except such part ~~as~~ of it as my son William L Turner has in his possession which which I give to Isaac H Turner, William R Turner Carolina S Turner & Samuel Turner children of said William S Turner.

I bequeath to my wife one horse and to cows and calves.

I give to my children Salley Coffey Twasher Turner, Polly Read, James Turner & William L Turner the sum of one dollar & no more.

Likewise to the children of my deceased daughter Betsy Tinsley - I give one dollar equally divided between them -.

The sum of Seven hundred Dollars due me by James Eidson & John Spain - I give & Bequeath to my wife together with all other demands which I may hereafter my just debts are paid.

And I appoint my wife Elizabeth & Kader Harrell commissioners to execute the above.

I hereby ~~make~~ revoke all former wills which I have made.

In testimony whereof I have affixed my seal this 24th day of August 1827.

At the request of John Turner we have affixed our names as witnesses of the above

John Turner (Seal)

Charles H. Stone
James B Harrell
Jacobb F Eitell

(P-37) State of Tennessee)
April Session A.D. 1832
Shelby County Court)

This the last Will and Testament of John Turner, deceased was produced in court and proven by the oaths of James R Harroll and the non-residence of Charles H Stone and the other witness thereto and his signature proven by the oath of B. H. Hawkins and ordered to be recorded.

Recorded January 27th 1833. Ro Lawrence C S C C

Ro Lawrence Clk

(P-38) JAMES KIMBROUGH

Being of sound and disposing mind and considering the uncertainty of human life I am disposed to make a will to dispose of my real and personal estate. Therefore I do hereby ordain & constitute and confirm this to be my last will and Testament Revoking all others heretofore made.

I will that all my just Debts be first paid out of my estate before disposition shall be made of it hereafter directed.

1st I give and bequeath to my beloved wife Margaret Kimbrough the following named negroes Stafford Tom Dave Lemuel Joe Pat Ginney Silvey Cass Finney Turneaver Tinley Willie Jefferson Walter John and Minder to her proper use and benefit to her and heirs forever with all the increase and of the before mentioned negroes also all the household and Kitchen furniture the stock on the farm of every description whatsoever.

I give to my wife Margaret Kimbrough also all the whole of my plantation tools of all description that may be on the farm at my Death. Also I will to my wife the use and possession of one third of the land on which I am now living during her natural lifetime so that the one third part shall include the mansion house and the buildings appertaining to my present Residence.

2nd I will to my daughter Martha Kimbrough Iris Cog and Milley and all their increase to her and her heirs forever.

3rd I then to my daughter Nancy Jones ~~Kimbrough~~ Carr three negroes namely, Nancy Carrell Ader to her heirs forever.

3rd I then give to my son William Ashbray Kimbrough the tract of land I am now living on in Shelby County Five miles from Memphis containing four hundred and ninety one acres Including the one hundred (P-39) and ten acres purchased with all the appurtenances thereto to him and his heirs forever.

Also I give to my son William A Kimbrough three negroes namely Edwin Malvina Ellen and their increase to him and his heirs forever.

5th Item My will is that my executor sell the tract of land I am now possessed of in Fayette County Tennessee containing Three hundred

(P-39 cont.) Thirty seven and a half acres be sold on One and two years for Two thirds of the sale money and the other third to be paid in hand when the sale is made, the proceeds of the said land when sold I do hereby give to my wife, Margaret Kimbrough in addition to what I have given her in the first item.

Having full confidence in the integrity and competency of Anderson B Carr, Buckley Kimbrough and my son William A Kimbrough, I do nominate and appoint them my Executors to this my Last Will and testament.

As witness whereof I hereunto set my hand affixed my seal this 15 day of March 1833

Witness Jas. Kimbrough (SEAL)

David Dunn

J V Williams

Thomas White

State of Tennessee)
April Sessions A.D. 1833
Shelby County)

This instrument purporting to be the last will and Testament of James Kimbrough decd. was produced in ~~[illegible]~~ open Court and David Dunn and Thomas White subscribing witnesses thereto being first sworn say, that they saw the said Jas. Kimbrough sign the same and that he was of sound mind and disposing memory. And thereupon Court ordered the said instrument to be recorded as the Last Will & testament of the said Jas. Kimbrough. Recorded May 15 1833

Ro Lawrence C.S. C.C. Ro Lawrence C S C C

(P-40) JAMES ROBB LAST WILL & TESTAMENT

My last will & testament is that my worthy and confidential friends L Wl Baldwin and Wm Hull be my Executors, and after canceling my just debts that the balance left be equally divided between my four children Francis Charlotte and Elizabeth in the way they in their discretion may devise. *

Memphis T. Jas Robb

March 7 1833

State of Tennessee)
July Sessions 1833
Shelby County Court)

Then came into Court F A Young Robertson Lapp and Wm C. Hull and

* William

(P-40 cont.) proved the above to be the signature of James Robb and also the writing to which said signature is attached to be his which is ordered to be recorded.

Ro Lawrence C.S.C.C.

Recorded 24 Sept 1833

Ro Lawrence C.S.C.C.

(P-41) THE LAST WILL & TESTAMENT OF ANDREW BELL

In the name of God; I Andrew Bell of the County of Shelby & State of Tennessee, being in perfect mind and memory but old age admonishes me to set my house in order do make this my last will and testament.

First, I give my soul to God and my body to its native earth.

Item first. I confirm to my daughter Esther D Brown all the property that I advanced to her and make no further provision for her.

Item 2nd. I confirm to my Daughter Jane Bond all the property I advanced to her, and make no further provision for her.

Item 4th I confirm to my son William Bell all the property I advanced to him and make no further provision for him.

Item 5th I confirm to my son James P Bell all the property I advanced to him and make no further provision for him

Item 6th I confirm to my daughter Martha Owen all the property I advanced to her and make no further provision for her

Item 7th. I confirm to my beloved Daughter Alvira Duff all the property I advanced to her and property advanced . . . .

Item 8th I confirm to my daughter Rebecca Burlinson all the property I advanced to her and make no further provision for her.

Item 8 & Last. I will and bequeath to my two youngest and last children viz Minerva S Bell and Betsy L Bell all the residue of my property after my debts is paid to the two above named children who has been the only ~~people~~ (P-42) prop under God in my old age, the property is to be divided by Lott & appraisement; And if either of them due under 21 and without Heirs the survivor is to have all my property and if both should depart this life the whole of the property is to be divided between my three Grand children, viz. James J. Bond and Andrew Bell Bond and Andrew Bell the son of my beloved son John M. Bell.

It only remains for me to appoint Esquire McAlpin Attorney at Law living in Memphis & Colonel John Brown of Sommerville, Attorney at Law & Minerva S. Bell and Betsy L Bell my executors and executrix and I do nominate and appoint them for that express purpose

Witness my hand and Seal this 16 Sixteenth of April 1831, wrote with my own Hand in the presence of us

Andrew Bell(Seal)

Joab Bean Tilman his X mark Bettis Margaret her X mark Bean

(P-42 cont.) State of Tennessee)
Sessions A.D. 1833
Shelby County Court)

The foregoing writing purporting to be the last will & testament of Andrew Bell was produced in Court and the same together with the signatures thereto proven by the oath of Tilman Bettis and Joab Bean to be the act and deed of the said Andrew Bell that the said Bell was in sound mind and disposing memory at the execution thereof which is ordered to be ~~ti~~ recorded.

Ro Lawrence Clk S.C.C.

Codicil to the foregoing Will

I Andrew Bell of the County of Shelby & State of Tennessee having further considered my Last Will & testament made the 16th day of April do make the following alteration or amendment I give and bequeath to my daughter Malvina Duff the following (P-43) property Towit. I give her my carryall; cart and Rifle gun & my bed. Also I give her one hundred and twenty dollars to be raised out of the hire or labour of my four negroes. Viz. Dick Esther Harry & Delphy in two years after my death. It is my will that the above 4 Slaves be hired unto persons known to be good to poor Slaves and at the end of every year to have ten dollars each and this to continue through life of the above four Slaves, with Rachel Jackson Miliby & Jerry is all the Slaves I have willed to Minerva Shelby Bell and Betsy L Bell with all the property I die possessed of the other children having already got their full shares with the above addition to Malvina Duff.

It is to be understood that Minerva ~~Shelby Bell~~ & Betsy L is to be equal in profit & loss until there is a legal divide. Again I press the greatest tenderness to the above and poor blacks all persons forbid by me to take any of the above blacks' property from them. If I should depart this life before the term of my lease is out it is my direction for it to sold, but until the first ~~day~~ of January next - I hope I will hold that that none of my children will murmur at this codicil........ with my Last Will & Testament. I place great confidence in Lawyers Mcalpin & Brown. My dear sons when you and others these lines I shall care little about the trash of this world written with my own hand in the 75 year of my age and tested in the Town of Raleigh this 9th day of January 1832.

Test Andrew Bell (SEAL)

J C Rudisill

Wm Lakey

State of Tennessee)
Sessions A.D. 1833
Shelby County Court)

The foregoing codicil to the Last Will & Testament of Andrew Bell was produced in open Court and the execution of the same (P-44) by the said Bell duly & regularly proven by the oaths of J C Rudisill & W Lakey witnesses thereto Also that the said Bell was of sound mind and disposing memory which is ordered to be ~~so~~ certified for Record

Ro Lawrence Clk S.C.C

(P-44 cont.) The foregoing Will & Codicil thereof of A. Bell was duly Recorded the 1st day of October A D 1833.

Ro Lawrence C. S.C.C.

Compared with original Apl 18th 1860

(P-45) JAMES WILLIAMS' LAST WILL & TESTAMENT

In the name of God Amen.

I James Williams of the County of Shelby and State of Tennessee being weak in body but of sound and perfect mind and memory considering the uncertainty of this mortal life do make and publish this my last will & Testament in manner and form following (that is to say) First that all my just debts be paid.

Secondly; I give to my beloved wife Martha Williams the tract of land containing 200 acres whereon I now live during her natural life and at her death to be sold at the discretion of my executors. I also give and bequeath to my wife aforesaid One bed bedstead & furniture. I also give & bequeath unto my daughter Mary Williams One Bed bedstead & furniture. I also give and bequeath unto my daughter Susan Williams One Bed Bedstead & furniture. I also give and bequeath unto my daughter Eliza Williams One Bed Bedstead & furniture. I also give unto my son Greenberry Williams One Bed bedstead & furniture.

Item I give in trust to Doctor Samuel Bond for the use & benefit of my Daughter Martha Bass One Bed Bedstead & furniture also one ninth part of my Estate not heretofore disposed of, not for his use but for the especial use & benefit of the said Martha Bass during her natural life & then to be equally divided among the Heirs of her body, if she should have any; if not to be equally divided among her brothers & sisters or their Heirs.

I also give each of my children above named one cow & calf. I also give my wife aforesaid the cow & calf which she already claims as her own.

Item It is my wish & will that the balance of my estate not heretofore disposed,of to be equally divided among my wife Martha Williams & my daughter Matilda Williams my daughter Cynthia Reddit My son Lewis Williams My Daughter Mary Williams my daughter (P-46) Susan Williams my daughter Eliza Williams & my son Greenberry Williams Share & Share alike.

Item. It is my wish that, at the sale of my Land given to my wife which will be after her death - that the one eighth part be given in trust to Dr. Samuel Bond for the special use & benefit of my daughter Martha Bass during her natural life, and then to be divided among the Heirs of her body, as aforesaid

Item. It is my wish that the balance of the sales of the Land as aforesaid be equally divided among my other seven children named above

Item. It is my wish & will that if any of my children heretofore named should die without having any Legal Heir or Heirs then and in that

(P-46 cont.) case the part of my Estate they were or would be entitled to, to be equally divided among the balance of their brothers & sisters share & share alike

Lastly I do hereby nominate & appoint Doctor Samuel Bond and Francis M. Weathered Executors of this my last will & testament hereby revoking all former Wills by me made.

In witness whereof I have hereunto set my hand and seal this 11th day of August 1833

his
James X Williams (Seal
mark

Signed Sealed & published & delivered

in presence of us H. Bates W.M. Kerr

State of Tennessee)
October Sessions 1833.
Shelby County Court)

This paper purporting to be the Last will & Testament of James Williams Decd. was produced in open court and the execution thereof proven by the oath of H Bates and W.M. Kerr to have been done by the said deceased with a sound mind and disposing memory and ordered to be recorded.

Given under my hand at office the 17 day of October 1833.

Recorded Nov. 21st 1833 Ro Lawrence C.D.C.C.

R. Lawrence Clk.

(P-47) In the name of God Amen. I Joel B Sanders of the Town of Memphis Shelby County Tennessee knowing that there is a time appointed for all to die and after death a judgment, do hereby constitute this my last will and testament hereby revoking all former wills whatsoever and being of a sound mind and disposing memory.

Item first. It is my will and devise that my body be buried in a plain and decent manner no _ how no parade made over my remains -

Item second. I will that all my just debts be paid and no claim is paid unless legally adjusted -

Item third. I will all my property both real and personal to my beloved wife Marian L Sanders during her widowhood for the purpose of educating my children in a moral & Christian like manner - In case of my wife's marriage it is my will that she take her third of all that I have both real and personal during her natural life after which I will it to my children -

Item fourth I will that my children Sarah G K Sanders, Eliza M Sanders Napoleon B Sanders, Xenophan B Sanders & Leonadas Sanders all those equally alike in the distribution of my property both real and personal. It is clearly my will that no account be taken of the expenses of their Education as I want them all to have a good English Education

(P-47 cont.) and then to share equally in the property. It is my ardent desire that my three sons, Napoleon, Xenaphon & Leondas be Educated at the Manuel Paliver Academy Located in Maury County, Tennessee.

Item fifth it is my will and desire that in case either of my children becomes of age or marries that my wife give to the same on the day of marriage or as soon thereafter as practicable her or his portion of the property (P-48) and take a receipt for the same -

Item 6th It is my will that at any time my wife thinks it prudent or in the interest of the family to sell any of my real or personal property to do so. I also wish her to consult William E Kennedy Williams or John H Sanders on all matters of much importance as to the interest of the family particularly as regards the sale of any property and their advice -

It is my will that my medicine Medical Books Instruments & Shop Furniture be sold for the benefit of the family - I also wish my wife to give my son Napoleon as he is my first born son my patent Lever silver watch as a suitable age and the others equal for the same -

In testimony I have hereunto set my hand & Seal this twenty fourth day of July 1833

J B Sanders

As my signature can be proven by William or John H S Lawby Col H Grove or other persons Tenn.

H Grove)
A Davis
Z Edmonds)

J B Sanders

State of Tennessee)
January Sessions A D 1834
Shelby County Court)

The foregoing said will & testament of Joel B Sanders Decd was produced in open court & the being no subscribing witnesses to it Hewson Grove Z Edmonds & Alexander H Davis men of respectable standing being sworn proved that the said will & signature is in the handwriting of deceased which ordered to be certified & recorded.

R Lawrence Clk -

(P-49) THE WILL OF HENRY F JAMES

In the name of God Amen:

I Henry F James of Memphis Shelby County Tennessee, being in unsound health but of perfect mind and memory do make this my last will and testament.

first At my death I give and bequeath to my wife Matilda James during her lifetime all the property of whatsoever kind I die possessed of or due me.

(P-49 cont.) Second. At the death of my wife Matilda James I give and bequeath the property left her during her lifetime to my children and to her two daughters by a former Husband Frances and Mary Lee to be divided equally among them.

third. I require and request my wife Matilda James to pay and settle all my debts.

fourth I appoint my wife Matild James sole executrix of my estate and do not require that she should give security in executing this my last will and testament.

In witness thereof I have hereunto set my hand & seal this the 19th day of May in the Year of our lord one thousand eight hundred and thirty three

H. F. James (Seal)

Signed Sealed and acknowledged

in presence of us W H Bolton W H Brown

Aug Smith

State of Tennessee)
April Sessions A.D. 1834 -
Shelby County Court)

The within will of Henry F James was produced in open Court and the execution of the same as well as his sound mind and (P-50) disposing memory duly proven by the oath of Wade H Bolton a subscribing witness thereto whereupon the Court ordered the same to be certified and recorded.

Given under my hand at office the 29th April 1834

Recorded 28th June 1834 Ro Lawrence Clk

R Lawrence Clk.

(P-51) ANDREW WHERRY'S LAST WILL & TESTAMENT

State of Tennessee

Shelby County

IN the name of God Amen.

I Andrew Wherry of the Sate & County aforesaid being of perfect mind and memory although in a very low state of health do make and declare these presents to be my last will and Testament VIZ) I give and bequeath my soul unto God that gave it and my body to be buried at the discretion of my executors in hopes they will unite at the Reserection of the Just.

First. I allow all my lawful debts to be paid and the remainder of my Estate both real and personal at the time of my decease I shall be possessed Of or of right appertain unto me I do give and bequeath in the

(P-51 cont.) way and manner following (viz) I bequeath to my wife Elizabeth M Reaves tract of Land her lifetime and at her death to my son Thomas J Wherry the Sloane or Roark tract of Land to my daughters Margaret & Dorcas to be divided equal so that Margaret shall have and hold the improvement she now occupies. My Negroes I bequeath to my wife Elizabeth her life time and at her death to be equally divided between my four named children (viz) Silas, Margaret, Dorcas & Thomas. I also bequeath to my wife Elizabeth all my Household & Kitchen Furniture, my waggon and Horses Farming utensils, cows & Hogs for her use and benefit. I furthermore bequeath to my wife Elizabeth all monies in hand and promissory notes for her use and benefit. I hold a note of hand on my soninlaw John L Neely for three hundred dollars which is to be given up as my daughter Mary S Neely's dividend of my estate.

And I do hereby nominate John Furgison Executor of my last will and testament hereby revoking all former Wills & Testaments by me heretofore (P-52) made and do declare this to be my last.

In witness whereof I have hereunto set my hands & affixed my seal this 4th day of Feby in the year of our lord one thousand Eight hundred and thirty four

Signed Sealed and delivered in the Andrew Wherry (Seal)

presence of Joshua L Sturgis James L

Dickey Wm. R Dickey

State of Tennessee)
April Sessions A.D. 1834
Shelby County Court)

The foregoing Will of Andrew Wherry was produced in open Court and the execution thereof as well as his sound mind and disposing memory was duly proven by the oath of Joshua L Sturgis and W R Dickey witnesses thereto and ordered to be certified for record

Recorded 28th June 1834 Ro Lawrence Clerk

R Lawrence Clk

(P-53) THE LAST WILL & TESTAMENT OF JOSEPH SMITH

As it is appointed unto all men to die it becomes necessary to take a disposition of our temporal matters In obedience to this duty being in proper mind and senses I acknowledge this to be my last will and testament

First I commend my immortal part to almighty God hoping eternal rest through atoning merits of our redeemer Amen.

Second For the love and regard I have for my wife, I give & bequeath unto her her heirs and assigns forever one half my property and I give & bequeath unto the heir in prospect for his or hers proper use of

(P-53 cont.) benefit the other half of my estate together with the cash capitol (or in other words whatever dues that call for money after paying all just debts this ballance to be put on Interest until it becomes sufficient to purchase a negro Girl for the benefit of the young child in prospect.

And in order that this my last will & testament should be more fully executed I must request & appoint Andrew Rembert my executor. So let it be Amen

Signed & Sealed this 2nd day of July 1834

Witnesses Joseph Smith (Seal)

Fielding Jeter Andrew Rembert

State of Tennessee)
July Sessions A. D. 1834
Shelby County Court)

The last Will & Testament of Joseph Smith deceased was produced in open Court and therein came Fielding Jeter and Andrew Rembert two sub scribing Witnesses to the same who being Sworn Say that the said Joseph Smith executed the same in their presence acknowledged the same to be his last will and testament and that he was at the time of sound and disposing memory. Ordered that the (P-54) same be recorded

A Copy
Test Ro Lawrence Clk
Recorded 6th August 1834

Ro Lawrence Clk. S.C.C.

JOHN BEST'S WILL

The State of Alabama Lauderdale County

I John Best being weak in body but of perfect mind and memory & calling to mind that is once appointed for all men to die do make ordain constitute this my Last will & testament revoking and disanulling all other will & deeds of such kind

Item first I leave all my property both real and personal to my loving wife Sally Best during her natural life by her taking good care of the same so as to return to my Heirs at her death

2 To my son Eben Best I give and bequeath one negro boy Charles one girl named Venda

3. To my youngest daughter Margaret Best one negro girl named Jin.

4th My three negroes to wit Bill Harry Liz I wish to be divided between my four sons namely Jonathan Charley Abijah & Elijah

(P-54 cont.) 5th, My three daughters to-wit Polly Hoad Jenny Hoad & Ellinor Macky I leave the sum of one hundred dollars each to be paid by my sons. I leave to my youngest son Eben in addition to the above one horse & saddle one bed & furniture two cows & calves & the Lot of Land Eighty Acres on which I now live To my daughter Margarett in addition to the above I leave one bed & furniture Two cows & calves

In testimony I have hereunto set my hand and affixed my seal this 26th day of September

his
John X Best (Seal)
mark

(P-55) Attest W W Garrard

Chs Bert

State of Tennessee)
January Session 1835
Shelby County Court)

The Last Will & Testament of John Best was produced in open Court and the death & handwriting of Ch Bert one of the subscribing witnesses thereto was proven to the satisfaction of the Court and the Handwriting of W W Garrard the other subscribing witness having been heretofore proven the said will is ordered to be certified for registration

Recorded 13 Feby 1835 Ro Lawrence Clk S C C
Ro Lawrence Clk

I Benjamin Luggett of Memphis Tennessee & formerly of or a native of Brunswick County Virginia having in mind the certainty of death and uncertainty of Life Knowing that I have to go the way of all the living make and leave on record this my Last Will and Testament. Viz After my death that my body be decently interred in the usual way and after the expenses thereof & all just debts ~~paid~~ are paid wish will and desire that my sisters eldest son Benjamin Preston may inherit & possess all my remaining Estate and also desire that John Kitchen and M B Winchester take said Estate and manage the same to the best advantage until said Preston becomes of Lawful age

his
Benjamin X Luggett
mark

(P-56) State of Tennessee)
Circuit Court December Term 1834
Shelby County)

On trial of the suit between John Kichin plaintiff and E Luggett defendant on a motion to establish the above as the Last Will & Testament of B Luggett decd. Twelve good & Lawful men upon their did say on the Testimony of W Yates, that it is the Last Will & Testament of said Luggett

(P-56 cont.) for personal Estate Whereupon the Court ordered the same to be certified for registration.

S.K. Brown C S.C.C.

The foregoing is a true copy of the original now on file in my office with the certificate of the Clerk thereto attached Feb 13 1835

Ro Lawrence Clk

J O E L B SANDERS' WILL

In the name of God Amen.

I Joel B Sanders of the Town of Memphis Shelby County Tennessee knowing that there is a time appointed for all men to die and after death a judgment do hereby constitute this my last will & testament hereby revoking all former wills whatever and being of sound mind and disposing memory.

Item 1st. It is my will and desire that my body be buried in a plain and decent manner, no show no parade over my remains.

Item 2. I will that all my just debts be paid and that no claim is be paid unless legally adjusted

Item 3rd. I will all my property both real & personal to my beloved wife Mariann L Sanders, during her widowhood for the purpose of educating my children in a moral and christian Like manner In case of my wife's marriage it is my will that she take her third of all that I have both real & personal during her natural life after which time I will it to my children

Item fourth. I will that my children Sarah, G.K. Sanders (P-57) Eliza M Sanders, Napoleon B. Sanders, Zenaphon E Sanders & Leonidus Sanders, all share equally alike in the distribution of my property both real and personal. It is clearly my will that no account be taken of the expenses of their education as I want them all to have a good english education and then to share equally in the property. It is my ~~//////~~ ardent desire that my three sons, Napoleon Zenaphon & Leonidus be educated at the manuel labor academy located in Maury County, Tennessee.

Item 5th It is my will and desire that in case that either of my children becomes of age or marries that my wife gives to the same on the day of marriage or as soon as practicable her or his portion of the property and take a receipt for the same.

Item Sixth It is my will that ~~//////~~ at any time my wife thinks it prudent or to the interest of the family to sell any of my real or personal property to do so. I also wish her to consult William Ekeridge William or John A Sanders on all matters of much importance as to the interest of the family particularly as regards the sale on any property and have their advice I also wish my medicine medical Books, instruments and shop furniture be sold for the benefit of the family. I also wish my wife to give my son Napoleon as he is my first born son my patent lever silver watch at a suitable age and the others equal for the same.

(P-57 cont.) In testimony I have hereunto set my hand and Seal this twenty fourth day of July 1833

Joel B Sanders (Seal)

N.B. My signature can be proven by William or John H Sanders H Tandy Col H Grove or divers other persons in Columbia Tenn.

Jo B Sanders (S)

State of Tennessee)
January Sessions A.D. 1834
Shelby County)

The foregoing last will & testament of Joel B Sanders decd was produced in open Court and being no subscribing witnesses Herman Grove Z. Edmons & Alexander H Davis men of respectable standing being sworn proved that the Seal and Signature are in the Handwriting of (Editor's Note: rest torn off, probably is "deceased.") which is ordered to be certified and recorded Recorded March 1835

H Lawrence   Ro Lawrence C.S.C.C.

(P-58) JOSEPH BROOKS WILL

State of Tennessee Shelby County the twenty second day of May 1832.

In the name of God Amen.

I Joseph Brooks being in good health & sound mind and memory do make this my last will & Testament in the following form as follows: Viz.

First I leave all of my store of good to be sold on a credit of twelve months and all of my just debts payed by my executors hereafter named I leave also all of my notes and accounts to be collected by the same executors

Item I give to my beloved daughter Sarah C Brooks one negro girl by the name of Firby to her Heirs & assigns forever.

Item I now give to my beloved wife Jiamima Brooks all of the residue of my property during her widowhood consisting of Land negroes household & Kitchen furniture & stock of horses cattle hogs & all other property which I possess to her proper use but not to be sold and at her decease I leave it to be sold and equally divided between all of my children that is then surviving or equally divided as my executors may think proper. And what moneys there may be after settling my debts out of the store and notes and accounts I wish to be kept on interest or laid out for young negroes for my heirs which is to be divided equally among all after paying executors for their trouble & I make & appoint my beloved sons Henry Brooks & Lewis Brooks & my beloved friend Andrew Rembert my executors to this my Last Will & Testament.

In witness whereof I have hereunto set my hand and Seal.

Joseph Brooks(Seal)

(P-58 cont.) Attest. A Rembert

Thos Douglass

State of Tennessee Shelby County Court October Sessions

This the last will & Testament of Jos Brooks deceased was produced in open court & A Rembert & Thos Douglass witnesses thereto being sworn (Editor's Note: page torn) the signature thereto is in the handwriting of said decd. (Editor's Note: Page torn off) at the time he executed the same was of sound mind (Editor's Note: page torn off) memory which is ordered to be recorded

Ro Lawrence C S. C.C.

(P-59) WILL OF NATHANIEL MOORE

I Nathaniel Moore of the County of Shelby and State of Tennessee planter being of sound Mind but infirm of Body, do make and publish this my last Will and Testament, hereby revoking and making void all former Wills by me at any time heretofore made, I dispose of the same as follows

First. I direct that all my Just Debts and funeral Expenses be paid as soon after my Death as possible Out of any Moneys that I may be possessed of or may first come into the hands of my Executors from any portion of my Estate Real or Personable

Secondly. I give and bequeath to my Wife Julia all my household & Kitchen furniture It is my will and Request that all my propperty both Real and Personal to remain together Under the care and management of the Executor & Executrix for the benefit and for the purpose of Raising & Educating of my Heirs Until they arrive to the age of Twenty one or Until Married. At which time it is my will and request that they should be put in possession of their due portion or dividend of my Estate - Consisting on One Hundred and fourteen acres of Land Five negroes names as follows- Ned, Samuel Fanny and her increase Peggy & her increase and Merrit Also all the Stock consisting of Horses cattle & Hogs that are remaining on my Plantation at that time together with one Bed and furniture. And also it is my Will and Request that all of the propperty of my wife Julia has been put in possession off by my last Will & Testament - at her Death that be equally divided between my Lawful Heirs - Also whatever Remains of the proceeds of the farm and Stock together with the Labor of the hands after rendering all necessary support shall be added to the Estate subject to an Equal Division - - With the above named propperty I do hereby make ordain and appoint my beloved Julia Moore My Brother Executor of this my last Will and testament in Witness Whereof I have the said (P-60) Nathaniel Moore Testator have to this my will written on one sheet of Paper Set my hand and Seal this the Sixth day of May in the Year of our Lord One thousand Eight Hundred and Twenty five

Signed Sealed and published in the presence of us who have subscribed in the presence of the Testator and of Each other

Nath Moore (SEAL)

Turner Dison Saml Bond James P Herald

(P-60 cont.) State of Tennessee)
July Sessions 1835
Shelby County Court)

This Instrument was produced in open Court & Samuel Bond & Jas. B. Hersol witnesses thereto being sworn say that Nathaniel Moore maker of the same was of sound Mind & Disposing Memory at the time he Executed the same & that we signed the same in his presence which is ordered to be Recorded

Recorded August 3rd 1835 Ro Lawrence Clk S.C.C.

(P-61) WILL OF BRIANT BANGUS

Tennessee Shelby County

In the name of God, I Briant Bangus now in the County & State first mentioned, being in my Rational and Common mind not Impaired by disease though my bodily strength & health has failed and believing from my Age & impaired Constitution that I cannot long exist here do make the following my last Will or desire about the division of my Earthly Substance of propperty freely without the influence or compulsion of any Person or Persons whatever - That is to Say

1st, That all my Just Debts be paid

2nd And then to my son Jack Bangus I do Give & Bequeath my Rifle Gun together with the Tract of Land by the name of Brown's Tract that is my Portion of the same I now live on the Land & lies in Shelby County Tennessee and on the State line Road & contains by survey 984 acres & Bounded by the old State or Winchester Line on the South & Thos McAns occupant in part of the West

3rd, And to my Daughters Mary Bangus Sally Bangus and Frances Bangus I give & Bequeath my Interest in two Tracts of Land one in Haywood County Tennessee and on the waters of Forkadeer River & Known by the name of Stewart - Brown & Allen's tract and contains about Five Thousand acres and the other Tract of Land is in Fayette County, Tennessee & Known by the name of Brown's Tract - & lies on the waters of Loosahatchie & which is undivided by survey is said to be five Hundred Acres All of the Lands when Divided I wish sold to the best Bidder on a twelve month credit Debt Secured by the Lands Security &c and the money when collected to be equally divided between the above named Daughters of mine also to the above named Daughters Each to have the Bed & furniture that they now claim and in my possession & if any money, propperty or valuables be Willed or Bequeathed to me or in any wise fall by rite to me (P-62) it be equally divided Between ~~the~~ John Bangus & the Three Daughters before named -

4th And to my sons Briant Bangus Vincent Franklin Bangus & my soninlaw John Moore & his wife Nancy I Give & Bequeath to Each One Dollar as their portion of my Propperty -

The foregoing is my last Will & Testament and wish it to be put in effect after my Death and in Testimony Whereof I have unto set my mark (as I cant write) and Seal in the presence of G Clark Wm.Renneck

* known

(P-62 cont.)

Briant his X mark Bangus

N.P. I Desire that George Clark & Doctor Cornelius be left as Executors or Administrators the day & Date not being part above I have insert it this the 16th day of June 1835

Clark

Briant his X mark Bangus (SEAL)

Wm Renick

State of Tennessee)
July Sessions A.D. 1835.
Shelby County)

The foregoing instrument of Writing was produced in open Court & proven by the oaths of G. Clark & Wm. Renick witnesses to the same to be the last will & Testament of Briant Bangus & that at the Time Said Bangus Made his mark he was of sound mind & Disposing Memory -

Which is ordered to be Recorded

Ro Lawrence Clk. B.C.C.

Recorded August 3rd 1835

(P-63 CHARITY MOORE'S LAST WILL & TESTAMENT

I Charity Moore being now of sound mind & memory but considering the uncertainty of this mortal life do make publish & declare this, my last will & Testament (that is) I will that my body be decently interred

I will & bequeath to my son Nathaniel Moore a negro woman by the name of Fanny a negro boy named Merit and one bedsted feather beds and furniture & one pair of car wheels, one pair of dog irons & one press & half the furniture that is in said press Except one Hundred dollars of the above property which I will, to, & require said Nathaniel Moore to pay to my son John K Moore or North Carolina

I will & bequeath to my son William Moore a negro man named Drake & a negro woman named Suckey & one pair of cart wheels & one work steer

I will & bequeath to my Grand daughters Josephine Sophrona being my son William's daughters a negro girl named Susan & Her children if she shall have any

I will & bequeath to my daughter Penny Thompson, one pided no Horned cow & calf & one half the furniture in the press, One Table & 4 chairs & one side saddle & one bedsted.

I will & bequeath to my daughter Gilly Locke, One pided short-tailed cow and calf.

I will & bequeath to my daughter Polly Warren One white cow with a red Head & calf

(P-63 cont.) I will that the balance of my bed clothes or furniture for beds be equally divided between my three daughters that Polly Warren Penny Thompson & Gilly Locke

I will that my Kitchen furniture be equally divided between my son Nathaniel Moore & my daughter Penny Thompson.

I will that my son Nathaniel Moore retain fifty dollars or one half the value of the mare he gave to Jno (P-64) Shipp for his interest in the Land on which I now live & that he Nathaniel pay fifty dollars being the other half of the value of said mare to my son William Moore or that they divide said Land equally between them

I will that my Stock of hogs & any other property not mentioned be equally divided between my two Sons Nathaniel & William Moore & my daughter Penny Thompson

In witness Whereof I have hereunto set my hand & Seal this 22nd day of August in the Year of our Lord one thousand Eight Hundred & Twenty nine

Signed & acknowledged in the presence of us
John Ralston J.D. Shaw, Alexander Snead Turner Person James Rembert

Charity her X mark Moore (Seal

I Charity Moore being now of sound mind make & publish the following codicil to the foregoing Will (that is) I will & bequeath to my son Nathaniel Moore Lylia a child of Fanny, which was before given to said Nathaniel & all children that said Fanny may have hereafter and in consideration of said child or children I will & require ~~that~~ my said son Nathaniel Moore to pay to my daughter Betsy Ship Ten dollars to be forwarded to her in No Carolina

I hereby appoint Wm. Andrew Rembert Executor of this my Last Will & Testament.

In witness whereof I have hereunto set my Hand & Seal this 1st day of November in the Year of our Lord One thousand Eight Hundred & Thirty one.

Signed & acknowledged in the presence of us Jno. Ralston Alexander Snead Jas R Harroll Turner Persons James Rembert

Charity Her X mark Moore

State of Tennessee)
October Sessions 1835
Shelby County court)

The foregoing will was produced & proven in open Court by the oath of J R Harrol A Snead T Persons & Jas Rembert & ordered to be recorded.

Recorded 10 Nov 1835 R.L. Clk

R Lawrence Clk

(P-65) LAST WILL & TESTAMENT OF MARGARETT KIMBROUGH

Being of sound & disposing I do hereby make & ordain this my last will & Testament.

In the name of God Amen. I give and bequeath to my daughter Martha Kimbrough Dave a negro man Slave Stafford, Ginny Linder Jefferson Hoally Nealey and Walter. The two children of Minders to her the said Martha Kimbrough with all the future increase of the aforesaid named negroes & to the said Martha & her Heirs forever.

2nd. I give & bequeath to my daughter Nancy Jones Carr the following negroes namely Lemons, Joe Sylvia Siraner Ridley, Eliza, Tom and Patty with all their future increase to her the said Nancy Jones Carr and her heirs forever.

3rd. I Give and bequeath to my son William Asbury Kimbrough the following negroes namely, with all their future increase Jack & Eady to him & his Heirs forever, provided He the said William A. Kimbrough complys with a certain instrument of writing executed & Signed by me October 5th 1833 by conveying certain negroes therein named to Nancy J Carr, her heirs & assigns forever, which above mentioned instrument of writing I do hereby make a part of my Last Will & Testament

4th Item. My Will is I give to my Granddaughter Virginia Carolina Carr a negro girl Mary Ann, to her the said Virginia C. Carr & her heirs & assigns forever with all future increase of the said negro Girl Mary Ann

5th Item I give & Bequeath to my daughter Martha Kimbrough in addition to what I have above bequeathed One Yoke of work oxen, One Waggon, all the Stock of hogs on the farm at my death. The balance of all my stock (except One Yoke of oxen which I give to my daughter Nancy J Carr,) I give to my daughters Marth Kimbro (P-66) ugh & Nancy J Carr. And further my Will is that after all the debts of the Estate are settled the residue if there be any Shall be equally divided between my Two Daughters Martha Kimbrough & Nancy J Carr equally

I do appoint Anderson B Carr and Buckley Kimbrough my executors to this my last will and Testament revoking all others & substituting this instead of all others with all its Items meanings and expressions as my Last Will & Testament.

Witness whereof I have hereunto set my Hand & affixed my Seal this 29th day of June 1835.

Farm and son interlined before Margarett M X Kimbrough (Seal)

Signed Witnesses

David Dunn Ezekiel Hendricks

State of Tennessee)

Sessions 1835

Shelby County Court)

David Dunn & Ezekiel Hendrick witnesses to the above will & Testament

(P-66 cont.) of Margarett Kimbrough decd being first sworn in open court say that the said Margarett executed the said Will in their presence & that she was of sound mind & disposing Memory which was ordered to be certified & Recorded

Ro Lawrence Clk, S.C.C.

Codicil to the Last Will & Testament of Margarett Kimbrough decd. To wit.

State of Tennessee Shelby County this 6th day of August 1835

I Margarett Kimbrough do hereby make & constitute this my codicil and alteration to my former Will & Testament bearing date the 29th day of June 1835, there being some alteration in One Item of the said Will which I intend to make by this codicil substituted instead thereof but is not intend to alter or abolish any part of my said last Will & Testament above alluded to except in Items specified in this my codicil, the residue of said Will above alluded toto remain in full force & virtue agreeable to all its Items & specified gifts (P-67) therein except the alteration herein named. In my said Will Lemon was given to Nancy J Carr, in this codicil I intend a change in that Item. I give said negro man, Lemon to Martha Kimbrough & the boy named Jefferson in said Will before that is given to Martha Kimbrough, my will is that he be given to Nancy J Carr. And the negro woman Eady given to William A Kimbrough be given to my daughter Martha Kimbrough & her heirs forever and the said above alteration I wish & intend to be a part of my former last Will & Testament before mentioned in this my codicil bearing date the 29th day of June 1835.

In witness whereof I have hereunto set my hand and affixed my seal this 6 day of August 1835.

Test.

M. Kimbrough (Seal)

D. Dunn

W.W. Tucker

State of Tennessee)

Shelby County Court)

D Dunn & W.W. Tucker subscribing witnesses to the foregoing codicil to the Last Will & Testament of Margaret Kimbrough decd. being sworn in open court say that the said Margaret signed the said Codicil in their presence & that they believe that she was of sound mind & disposing memory at the time of executing the same. Which is ordered to be certified & recorded in the Book Kept for the Registration of Wills.

Ro Lawrence C.S.C.C.

Recorded 20 Nov. 1835

Ro Lawrence Clk.

(P-68) WM HOWERTON'S WILL

In the name of Almighty God. I William Howerton of the county of Shelby State of Tennessee being of sound mind & disposing memory make & ordain this my last Will & Testament.

In primis. I loan unto my beloved wife Catherine E Howerton during her widowhood all the property I possess or have any title to for her support & education of my children of my children. Should my wife marry then my will & desire is that she shall have allotted to her one-third of all my Estate to be held in Lieu of right of dower to be divided equally between my children at her death

My will & desire is, that, as my children become of age or marry they shall have allotted to them their share of my Estate in equal portions

My will & desire is should both my children die before they marry or become of age then I will all my estate to my brother Thomas Jefferson Howerton to him & his Heirs forever.

I will & devise unto Thomas C Coates when my daughter becomes of age should said Coates be then living One Hundred & thrity dollars, to be paid out of the joint property of my Estate.

I constitute & appoint my wife Catherine E Howerton sole Executrix to this my last will & Testament revoking all others by me heretofore made.

In witness whereof, I have hereunto set my name & affixed my Seal this 6th day of July 1835

Signed Sealled & declared as William Howerton (Seal)

his last Will in presence of us witnesses

W A Bowers Wm Campbell

(P-69) State of Tennessee)
October Sessions 1835
Shelby County Court)

The within Last Will & Testament of William Howerton was produced in open Court & the execution thereof proven by W.A. Bowers one of the subscribing witnesses & it appearing to the satisfaction of the Court that William Campbell the other witness is dead & his handwriting to the same being sufficiently proved the said Will is admitted to be fully proven & ordered to be recorded

Recorded 20 Aug 1835 Ro Lawrence Clk

Ro Lawrence Ck.

NONCUPATIVE WILL OF WILLIAM COBB DECD TOWIT

(P-69 cont.) State of Tennessee Shelby County

We the undersigned Hezekiah Cobb and Nancy Cobb do declare and make known, that on or about the 27th day of April last (1831) William Cobb being then confined in his last sickness at his residence in Shelby County & said State of which sickness he the said William Cobb died on on the 13th of May instant in the county & State aforesaid being in sound mind & of disposing memory, did make & publish a noncupative or verbal Will to the effect & in the manner following towit

I make my wife Mary Cobb executrix of my Will.

And my Will & desire is that she shall have full power & control of my whole Estate & that she shall make settlement with Hezekiah Cobb & that he pay over to her all the neat ballance of my Estate that shall remain in his hands after making provision for the debts that now stand against H & W Cobb. I also want my wife to take my two children Humphrey and Columbia Ann, to keep & raise them & that she (P-70) dispose of the property that I leave her for their use & benefit as she may think best.

We the said Hezekiah Cobb & Nancy Cobb also declare & make known that the said William Cobb deceased at the time of making the said Will expressed a wish or gave an intimation that he did not wish security required of his wife for the performance of her duty as Executrix. We also State that said William Cobb died in his own habitation or dwelling House in the county aforesaid & that we were specially requested by him to bear witness to his said Will and desire as above written.

In testimony whereof we have hereunto set out Hands this 30 day of May 1836

Hezekiah Cobb

Nancy B Cobb

(Editor's Note: In the margin of O.MS is written "WILLIAM COBBS VERBAL WILL".)

State of Tennessee)
June Sessions 1836
Shelby County Court)

This the noncupative will of W Cobb was produced in court & legally established by the oath of Hezekiah Cobb & Nancy Cobb witnesses to the said noncupative or verbal will. Which is ordered to be certified & recorded

Recorded 18 July 1831 J W Fuller Clk

J.W.F. Clk.

(P-71) Know all ye whom it may concern that I William - Bell of the town of Memphis late of the State of North Carolina being low in health but sound in mind do make and ordain this my last will and testament -

Item 1st To my friend Marcus B Winchester of the town of Memphis I give and bequeath my black people to Wit. Sarah and her four children Adam,

(P-71 cont.) Joseph Mary & Caroline and Barbara & her infant Lucy in the full faith and under the Injunction that he will forwith send them into a free State and there emancipate and give them their liberty & freedom

Item the 2nd I also give and bequeath to said Winchester all the cash which I may have with me at my death and bills bonds notes debts, dues and accounts owing to me in the State of Tennessee in trust that he will apply the same to the removal of my black people as aforesaid and to their benefit after removal as he Shall deem best

Item the 3rd to my Mother from the money due me in North Carolina when collected, I give and appropriate and desire that the same may be paid according the Sum of five Hundred dollars. —

Item 4th All the rest and residue of my Estate whether real or personal, I give and bequeath in trust to M.B. Winchester to be applied for the benefit of my black people as aforesaid

Item the 5th I do hereby nominate and appoint the said M.B. Winchester executor of this my last will and testament requiring no security from him for the performance of the same

(P-72) In Witness of which I have Set my hand and Seal thereto July the 4th 1836

Witnesses present Wm. Bell (SEAL)

Wyatte Christian

Levi Prescott Arch McLean

State of Tennessee)
August Sessions 1836
Shelby County Court)

This the last Will and Testament of Wm. Bell was produced in open Court & Wyatt Christian and Arch McLean Witnesses to the Same being sworn say that they saw said Wm. Bell sign Will and thathe declared the same to be his last Will & testament and to the best of their knowledge & belief he the said Bell was at the time of signing the same in sound mind & memory which is ordered to be certified and recorded

J.W. Fuller Clerk

THE LAST WILL AND TESTAMENT OF TURNER B. HENLY

of the County of Shelby and State of Tennessee

I Turner B. Henley considering the uncertainty of this mortal life and being of sound mind & memory (blessed be Almighty God for the same) do make and publish this my last will and testament in manner & form following;

And first I direct that all my debts and funeral expenses be paid as soon after my decease as possible out of any moneys that I may die possessed of or may first come into the hands of my Exutr. from any portion of my estate real or personal

(P-72 cont.) Secondly I desire and direct that my faithful friends Wyatt Christian, John R Frayser and William H Bryant Should act as the agents of my beloved wife, who I hereby appoint executrix of this my last will & testament in the disposal of all the property purchased by (P-73) me of Thomas G Johnson in the town of Memphis saving only such as she may wish to reserve for herself

Thirdly I direct that my blood stock of Horses now in the hands of Dr. Alexander Goode be disposed of it the sum of twenty five hundred dollars can be obtained for them if not I direct that they should be carried back into the middle part of the State

Item. I give and bequeath unto my beloved wife Rebecca S Henly all my estate consisting of negroes horses and everything whatsoever of a personal nature to hold to her the said Rebecca S Henly during her natural life and at her death to be equally divided between my children, Mary, Amanda, Susan, Isaac, Kaleb, John Thomas Jefferson & Richard. I direct that so much of my estate as may be necessary for the purpose be spent in the Education of my children above named leaving the same to the discretion of my beloved wife, & I hereby commit the guardianship of all my children untill they Shall respectively attain the age of Twenty one years unto my said wife during her life their maintenance and education as before said to be provided for by my said wife Out of the money and estate given and bequeathed to her in and by this my last will and testament - I also desire and direct that my said wife should have complete control of all my estate hereby bequeathed to her the power to dispose of any negroes who may fall into her ~~hands~~ possession by this my will and purchase others in their stead and to do all things in regard to the same as may seem to her best, lastly I appoint her my said wife sole executrix of this my last will and testament hereby all former wills by me made.

In witness whereof I have hereunto set my hand & Seal this twenty Second day of August in the year of our Lord One Thousand Eight Hundred & Thirty Six.

Signed Sealed published & declared by T.B. Henly (Seal)

the above named Turner B Henly to be his

last will and testament in the presence of us who have

hereunto subscribed our names as witnesses in the

presence of the Testator

W.F. Young Jno. R. Frayser A Smith

(P-74) State of Tennessee)

September Sessions 1836

Shelby County Court)

This the last will & testament of Turner B Henly was produced in open Court William F. Young and John R Frayser witnesses thereto being sworn say that the said henly signed the same in their presence & acknowledged and declared the execution thereof to be his own proper act and deed & that the said Henly was of sound mind which is ordered to be certified

J.W.Fuller Clerk

(P-74 cont.) In the name of God I, Lynch Cockran of the County of Shelby and State of Tennessee do solemnly make & the following will and testament of all my property real and personal goods and chattles

In the first place I do will & bequeath unto my loving wife Nancy Cockran all my real ~~Estate~~ personal property with all my goods & Chattles household furniture &c to have and to hold for her own exclusive benefit during her life time -

In the Second place I do will and desire that my loving wife the Said Nancy Cockran Shall appropriate a Sufficient portion out of the proceeds of the above described property - to support and education of her son untill he becomes of legal age -

In the 3rd place it is my Solemn will and testament that the above bequeath of my property to my loving wife Nancy Cockran is so conditioned and modified that so soon as the aforesaid child, Wm.O.King becomes of legal age that then at that time he shall be entitled to an equal division of one half of all of the above bequeathed property & at the death of his mother to all the balance -

In the 4th place I do will & desire that the above bequest shall in no respect bar the payment of my honest debts or claims against me (P-75) out of the proceeds of my Estate.

In Testimony of the above will & testament I have this day subscribed my own proper signature May 8th One Thousand Eight Hundred Thirty Six.

In presence Wm. W. Tucker — Lynch Cockran

John Pope.

~~Know ye all men by these presents that I George (Editor's Note: next two words obliterated) of sound & disposing mind but conceiving that the time of my dissolution is drawing near & being anxious to make some disposition of my property in Memphis and having confidence in Silas Toncray - do hereby appoint him my executor with full power to take possession of all my property in Memphis Golconda & Vicksburg real & personal & in his discretion to use the same and make such disposition of it as to him may seem best for the interest of my heirs & it is also understood that no security shall be required of him as my executor and I hereby revoke all first and former wills that come within the (Editor's Note: obliteration) purview and meaning of this my last Will & Testament -~~

~~Witness my hand and Seal this 30th of March 1836.~~

~~Joseph Kirk~~ — ~~George Aldridge (Seal)~~

~~James X Snow~~ (his mark)

(Editor's Note: The following Jurat is written on a separate sheet of paper and is pasted over the above VOIDED Will.)

(P-75 cont.) State of Tennessee)

Shelby County Court) August Sessions (Editor's Note: date gone.)

This the last will and testament of Lynch Cockran and was produced in open Court Whereupon John Pope & W W Tucker witnesses to said Will being sworn say that said Cockran Signed said Will in their presence & declared the same to be his act & deed & that to the best of their knowledge & belief the said Cockran was of sound and disposing mind which is ordered to be certified and recorded

J W Fuller

(P-76) THE LAST WILL & TESTAMENT OF BENJ MAY DECD.

State of Tennessee)

Gibson County)

I Benjamin May of the county of Shelby and State of Tennessee being of sound mind & memory do make & establish this my last will and Testament in manner & form following

First I give & bequeath my soul to God who gave it and my body to be decently buried to return to dust from which I sprung.

After the payment of my just debts I will & bequeath to my beloved wife Deletha M May all my property both real & personal Estate during her widowhood wishing Her to keep our child Keturah H May and in the event of my wife's second marriage I will unto my beloved daughter Keturah H May two of my Slaves known by the name of Phillip and Lovelace also I will unto Her the plantation on which I live in Shelby County Tennessee reserving to my wife the use of the ~~farm~~ one half of the farm including the Houses during her natural Life all the above property bequeathed to my beloved daughter Keturah H May I wish equally divided among the two brothers & sisters of my beloved wife Deletha & those of my own in event of my daughter Keturah dying without issue

And lastly I do hereby appoint my wife Delitha M May my executrix and Hugh W Buck Executor of this my Last Will & Testament.

Hereby revoking all wills by me made

In Witness Whereof I have hereunto set my hand and affixed my Seal this 25th day of July 1836

Benj May (Seal)

Signed Sealed and delivered by the above named Benj. May to be his last Will & Testament in the presence of us who have hereunto subscribed our names in presence of as witnesses in presence of Testator

Wm B G Killingsworth

T S Sharpe & Edwin Sharpe

(P-77) JOHN PARK'S LAST WILL

I John Parks of the county of Shelby & State of Tennessee Planter do make & publish this my last will & testament Hereby Revoking & making void all former Wills by me at any time heretofore made

And first, I direct that my body be decently interred in the grave-yard at Raleigh in said county

And as to such worldly Estate as it hath pleased God to entrust me with I dispose of the same as follows

First. I direct that the place whereon I now live containing one hundred & seventy two acres be divided equally between my two sons Symes & Robt. N Parks

Second, I will & bequeath to my son Robert N and my daughter Jane & my granddaughter Martha each one horse saddle & bridle the horses to be worth seventy five dollars each

Third I will that the balance of my Estate including five Black people be sold at public sale to the highest bidder and the proceeds to be equally divided between the following children Alexander C, John, Samuel, Jane & Martha.

Fourth. I will unto my beloved wife, one negro woman named Hannah one of the above written five Also my mare Bet also one cow & calf with five Head of my best Hogs together with house & farm - adjoining the House wherein I now live with farming tools sufficient to cultivate the said place, together with household and kitchen furniture sufficient for her comfort during her life time, and at her death the place and property is to be disposed of as above stated

Fifth I will that before the division of my person (P-78)al property to the above named children that all my just debts be paid. I do hereby make ordain and it is my will that David and Rebecca L my son and daughter have the property that they have heretofore received from me and no more and I do hereby make ordain and appoint my esteemed ~~friend and~~ neighbor and friend Adam R Alexander Executor of this my last will and testament.

In Witness Whereof I John Parks the said testator have to this my will written on one sheet of paper set my hand & seal this 1st day of December in the year of our Lord 1836

Signed Sealed in the presence of John his X mark Parks

J.C.Rudisill

D.S.A Walker

State of Tennessee)
Shelby County Court) January Session 1837

(P-78 cont.) This Last Will & Testament of John Parks dcd was produced in open Court and J.C. Rudisill and D S A Walker Witnesses thereto being sworn say that they saw the said John Parks Execute the same by making his mark thereto & that he was of sound & disposing mind & memory Ordered to be recorded

Recorded 17 January 1837 John W Fuller Clk

J.W. Fuller, Clk

(P-79) GERALD IRBY LAST WILL & TESTAMENT

I make this my last Will and Testament and revoking all others after paying all my just debts, I give and bequeath to my beloved wife Martha, during her life or widowhood the following named negroes Hannah and her increase Squire Charles, Ned, Nancy & Bartlett and all of my other property which may be left after paying my just debts. At the death of my wife Martha or widowhood I give and bequeath to my beloved son Nathaniel P Irby Hannah and her increase Squire Charles Ned & Bartlett and all the other property and proceeds. I give and bequeath to my daughter Eliza Adams Nancy & her increase, at the death of my wife Martha or widowhood If my daughter Eliza Adams should die before my wife Martha I give unto my son Nathaniel P Irby the said Nancy & her increase

I appoint my brother Edmond P Irby my executor and my wife Martha my Executrix.

WITNESS my hand and Seal this 23rd day of March 1836

Test Gerald Irby (Seal)

William T Wilson Isaac Jenkins

J.W. Royster

State of Tennessee)
January Session 1832
Shelby County Court)

This the Last will and testament of G Irby was produced in open court & William L Wilson & Isaac Jenkins witnesses thereto being sworn say that the said Irby when he executed said Will was of sound mind and disposing memory. Ordered to be certified & recorded.

Recorded 17 January 1837 J W Fuller Clk

J W Fuller Clk

(P-80) ELIZABETH WARD'S WILL

As life is uncertain and knowing that we all have to die I make this my last Will and Testament, with the consent and agreement of my Husband Mathias Ward to it - It is my Will that my Husband Mathias Ward

(P-80 cont.) have George and One Hundred & Sixty Dollars due me by Thos. A. Sanders, Elizabeth Martin the daughter of William Martin to have Harriett and her child Elenor Wagnor the daughter of Jno J Wagnor to have Dice and her child, provided there is not another daughter cald after my name if theres should be one named after me she is to have the above named negroes Dice & her child - My Mother Locky Sanders to have Rachel and her children during her lifetime, at her death, my brother William T Sanders is to have Joe & Angeline his life time, after William T. Sanders' death Joe & Angeline and issue to be equally divided between my Brother & Sister - to my Brother James I give Alford, the above property I give and bequeath agreeable to the above donations there is to be no exceptions or advantage taken of this Will or gift or property on account of form or diction being done in haste this 2nd day of September 1836, as Witness my hand & Seal in Presence of

William Ward Edward Sanders — Elizabeth her X mark Ward (Seal)

(P-81) I bind myself to adhere and do relinquish all my claim or claims to the above property as named by my wife Elizabeth Ward, as Witness my hand & Seal this 2nd Sept. 1836, except George which is given me & $160

Test as above — Mathias Ward (Seal)

One of the children of Rachels by the name of Granderson I wish my Mother to give to my Brother Daniel Sanders, and further understood if William T Sanders has heirs the two named negroes shall belong to them if not to be returned to my Brothers & Sisters

State of Tennessee)
February Sessions 1837
Shelby County Court)

This the last Will and testament of Elizabeth Ward, was produced in open Court and having been heretofore Proven by the Oath of Edward Sanders a witness thereto, William Ward the other Subscribing Witness being Out of the State and a resident of another government and Oath having been made by Alanson Trigg & James Sanders to the fact that the said A Trigg & James Sanders saw the said William Ward Sign the said Will as a Witness. It is ordered to be admitted to record as fully proven.

Recorded 10 May 1837 — John W. Fuller Clk

Test John W. Fuller Clerk.

(P-82) ELIZABETH SANDERSON'S WILL

February 1st Eighteen Hundred and Thirty Seven. In the Name of Our Lord Jesus Christ, Amen. Now I Elizabeth Sanderson, Being Sound of Mind but Weak in Body and about to die, and leave this World do in my last Will and testament will and bequeath that all my just debts be paid out of Monies now held by my son Overall Sanderson belonging to me, then after my just debts are paid I also will and bequeath to my Son William Sanderson two Dollars in Cash. To my Son John Sanderson Two Dollars in Cash. To my Son James Sanderson Two Hundred Dollars in Cash. To my Son

(P-82 cont.) Jacob Sanderson Two hundred Dollars in Cash. To my Daughter Jane Cock two Dollars in Cash. To my Daughter Sally Barney two Dollars in Cash. To my Daughter Elizabeth Cock Two Dollars in Cash. To my Son Overall Sanderson a negro man named Core- Also I will that my negro man named Lawson be hired out from year to year, for four Years then at the expiration of Said time that my Executor Pay to each child the amount willed to him or to her, then the Said Negro Man Losson is to be sold and the money arising from the Sale of the Said Negro Man Shall be equally divided between my Grand Daughters Jerusa Ann Sanderson and Elizabeth Sanderson and my Grand Sons Robert Sanderson and William Sanderson they being the sons of my Son Overall (P-83) Sanderson- And if there Should be an Overplus of money, arising from Losson's hire, Then it shall be equally divided between my four grand children above named and now living with me - Also I will and bequeath to my Grand Daughters Jerusha Ann Sanderson and - Sanderson two feather Beds & bed clothes two bedsteads, one table one Safe, and my Kitchin furniture To be equally divided between them- Also that my Cow be sold and t the money equally divided between my Grand Daughters Jerusha Ann Sanderson and Elizabeth Sanderson, Also I choose and Appoint Milton Estill my Executor to this my last Will and testament.

Signed in the Presence of

Elizabeth her X mark Sanderson

Jared S. Edwards E W Brookshire

State of Tennessee)
April Session 1837
Shelby County)

This the last Will & testament of Elizabeth Sanderson, was produced in open Court and Jared S. Edwards a Witness thereto being sworn says that the said Elizabeth Sanderson Signed the Said Will by making her mark thereto & that She was of sound & disposing Mind and Memory and said Will having heretofore been proved by the oath of E.W. Brookshire another Witness thereto is Ordered to be recorded.

Recorded 10 May 1837 John W. Fuller Clk

Test John W Fuller Clk.

(P-84) HOWELL EASON'S WILL

The last Will & testament of Howell D. Eason. In the Name of God I Howell D Eason of Madison County in the State of Alabama do make this my last Will & testament that is.

Item. 1. I will that all my just debts be paid out of my property first.

Item 2. After all my debts are paid it is my Will & desire that my Wife Mary Eason shall have and enjoy all my property whether personal or real in possession or expectancy and I will & bequeath the same to her -

Item 3. I hereby constitute and appoint my beloved Wife Mary Eason my Sole Executrix of this my last Will & testament.

(P-84 cont.) In Testimony whereof I have hereunto Set my hand & Seal this the 29th day of March 1830.

Signed Sealed published & declared in presence of L Mead Wm. H.T. Browne Asa Pryor — Howell D Eason (Seal)

State of Tennessee)
May Sessions 1837
Shelby County Court)

The Last Will & testament of Howell D Eason was produced in open Court and the depositions of Wm. H.T. Browne (P-85) taken in conformity with a Commission issued from this Court being also produced and the Signatures of the said Howell D Eason to the said Will being proven by the said Brown and the Signatures of Asa Pryor another Witness to the said Will being proven by the said Brown and the said Pryor has departed this life It is ORDERED that the said Will be Admitted to record as fully proven.

Recorded 10th May 1837 — John W. Fuller Clk.

Test John W. Fuller Clk

J O H N K B A L C H ' S W I L L

I John K Balch of Shelby County, State of Tennessee, being weak and debilitated in body but of perfectly sound & disposing mind and memory, do make publish and declare this my last Will and testament, hereby revoking all others by me at any time heretofore made, that is to say.

Item first. It is my will and desire, and I hereby direct that my Executrix hereinafter named do proceed as speedily as practicable to the settlement of the business of my Estate by the collection of all debts and demands due to me and the payment of all my just debts.

Item 2nd. I give and bequeath to my beloved wife Amanda Balch all the property of what Nature ~~of~~ Kind or description, soever, real personal and mixed, that I possess during her widowhood, or during her natural life provided she remains unmarried, and in the (P-86) event of her marriage, I I hereby direct that She have and possess one third of all my property, and that the remaining two thirds be equally divided amongst my three children, Nancy Brown, Hugh Wheatley and Samuel Y Balch. And in the event of the future marriage of my wife Amanda it is my Will and desire and I hereby direct, that so soon as Such Marriage may take place, a division of my Property and of the increase thereof may be made between her and my three children as above stated

Item 3rd. It is my Will and desire and I hereby further direct that my Executrix use so much of my Property or the annual Proceeds thereof as will be necessary to maintain and educate my children above Named, in a proper manner, that is and I hereby mean that my said children shall be maintained and educated out of my entire Estate until the Marriage of

(P-86 cont.) my said Wife Amanda in the event she should marry again; and in such event, it is then my Will & desire and I hereby direct that my said children should after that event be maintained and educated by their respective Guardians after a division of my Property is made between my Wife and children as contemplated by a previous item in this my last Will & testament.

Item 4th. I hereby authorize and empower my Said Executrix hereafter named, to Sell and Convey at any time during her Widowhood the tract of land and premises on (P-87) which I now reside, and also any of my Slaves that She may think it best or most to the interest of my Estate to sell. And should my Said tract of land not be Sold at the termination of the Widowhood of my Said Wife I still wish & desire that she sell the same at any Time that she and the guardian of my children may agree & think it best to sell and convey the same.

Item 5th It is my will and especial desire that my Children be well educated, and I leave it at the discretion of my Wife Amanda to make such a division of the Property amongst them I have herein given absolutely to my said Wife as she may think best and most advisable, either by deed of gift in her lifetime or by last Will & testament at her death

Item 6th. And last I hereby appoint my beloved wife Amanda, the sole executrix of this my last Will and testament, and I desire and direct, that She be permitted to qualify and act as executrix without being required to give any Bond or Security whatever as Such, hereby expressly releasing her from giving Bond and Security as Executrix of this my last Will and testament MARCH 20th 1837

Signed, Sealed, and Published John K Balch (Seal)

in presence of us subscribing

Witnesses this 20th March 1837

Test B.H. Hawkins Z.C. Alexander

(P-88) State of Tennessee)
April Sessions 1837
Shelby County Court)

This the last Will & testament of John K. Balch, was produced in open Court and B.H. Hawkins and Z.C. Alexander, witnesses to the same being sworn say that they said Balch, Signed Sealed declared & published the Same to be his last Will & testament and that he the said Balch was of Sound Mind & Memory, & ordered to be recorded.

Recorded 10th May, 1837 Test. JOHN W. FULLER, Clerk

Test John W. Fuller Clk

D A V I D D U N N ' S W I L L

I David Dunn of Shelby County and State of Tennessee, being of

(P-88 cont.) sound mind, do ordain and constitute this my last Will and testament this 12th day of September One Thousand Eight Hundred and thirty Six hereby revoking all other Wills heretofore written -

It is first my Will that all my just debts be paid by my executors to be hereafter Appointed.

It is my Will that my beloved Wife Sarah Dunn have and use for her benefit, during her natural life time three hundred and twenty five acres of land to be taken off the West end of the land I now live on, designated by a line running due South from a point on the northern line, to include (P-89) the /// named 325 acres of land, also to have the use of my negro man Nelson during her natural life time.

I hereby give my Wife Sarah Dunn all the property hereinafter named to wit, the carriage and two Horses all the property got by her of every description whatever four mules, a propertion of all other Stock agreeably to her force, to Judged of by my executors all the Household and Kitchen furniture, plantation utensils sufficient for her use, one yoke of oxen and a waggon if they be on the plantation at my death I also give One thousand dollars to her out of the growing crop at the time of my death. I further give to her One year's provision for her and family -

It is my Will that my daughter Eliz G.E. Deadrick have and possess during her natural life time, all the balance of my Estate both real and personal except such parts as may be hereafter otherwise disposed of at her death, it is my Will that the property be equally divided among all her children then living - as well all her present children as those she may have in case of after Marriage or Marriages.

It is further my Will that Liza my yellow girl, with her offspring, and Madison a yellow boy, the children of Negro woman Casey, be freed, if the laws of this State will not admit of their remaining here as free persons, it shall be the duty of my executor to have them removed from this State to some (P-90) other State where the laws will admit of their freedom, they having the Choice of place or State to which they will be removed - after defraying the expenses of removing them, they shall each have One hundred Dollars which shall be paid to them when they arrive at their place or destination - the above donation of One hundred Dollars is intended to apply to Madison and Liza and Not to Liza's children as might be supposed from the wording of the above donation.

It is my desire that each of my grand children have Two Hundred Dollars as they arrive at the Age of twenty years or marry, to be taken from the profits of my estate, or otherwise to be paid to them by my daughter, Eliza G E. Deadrick.

I do hereby appoint my Brother Dudley Dunn and Littleton Henderson my executors to this my last Will and Testament, I do hereby acknowledge this my last Will and testament to which I have hereunto Set my hand and Seal the day and date above written.

David Dunn (Seal)

Test J.G. Dunn Isaac Rawlings Wm. W. Tucker

The word dollars will be found interlined in or above the 25th line before signed

(P-90 cont.) Shelby County Septr. 17th, 1836.

Addition to the foregoing Will. I hereby bequeath to my Wife Sarah B. Dunn in addition to what I have already bequeathed in the foregoing Will the further (P-91) Sum of Six Hundred Dollars in cash to be expended by her in the purchase of a carriage & to be paid out of my Estate in the same manner, which the other money given her in the aforesaid Will is provided to be paid - I also hereby bequeath to my Grand Daughter Mary E Deadrick in addition to what I have given her in the foregoing Will, two negro girls, Phillis the Daughter of Mary about four years old, and Fanny the Daughter of Maria aged about four years old.

In testimony whereof I have hereunto set my hand & Seal this the 17th Sept in the Year One thousand eight hundred and thirty six

Witness David Dunn (Seal)

Isaac Rawlings S.C. Dunn

Wm. W. Tucker

State of Tennessee)
April Sessions A.D. 1837
Shelby County Court)

This the last Will & testament of David Dunn, was produced in open Court and Samuel G Dunn & W.W. Tucker Witnesses thereto being sworn say that the Said David Dunn signed said last Will & Testament in their presence and declared and Published it as such & that he was of Sound & Disposing Mind & Memory & Ordered to be recorded.

Recorded 10th May 1837 John W. Fuller Clk

Test John W. Fuller Clk

JAMES FRAZIER'S WILL

(P-92) Know all Men by these Presents that I James Frazier of the County of Shelby and State of Tennessee being now weak of Body but of Sound mind and Knowing all men must die, and with a view to Settle my Worldly affairs, make this my last Will and testament, I give to my Nephew D.D. Dickson all the money that is coming to me from my Estates of my deceased Mother and Brother Decatur that is yet unsettled. I give to my Nephew James D. Frazier Six Hundred Dollars and to my Niece Emeline Frazier four Hundred Dollars which Sums is not to be paid to them until they arrive at the age of twenty one Years nor untill my other Debts is paid. I give to my Much lovd wife everything else that I own on earth both real and personal during her life time at the Close of which it is to return to my legal representative. I also appoint my wife Rhoda my sole executrix to Settle all my business to collect & Pay over debts make and Sign Instruments of Writing where it becomes Necessary to do so on my Account, to give No Security Nor to Administer, but to transact business and Settle all things as though I still lived.

In testimony whereof I have hereunto Set my hand and Seal this 23rd

(P-92 cont.) day of January 1837

Witness Present
James Titus
Ebenezer Titus

James Frazier (Seal)

(P-93) State of Tennessee)
April Sessions 1837
Shelby County Court)

This the last Will & testament of James Frazier decd. was produced in open Court and Ebenezer Titus a Witness thereto being sworn says that said Frazier executed the same in his presence and that he was of Sound and disposing mind and Memory & the said Will having heretofore been proven by the oath of James Titus another Witness thereto is Ordered to be Certified & recorded

Test John W. Fuller Clk

February 18th 1837

This is to certify that I allow to my Nephew D.D. Dickson, five Hundred Dollars out of the Note due me from D Spanish in place of the Money due me from my Mother's Estate as I have disposed of that money otherwise

Test.
James Titus Senior

James Titus Junior

James Frazier

State of Tennessee)
March Sessions 1837
Shelby County Court)

This Supplement to the Will of James Frazier, was proven in Open Court by the Oath of James Titus Senr. & James Titus Jun. and Ordered to be recorded.

Recorded 10th May 1837 Test John W. Fuller Clk.

Test John W. Fuller Clk S.C.C.

(P-94) L E V I N A W H E A T L E Y, W I L L

In the Name of God Amen, I Levinah Wheatley of the County of Shelby and State of Tennessee, having perfect soundness of memory make & constitute the following to be my last Will & testament.

Item 1st Whenever it shall please the Almighty to take me from this Earth I desire to be decently buried & without Parade.

Item 2nd. I give and bequeath to my beloved Niece Charlotte Wheatley Haynie Two Negroes Amanda, a girl about Seventeen years of age & Will

(P-94 Cont.) a boy of about Twelve years of age; Also one feather bed & furniture, also one Trunk.

Item 3rd. I give & bequeath to my Nephew John W. Haynie, one negro girl of the age of 10 years named Lucinda.

Item 4. I give & bequeath to my Nephew Wesley Haynie One Negro Girl Sarah Susan about 7 years of age.

Item 5. I give & bequeath to my Nephew Thornton Haynie a negro boy of the name of Spencer aged Sixteen years.

Item 6th. In the event of the death of either of my Nephews herein mentioned without heirs by marriage it is my Will that the bequests herein made to him or any one of them, so dying be & is hereby made the property of my Niece Charlotte Wheatley Haynie & should my Niece Charlotte W. Haynie, die without heir I will the property herein bequeathed to her & hereby make it the joint property of my Nephews John W. Haynie, Wesley (P-95) Haynie and Thornton Haynie, each having an equal interest in it.

Item 7th. I hereby enjoin upon the four children to whom I have made the above bequests to maintain & support during their natural lives their father George Haynie & their Mother Celia Haynie.

Item 8th. I appoint my Nephew John W. Haynie Executor & my Niece Charlotte W. Haynie Executrix of this my last will & testament & require Not that either of them give security for the faithful execution of their duties as such, having full confidence in their rectitude and qualifications.

In testimony of all of which I hereunto Set my hand and Seal, this thirtieth day of May in the Year of Our Lord Eighteen Hundred & Thirty Six.

Witness Levinah Wheatley (LS)

Hugh Wheatley Jno. K. Balch)
James S. Faris)

State of Tennessee)
April Sessions 1837
Shelby County Court)

This the last will & testament, of Levina Wheatley, was produced in open Court, and being heretofore proven by the oath of J.L. Faris, a witness thereto, then came Seth Wheatley and S.R. Brown and being sworn say that Hugh Wheatly and John K. Balch, two other witnesses to the Same have departed this life and that their signatures is in their own proper hand. It is ordered that the (P-96) Said Will be recorded fully Proven,

Recorded 11 May 1837) Test John W Fuller Clerk

Test John W. Fuller Clk)

(P-96 cont.) B E R T H I E R J O N E S ' W I L L

I Berthier Jones of sound mind and memory do make and ordain this my last Will & Testament -

1st. It is my will and desire that all my just debts be paid-

2nd It is my Will and desire that my estate be Kept together until my Daughters become of age or get married at which time I wish it to be equally divided between them- I hereby appoint my brothers Lafayette Jones Chamberlayne Jones & Ceasar A Jones Executors of this my last Will and Testament and Guardians of my Children- It is my Will and desire that my Daughters should be put under the care and protection of my Aunt Chatham Greenhill until they are old enough to go to school-

In Witness Whereof I have hereunto set my hand and Seal this 28th April 1837

In presence of P G. Gaines Berthier Jones (Seal)

J.R. Frayser

CODICIL It is my Will and desire that my brothers abovementioned, should have the right and liberty to manage my estate precisely as they would their own; that is to dispose of property whenever it will be to the interest of the children, and in fact to do anything in relation to the Estate which they think will promote (P-97) the interest of my children-

In Witness Whereof I have hereunto Set my hand and seal this April 28th 1837.

P G. Gaines J.R. Frayser Berthier Jones (Seal)

State of Tennessee)
June Sessions 1837
Shelby County)

The last Will & Testament of Berthier Jones was produced in open Court and J.R. Frayser a Witness thereto being sworn, says that the said Jones executed Published and declared the same to be his last Will and Testament- and that he was of sound disposing mind & memory and ordered to be filed for further probate.

Recorded June 2nd 1837 Test J W Fuller Clk.

Test John W Fuller Clk

* (Editor's Note: This is a new page but is numbered also "97" really being 98)

* (P-97 -A)

(P-97 A. cont.) L U C Y T R I G G S W I L L

State of Tennessee)

Shelby County)

Whereas life is uncertain I Lucy Trigg of the County and State aforesaid do make this my last Will and Testament-

Whereas I have in pursuance of a decree of the Chancery Court at Carthage sold the Land on Drakes Creek which was decreed by my decd husband to my Son Alexander for the sum of Six thousand dollars. And further in pursuance of said decree I have sold the land on Bartons Creek in Wilson County for $3510 which property belonged by said will jointly to my two sons Henry and Stephen Trigg And also one tract on Spring Creek for $2500 belonging to H. & S. having sold said lands for the purpose of investing the money in lands which would ultimately be more profitable. In pursuance of such purpose, I have purchased in Shelby County near Memphis two tracts of Land To Wit. One tract which I purchased of John C McLemore, at $10.29/100 per acre or $7,498 which is to be divided between Henry and Stephen as to quantity and quality, agreeably to the amount of money this land sold for in Wilson County, they paying $10.29/100 per acre there will be a balance coming out of the above land after paying Henry and Stephen. The other tract I purchased of Charles Lewis at $15, per acre which my son Alexander is to have in part for said six thousand dollars abovementioned the balance is to come out of the McLemore tract after paying Henry & Stephen - -

(P-98) There will be a balance left after paying Henry Stephen and Alexander - purchased by my own money - which they can have after paying my three daughters Nancy Shanault, Jane Rent and Mary Trigg $10.29/100 per acre to be equally divided between them the said three daughters- And further give and bequeath to my daughter Mary Trigg my carriage. And it is my wish will and desire that my children acquiesce in and be satisfied with this my last Will & Testament and take no exceptions to it on account my informality in the wording of it-

In testimony whereof I have hereunto set my hand and affixed my Seal this 31st day of July 1836

Test

L P Wagnor

Lucy her X mark Trigg (Seal)

Leonidas Sanders Sworn to in open Court

Test J.W. Fuller Clk S.C.C. Recorded Oct. 26 1837.

(P-99) E L I Z A B E T H B R O W N ' S W I L L

In the Name of God Amen. I Elizabeth Brown being weak in body but in my proper mind, Knowing that I am born to die, doth make this my last will and Testament.

First. I will my Soul to my God who made me, and my body to be de-

(P-99 cont.) cently buried. As to my worldly Estate My Will is that the land I now ~~live on~~ am seized and possessed of shall be equally divided between my two Sons Benj. Brown and Jesse Brown, which I give unto them and their heirs forever. I also give unto my daughter Louisa, one Brown Heifer by the name of Cherry. I moreover give unto my son Jesse one bay mare, one milch Cow & Yearling - I give unto my Daughter Amantha Hoffman one spotted cow & one bed blanket or counterpane. I give unto Louisa one Blanket or coverlet. I give one bed blanket or coverlet to Jesse And also one Sow & eight pigs.

All my household property my Will is Shall be Equally divided between Benjamin Jesse and Louisa

Witness I hereunto Set my hand & Affix my Seal the 3rd day of March 1837

her
Elizabeth X Brown (Seal)
mark

In presence of R.B. Daniel
her
Sarah X Phillips
mark

State of Tennessee)
Nov Sessions 1837
Shelby County Court)

A competent Court present, A paper purporting to be the last will and testament of Elizabeth Brown was produced in open Court, and proven by R.B. Daniel & Sarah Phillips. It is therefore ordered to be recorded

Test J W Fuller Clk

(P-100) ~~LAST WILL & TESTAMENT OF EDWARD WARD~~

~~In the name of Almighty God, Amen - I Edward Ward of the County of Shelby & State of Tennessee being of sound mind and disposing memory, make and ordain this my last Will and Testament, in manner and form following, viz,~~

~~In primis, I will and devise to my nephew John W. Jones all my landed Estate & all my negroes that are not herein hereafter specially disposed of to other persons. All my stock of horses, cattle sheep & Hogs All my plantation implements, my riding carriage & Sulkey and Waggons and two thirds of my household furniture~~

(P-101) LAST WILL & TESTAMENT OF EDWARD WARD

In the name of Almighty God Amen -

I Edward Ward of the county of Shelby & State of Tennessee being of sound mind and disposing memory make & ordain this my last will & Testament in manner and form following, viz

(P-101 cont.) Inprimis. I will and devise to my nephew John W. Jones, all my landed estate and all my negroes that are not herein hereafter specially disposed of to other persons - All my stock of horses cattle sheep and hogs. All my plantation implements, my riding carriage & Sulky and waggons, and two thirds of my household and kitchen furniture - all the provisions for man & beasts & the crop that may be on hand or growing on my farms at the time of my death, Together with all money on hand or that may be owing me, bonds, or open account ~~or otherwise~~ To him and his heirs forever - - I will all my just debts to be paid by John W Jones out of the above Legacy left him - - - - Secondly, I will & devise to my nephew Robert B Jones, the following negroes Hall, Janey, Powell, Alboa, Molly, Armin, Polly, (w Mary, Margarett, Dorcas & Lilly, with the children they now have with them, and their future increase to him and his heirs forever - Thirdly I will & devise to my nephew Peter Munford Jones, son of Prudence Jones, the following negroes. Emanuel, Edmund, little Ben, Drury, John (Isaac) Joe, Billy, Sally, Ervin & Harriette and their past and future increase, to them and their heirs forever- Fourthly, I leave to my niece Virginia Upshaw during her natural life the following negroes (P-102) Melville, Nancy Pallas & Lucy with their past & future increase, to be divided at her death among the heirs of her body as She may see cause, to them and their heirs forever. I leave her in the same way (a piece) a piece of land, quantity unknown, on the North East corner of the Alexander tract bounded on the South by a line and marked by myself. I also will to my sd. niece Virginia Upshaw the one third part of my household and Kitchen furniture to her and her heirs - Fifthly, I devise by way of loan to my niece Martha Jane Jones, daughter of John W. Jones the following negroes during her life. - Peter, Susan, Anthony & Patsy, Elizabeth & child, Matilda (S) Rhoda & Emily to be divided among the heirs of her body should she have any at her death, as She may see cause, But should she die without issue, that it is my will that they and their increase shall be equally divided amongst her brothers & sisters, to them and their heirs forever. Sixthly, I will and devise to my niece Alethea Munford Jones by way of loan, the following negroes, Lucilla- Franky, Marcia, and Peggy, during her life to be divided amongst the heirs of her body(should She have any at her death) as she may see cause, but should she die without issue, then it is my will that they and their increase shall belong to her father John W. Jones, to him and his heirs forever Seventhly I will and devise to my nephew Albert G Ward a negro girl by name of Malinda with her future increase to him and his heirs forever - - Seventhly, my will & desire is that Tony & Kever, Old Israel & Ussa, Davy & Nan Surry & Sally his mother, and Sam be considered as five separate & distinct families, to be provided for as such, and are not to be esteemed or held as personal property to descend to any of my relations. I will to each of these five families a lifetime Estate(Editor's Note: (P-102) is here duplicated) of eighty acres of land to be selected out of my Brownland estate, convenient to a spring or springs to each family. I further will that my Executors have built for each family one eighteen feet square Cabin with plank floor, 2 smaller houses for crib & poultry that each family be furnished with a good sixty dollar horse or mare or mule, one cow & calf and a two year old heifer, one sow and five or six pigs, twenty barrels of corn & a stack of fodder & 100 lb. of pork one good turning plough and necessary gear, one good axe, 2 weeding hoes, one wedge, one drawing knife, 2 augers, one handsaw, four good new blankets, winter and summer suit of clothing, shoes socks & hat, 2 bushels of Salt, one pot & kettle, one pail & Tub, and twenty yards of good strong plain domestic cloth. It is my will that the different

(Duplicate (P-102) cont.) families of the old people die that their portion of the land revert to John W. Jones & heirs- The portions allotted to Sam & Surry I will to them in fee simple - Should they wish to sell & John W. Jones or any, other regularly appointed agent shall consent for them to sell, then I will that the aforesaid John W. Jones or aforesaid agent as the case may be shall make title to said land as my executor, or as agent acting in accordance with this provision of my will-

I constitute and appoint John W. Jones Robert B Jones & Peter Munford Jones, Executors to this my last will and testament, revoking and making null and void all others by me heretofore made.

In witness in Witness whereof I have hereunto set my hand and affixed my seal this 30th day of September in the year of our Lord Christ 1837

Acknowledged before us Edward Ward (Seal)

(P-103) It is understood that what is written on this page has been written before the body of this will had been signed or witnessed and therefore is to be considered as a part of my last will and Testament--

I will and desire that my two old servants Isaac the Smith & Charles the carriage driver be liberated & each given fifty dollars cash and a full suit of respectable clothes. Isaac will be fully able to provide for himself by his trade, and Charles will be fully provided for by his Children in or about Nashville. Signed as within Sept. 30th 1837.

Edward Ward (Seal)

Acknowledged before us

State of Tennessee)
January Term 1838
Shelby County Court)

A competent Court present This day was produced in open Court a paper writing purporting to be the last will and Testament of Edward Ward deceased, and having the name of said Ward subscribed thereto - And thereupon came into Court A.D. Hunter & J P Thompson, who being duly sworn said that said paper writing was found among the valuable papers of said Ward and thereupon also came into Court, A D Hunter, James P Thompson and J.E. Munford creditable witnesses who being sworn said that said paper writing is in the handwriting of said Ward, and that the said handwriting is generally known by the acquaintances of said Ward, and that they believe said paper writing and every part thereof to be in the handwriting of said Ward, Said will is therefore ordered to be recorded. -

I John W. Fuller Clerk of the County Court of Shelby County in compliance with the requisition of the above order have recorded the said Will this 11th day of January 1838

John W Fuller Ck S C C

per T H Hayden Dpty

(Editor's Note: On Original MS Page No. is 105 should be 104)

(P-105) M R S A M A N D A B A L C H' S W I L L

State of Tennessee)

Shelby County)

To all whom it may concern.

Know ye that I Amanda Balch widow of the late John K. Balch of the County and State aforesaid do make publish and declare this my last will and testament being weak and debilitated in body but of perfectly sound and disposing mind and memory that is to say

Item 1st I hereby give and bequeath unto my two children Nancy Brown and Hugh Wheatley Balch all and every part and particle of the property real personal and mixed which I have hold and possess and which by the last will and testament of my said husband I am authorized and empowered to give and bequeath by my last will and testament to be equally divided betweem them and the survivors of them, in the event of the death of either of them without lawful heirs, but should they or either of them die leaving lawful issue, then all the property herein bequeathed and given to belong and to rest absolutely in my children and their heirs forever or to the survivor of them should either die without issue.

Item 2nd In the event of the death of both of my children abovenamed without lawful heirs by either of them. Then and in that case I hereby give all the property abovementioned to my two sisters Marie Louisa & Susan Charlotte Wheatley and to my two nieces Mary Ann and Frances Adelaide Brown to be equally divided between my two Sisters and two nieces. At the death of the last one of any(P-106) children without issue - - -

Item 3rd I hereby expressly authorize and empower my Executor hereinafter named to sell and convey at his discretion the tract of land mentioned in the last Will and Testament of my said husband and by him authorized and requested to be sold being the same tract on which I now reside also any of the Slaves mentioned in my said husband's Will and which pass to my legatees by his Will it being intended by me to give and confer upon my executors hereinafter named all the powers and authority to sell and convey said land and negroes that I in my own right as executrix of the last will and Testament of my said husband have and possess, and am capable and authorized by law to give & confer and should my executor hereinafter mentioned sell said land and Slaves or any or either of them I hereby give and confer upon him full power and authority to vest the funds of such sale or sales in any manner whatever that he may think best at his discretion for the benefit of my said children and those interested in the event of their death

Item 4th I hereby further will devise and direct that my executor sell as speedily as practicable all my household and Kitchen furniture farming utensils & stock of every description and whatever other property he may think proper either at private or at public sale and apply the proceeds to the payment of my debts and those of my late husband.

(P-107) Item 5th and last I hereby appoint my only surviving brother Seth

(P-107 cont.) Wheatley, Executor of this my last Will and Testament. And I also hereby appoint my said brother Seth Wheatley Sole Guardian of my two children and I do hereby will and direct that he be permitted and authorized to qualify & act as sole executor of this my last will and testamant and guardian of my children without being required to give bond or security either as executor or as guardian as aforesaid, and having full confidence and trust in my said brother I leave at his direction to manage and employ all and every part and particle of the property that may come into his hands as Executor and guardian any way or manner that he may deem best and that may in his judgment be most advisable for the interest of all concerned only enjoining upon him that he have my children raised & educated in the best and most approved style and manner sparing no reasonable expenditure that may in his judgment be necessary for that purpose.

In testimony whereof I have hereunto set my hand and affixed my seal this the 25th day of December 1837.

her
Amanda X Balch (Seal)
mark

Signed Sealed and published in the presence of the undersigned Subscribing Witnesses the 25th day of December 1837

Test
B H Hawkins
G.C. Aledander
John Dixon

(P-108) I Amanda Balch, since making and signing of the foregoing last will and Testament have concluded and determined to change and alter the same so far as relates to my interest I have and am entitled to in the estate of my deceased brother Hugh Wheatley and by way of codicil to the above and foregoing will I hereby give bequeath relinquish and devise to my two Sisters Alma Louisa Wheatley and Susan Charlotte Wheatley and to the Survivor of them should either die without heirs all the right, title claim and interest that I have or am entitled to in the estate of my said deceased brother Hugh Wheatly - real personal and mixed - My interest and claim in and to said estate be equally divided between my two sisters abovementioned - - and I hereby confirm the above and foregoing will in all respects except so far as same is changed and altered by this codicil pertaining only to my interest in the estate of the said Hugh Wheatly Deceased

In Witness Whereof I have hereunto set my hand and affixed my Seal this 25th day of December 1837-

her
Amanda XBalch
mark

Signed Sealed and delivered in presence of us subscribing Witnesses.
Test
B H Hawkins Z C Alexander
John Dixon

State of Tennessee)
April Term 1838
Shelby County Court)

A paper purporting to be the last Will and testament of Amanda

(P-108 cont.) Balch (P-109) was produced into Court, and B H Hawkins and Z C. Alexander Subscribing Witnesses to the same being duly sworn depose and say that they were present at the execution of the same and that the said testator was at the time of sound and disposing mind and memory, ordered that the Same be recorded - and Seth Wheatley the Executor therein named came into Court and qualified as Executor thereto ordered that he have letters accordingly-

I John W. Fuller Clerk of the said Court do hereby certify that the foregoing is a true copy of the Will and order relating thereto-

Recorded this 4th day of June 1838

John W Fuller Clk

F R A N C I S M C M A H A N S W I L L

I Francis McMahan of Memphis Tennessee do make and publish this my last Will and Testament hereby revoking and making void all other wills by me at any ~~other~~ time made. First it is my desire and do direct that my funeral expenses and all my honest debts be paid as soon after my death as possible out of any monies that I may die possessed of or may first come into the hands of my Executor

2ndly. I give and bequeath to my Sister Elizabeth (wife of Arrington Howard) and her heirs one thousand dollars.

Thirdly. I give and bequeath to my niece Minerva Lemon one thousand dollars

Fourthly. I give to my brother Cornelius C McMahan all of the balance of residue of my (P-110) Estate both real and personal after paying over as provided for in the first second and third provisions of this instrument

Lastly I do hereby nominate constitute and appoint Cornelius C McMahan (my brother) my Executor

IN WITNESS WHEREOF I do to this my Will Set my hand Seal this 28th day of January 1838

Signed Sealed and published Francis McMahan (Seal)

in our presence.

James D Currin

J W Fowler

State of Tennessee)
March Term 1838
Shelby County Court)

A paper purporting to be the last Will and Testament of Francis

(P-110 cont.) McMahan Deceased was ~~brough~~ produced into open Court & John W. Fowler a Subscribing witness thereto being sworn says that he was present at the Execution of the Same and that the said Testator was of sound mind and disposing memory and that he Signed and Sealed and delivered the same in his presence on the day it be and date ordered that Said will be filed for further probate-

State of Tennessee)
April Term 1838-
Shelby County Court-)

James D Currin a Subscribing Witness to the last Will and Testament of Francis McMahan Deceased came into Court and being sworn said that he was present at the time of the execution of said will and that the said Testator was of sound mind and dispos (P-111) ing memory, at the time he Signed Sealed & published the same as his last will and Testament Ordered that Said will be recorded.

The foregoing is a true copy of the Last Will and Testament of Francis McMahan and the probate thereof- WITNESS

Recorded June 7th 1838 J W Fuller Clk S C C

J O H N B O W E N ' S W I L L

By this my last Will and Testament I appoint my friend James Blasingame the Executor of my Estate

Article 1st I Wish Mr. Blasingame to collect an open account due me by M.B. Winchester the amount four hundred and thirty five dollars for services on the ferry boat- I also request my Executor to collect the following open account - by one Joshua Hicks for some fifteen dollars. Also an account on G Joiner for some twenty seven dollars -

Article Second. I desire my Executor to collect all monies that he may find due me & to liquidate all just claims against me-

3rd. I wish my Executor to pay out of the funds thus collected as above to pay to my brother James one hundred dollars, which I bequeath him and to my Sister Anna a Similar amount that is to say one hundred dollars The residue I desire my Executor to hand to my wife-

(P-112) Signed in the presence of

the Testator. Witnesses Samuel Mosby
W O Kimbrough

his
John X Bowen
mark

Codicil

Myself and O.B. Knickerbocker are trading at the ferry landing on the ferry wharf boat in copartnership - I desire my Executor at my death to have a settlement with Lard Knickerbocker and collect and pay over my portion of the profit or loss as the case ~~may~~ be. I have ~~more a hundred~~ on

(P-112 cont.) hand of monies belonging to the concern one hundred and Seventy one dollars which I wish taken into consideration in the settlement any monies thence accruing I leave to my wife.

his
John X Bowen
mark

WITNESSES Saml. Mosby

Wm. Kimbrough

State of Tennessee)
July Term 1838.
Shelby County)

It appearing to the satisfaction of the Court that at the April Term of this Court a paper purporting to be the last Will and testament of John Bowen was produced into open Court and was proven in due form of law by W. Kimbrough one of the Subscribing witnesses thereto, and date said probate had failed to be heard, it is ordered that the same be entered upon record as of that term.

Recorded July 9 1838. John W Fuller Clk S C C

State of Tennessee)
May Term 1838
Shelby County Court)

The last Will and Testament of John Bowen deceased was produced in open Court and Samuel Mosely as Witness to the Same says that he saw the said John Bowen deceased sign Said will in his presence and declare the same to be his act and deed and to the best of his knowledge and belief the said John Bowen was at the time of Signing the same in sound mind and memory which is ordered to be certified and recorded-

Recorded (Editor's Note: writing obliterated) 1838 J W Fuller Clk

(P-113) W M T T H O M P S O N ' S W I L L

In the Name of God Amen! I William T Thompson of the town of Memphis Shelby County and State of Tennessee Being in good health but intending a journey to New Orleans, and aware of the uncertainty of life, Do make this my last will and testament. First at my death I will and bequeath all my property consisting of my lot in the town of Memphis Tennessee No. 170, as will be seen by reference to the plan of said town with all the houses and improvements thereon. And all my household furniture, and whatsoever else I may die possessed of, to my wife Catherine Thompson during her natural life - - Second - At the death of my wife Catherine Thompson I will and bequeath (should she outlive me) that the land property consisting of my lot No 170 in the Town of Memphis, Shelby County Tennessee with the improvements thereon all the household furniture then remaining, and whatsoever remaining which I shall die possessed of, equally between my son Daniel Washington Thompson and her son Wm. Ormsly.

Third Should I outlive my wife Catherine Thomson At my death I

(P-113 cont.) bequeath the aforesaid property equally to the said Daniel ..ington Thomson and William Ormsly-

Fourth At this time I am out of debt, I appoint my wife Catherine Thompson as my Executrix of my Estate - & that she be not required to give security in being so-

In Testimony Whereof I have hereunto affixed my hand and Seal this the 30th May 1834.

Witnesses: Isaac Rawlings, Wm. T. his X mark Thomson (Seal)

Thomas Dixon & Saml. Finley

(P-114) State of Tennessee)
Court April Term 1838
Shelby County)

Isaac Rawlings and Thomas Dixon Subscribing Witnesses to the last will and Testament of Wm. T. Thompson, who was duly summoned to appear and give evidence in relation to said came into Court and being first sworn depose and say that the said Thompson, was at the time of the execution of his said last Will and Testament of sound mind and disposing memory and that he published the same as such. Ordered therefore that the said Will be recorded - -

Recorded June 7th 1838

John W Fuller Clk

J A N E W I L S O N ' S W I L L

State of Tennessee)

Shelby County)

I Jane Wilson of the town of Memphis being of sound and perfect mind and memory do make and publish this my last will and Testament in manner and form following. That is to Say -

I give and bequeath unto my mother Rachel Tarlton, of said Town all and every part and portion of the property that I now own possess have or claim title to real as well as personal, or that I may herafter acquire either in said State of Tennessee or elsewhere especially I give bequeath and devise unto my Mother the said Rachel Tarltón, a entire lot or parcel of ground situate lying and being in (P-115) in the City of Cincinnati and State of Ohio being the same lot or parcel of ground conveyed by deed to me the said Jane Wilson bearing date the 21st day of December 1818. Executed by William Hood, John Hood, Eleanor Hood and Elizabeth Hood. Which said deed is duly registered in the recorder's office of Hamilton County in the State of Ohio in Book T. page fifty six (56) and for a more particular description of which reference is hereby had to the said deed on record as aforesaid and I do hereby appoint my mother the said Rachel Tarlton my sole Executrix of this my last will and Testament hereby revoking all former wills by me made-

In Witness Whereof I have hereunto set my hand and affixed my

(P-115 cont.) Seal this 13th day of August 1836

Witnesses present
Seth Wheatly)
Jos. Bohannon
Charles B. Murray)

Jane Wilson (Seal)

State of Tennessee)
May Term 1838
Shelby County Court)

The last Will and Testament of Jane Wilson deceased was produced into open Court and Seth Wheatly and C.B. Murray witnesses to the same being sworn say that they saw the said Jane Wilson sign the said Will, in their presence and declare the same to be her act and deed and to the best of their knowledge and belief the said Jane Wilson was at the time of the signing the same, of sound mind and memory which is ordered to be certified and recorded.

Recorded June 7, 1838

John W. Fuller Clk.

(P-116) T H O M A S A . R A S H ' S W I L L

Know all men by these presents that I Thomas A Rash being of sound mind but weak in body do make this my last Will & Testament

WITNESSETH that I give and bequeath unto my beloved wife Marilla T Rash & her heir (should she prove to be pregnant at my death) all the property money and bonds that I possess on earth, with the exception of one hundred dollars that I give to my uncle Robert Rash of Virginia, and forty dollars to John Sneed of Virginia for twenty dollars that I am owing him - - Given under my hand this 12th June 1838.

John W Stout

Henry McCallan

Thomas A Rash

State of Tennessee)
July Sessions 1838.
Shelby County Court)

A paper purporting to be the last Will and Testament of Thomas A Rash was produced into open Court and Henry McCallen, a Subscribing witness thereto being first sworn deposes and says that he was present at the execution of said Will and Signed his name thereto in the presence of the testator, and that the said Testator was of sound and disposing mind and memory and that he published the same in his presence to be his last Will and Testament. Whereupon it is ordered that said Will be established as to personal property & be recorded. And no Executor being therein named Richard Leake came into Court & Entered into bond and Security & qualified as administrator with the deed annexed upon the Estate of the said Thomas A Rash deceased

Recorded July 9th 1838

J W Fuller Clk S C C

(P-117) In the name of god amen. I Thomas Miller, a citizen of the United States of the State of Tennessee and County of Shelby, and a native of Ireland, being of sound mind and mindful of my mortality, do make, ordain, and declare this instrument to be my last will and testament, revoking all others.

Imprimis. I give and bequeath to my nephew William Miller, the son of my brother, James Miller, who is now and has been for some time absent to Indiana, the one half of a tract of land, lying and being in the State of Kentucky five miles from Casey's Landing on the Ohio river, opposite the mouth of Saline Creek, and eight miles from Shawneetown the State of Illinois which said tract contains Eleven hundred thirty acres more of less and formerly belonged to General Breckinridge - To have and to hold the said one half of the said tract of land to the said William Miller and his heirs and assigns forever.

Item. But whereas it is very uncertain Whether the said William Miller is alive at this time & if alive Whether he will ever return to take & to hold the above legacy herein bequeathed to him. Therefore I will and ~~bequeath~~ do hereby give and bequeath to Joseph Bohannan & Doctor Wyatt Christian of the town of Memphis & State of Tennessee the aforesaid one half of the eleven hundred and thirty acres to have and to hold to them their heirs and assigns forever, provided, the aforesaid William Miller Should never return from Indiana and Should he return at any time - whatever, then the aforesaid legacy to him is confirmed & that to the said Joseph Bohannan & Wyatt Charistian is to be null & void

Item I give and bequeath the other half Moiety of the aforesaid eleven hundred & thirty acres of land lying and being situate as aforesaid to Nicholas Casey, Junior James Casey, Samuel Casey and Peter Casey, four Brothers & the sons of Nicholas Casey, Senr. who is a citizen of the State of Kentucky.

(P-118) It is my will and desire that each of the aforesaid Brothers shall hold an equal share of the ~~aforesaid~~ one half of said tract of land viz. I give to each the one-fourth of the said one half of the eleven hundred and thirty acres of land to have and to hold to them and their heirs and assigns forever.

Item - I give and bequeath to Richard L. Bohannan, of the town of Memphis and Mary C. Christian, Sally F. Christian and Caroline W. Christian, who are the daughters of Doctor Wyatt Christian, of the town of Memphis,as aforesaid, a tract of land lying and being in the State of Ohio and written the Picaway Plains, containing twelve hundred acres more or less and which is now in Suit & is under the management of John Sergeant Esq. of Washington City, To have and to hold the aforesaid twelve hundred acres of land to the aforesaid Richard L Bohannan and Mary C & Sally F & Caroline W. Christian and to their heirs and assigns forever.

~~Item I give and bequeath to the said Dr. Wyatt and to the said son~~

Item. Whereas I hold and own the one half, and the one half of the one sixteenth (1/2 & 1/2 of 1/16th) of a tract of land lying and being in Chesterfield County Virginia and is commonly called the Black Heath tract,

(P-118)cont.) and Whereas the said interest in said tract is now in Suit and litigation & is not yet disposed of That I know of. Therefore I will and do give and bequeath all my interest - said tract of land to Doctor Wyatt Christian of the town of Memphis as aforesaid To have & to hold the said interest, whatsoever it may turn out to be - the said tract of land to the said doctor Wyatt Christian and to his heirs and assigns forever.

Item I give and bequeath to the said Dr. W Christian and to the said Joseph Bohannan the following personal estate, viz. one fine blooded Brood mare called Jane Shore, one dark bay filly sired, by Telegraph, now three years old, her dam being the said Jane Shore.(P-119) Also one horse colt foaled this Spring out of the said dam, Jane Shore, Sired by Marshal Ney. Also a Betrand Mare named Betsy Miller and also one fine Stallion named Highlander now standing - the vicinity of Memphis.

Item. I charge the last aforesaid legacy to Dr. Christian & Joseph Bohannan with the payment of a debt I owe Thomas Johnson, & Wm. Park and Co. of town of Memphis.

Item. To the aforementioned Nicholas Casey Jr. I give and bequeath my Brown filly, four years old her dam being my mare Jennet-

Item. To the aforementioned James Casey, I give and bequeath my sorrel Filly, three years old out of the same dam - Jennet-

Item I give and bequeath to the aforementioned Samuel Casey, my three year old filly out of the Polly Dobson Mare.

Item. I give and bequeath to the aforementioned Peter Casey, who is a cripple my Brood Mare named Jennet.

Item I will and desire that my two horses Dick & George, Dick being a three year old, and George a four and also a Brown filly, being a different filly from the one heretofore bequeathed to Nicholas Casey, Jr. may be sold by my executors hereinafter appointed to pay a debt to Mrs. Martin, a Sister Lewis R. Richards.

Item. All the rest & residue of my estate whether real or personal not disposed of - manner aforesaid - whatsoever, consisting whatsoever lying and wheresoever found, I desire may be sold by my executors at such time - Such manner and on Such terms as in their judgment Shall be most conducive to the interest of my estate, and the moneys arising thereform to be disposed of - the (P-120) first place, the payment of all my just debts not heretofore provided for, and secondly the residue after paying my debts whatsoever it may be shall be the property of said executors

Lastly, I constitute and appoint, Wyatt Christian, Joseph Bohannan my executors of this my last Will & testament.

In ~~Testimony~~ Witness thereof, and of all and each of the things herein contained, I have set my hand and Seal this 14th day of July in the year of our lord, one thousand eight hundred and thirty eight and of the independence of the United States the Sixty third.

Signed Sealed & delivered in presence Thomas Miller (Seal)

(P-120 cont.) of us who have Subscribed

in the presence of each other & in the

presence of the testator. James T. Leath Test)

John B Fenny   Recorded Septr. 5th 1838.

Justin Smith   J.W. Fuller Clk.

State of Tennessee)

September Sessions 1838

Shelby County Court)

A paper writing purporting to be the last will and testament of Thos. Miller, decd was produced in Court and James T. Leath, John B. Fenny and Justin Smith, Subscribing witnesses thereto, being sworn depose and say, that the said Thomas Miller at the time of Signing of same was of Sound mind, and disposing memory and that he made declared and published the same in their presence to be his last will and testament, which is ordered to be recorded and thereupon ~~same~~ Wyatt Christian & Jos. Bohannan executors therein named, came into court ~~and~~ entered into bond and Security and qualified as such as the law requires.

J.W. Fuller, CLK.

(P-121) In the name of God Amen. I Vivant Quinichett of the County of Shelby and State of Tennessee, do make and ordain this my last will and testament in manner & form following revoking all others heretofore made by me, To wit.

Item 1st. I give my soul to god who gave it.

Item 2nd I desire that all my Just debts be paid by my Extrs. hereafter named.

Item 3rd. My will and desire is that my estate be kept together as long as my white family remains together, thereby releasing my negroes from the Servitude of being hired out. Allowing however to my beloved wife the privilege at any convenient season, to hire out some of the negroes to the neighbors if she thinks proper for her convenience but they are by no means to be considered crop hands hired out in the usual way by the year as long as they as my Estate

Item 4th, Should either of my children marry after my death my will and desire is that my Extrs give to Said child or children the full proportion of that child or children's part of my estate reserving a portion in value in property, or money of two thousand dollars to aid my beloved wife and Extrs. in the ardous task of educating my youngest children. And at the close of the education of my beloved children, I wish this two thousand dollars with its increase of value, to be paid to my married childred and those of my younger children When they arrive to lawful age

Item 5th. My will and intention is that should please God to cause me to live a few years to purchase a portion of land for each one of my

(P-121 cont.) children Thereby my Extrs. will be enable to give to my children, a moiety of land without interfering with my beloved wife, wishing her to (P-122) remain on my mansion house tract of land if she likes best or going anywhere else in or out of the State, but the negroes with the exception of enough for her convenience, are not to be carried out of the State

It is my wish that my three youngest children be placed under the care and guardianship of my two esteemed and confidential friends hereafter named as my executors, and that they have the entire control of their education, in sending them to the best seminaries of the country or anywhere else, should my estate be sufficient adhering strictly to their morals

Item 6th. It will be necessary for my representatives to select for the good management of my estate, prudent, humane, careful, sober, industrious & honest men, who can come well recommended as such-

Item 7th. I nominate and appoint my worthy and esteemed friends William B. Hamblin & Jon F. Hamblin whom I have partially raised Extrs to my last Will and testament & friends to my beloved family, hereby revoking all and every other will heretofore made by me

Test. Geor. H. Wyatt)
Saml. D. Key John D. White) Vivant Quinichette (Seal)

State of Tennessee)
October Sessions A.D. 1838.
Shelby County)

A paper purporting to be the last will and testament of Vivant Quinichette was produced in open court, and John D. White and Samuel D. Key Subscribing witnesses thereto being sworn depose and Say that the said Vivant Quinichett at the time of the signing of the same was of sound mind and disposing memory and that he made declared and published the same in their presence to be his last will and testament which is ordered to be recorded.

Recorded October 15, 1838. J.W. Fuller

(P-123) In the name of god amen,

I Richard Anderson of the County of Shelby and State of Tennessee and now on a visit to the County of Wilson, and State aforesaid, being of sound ~~mind~~ & disposing mind do make constitute and ordain, this my last Will and testament.

Item 1st. It is my Will that all my just debts be paid so soon as practicable

Item 2nd. I will and bequeath unto my wife, Elizabeth Anderson, all the residue of my estate both real and personal, after the payment of my just debts to have and to hold forever for her own proper use and benefit

I appoint and constitute my wife Elizabeth Anderson, and my friend Joseph Kirkpatrick, my Executor to this my last will and testament

(P-123 cont.) In testimony whereof I have hereunto subscribed my name, and set my Seal, this 22nd day of June, 1836

In presence of Jas. H. Britton, Richard Anderson (Seal)

Johnathan Wallac

State of Tennessee)
October Sessions A.D. 1839.
Shelby County)

A paper writing purporting to be the last Will and testament of Richard Anderson, was produced in court, and James H. Britton & Johnathan Wallace Subscribing Witnesses thereto being sworn depose and say, that the said Richard Anderson at the time of the signing the same was of sound and disposing mind and that he made, declared and published the same in their presence to be his last Will and testament which is ordered to be recorded.

Recorded October 18th 1838 J. W. Fuller Clk

(P-124) W M. H Y N E S ' W I L L

I William Hynes of the county of Shelby in the State of Tennessee having in view the uncertainty of life & the certainty of death and being desirous of settling my estate upon my children according to my own wishes and being of sound mind and disposing memory, do make ordain and declare this my last will and testament revoking all former wills that I may have made to wit-

First. It is my desire that after my death, my body be consigned to Mother earth in a decent and christian like manner And out of my estate my just debts be paid

Second I bequeath to my daughter Susan T. Hynes a negro girl rose aged about sixteen years to her & her Heirs forever.

Third I bequeath to son John Donalson Hynes to him and his Heirs forever a negro boy named Jacob aged about twelve years

Fourth. I bequeath to my son Turner Williamson Hynes & to his Heirs forever a negro boy named Anthony aged about ten years

Fifth. I bequeath to William B. Hynes & his Heirs forever a negro boy named William aged about ten years

Sixth. I bequeath to my grandson Micajah Hines and his heirs forever a negro named Orange aged about eight years.

Seventh. I desire and direct that after my death all my negroes not named above and all the balance of my personal estate & all monies notes and accounts of which I may die possessed & which may at the time of my death be due & owing to me or that may after my death be due (P-125)Wm. Hynes) & coming to my Estate from any source whatever be equally divided

(P-125 cont.) between my four children, Susan T. Hynes, John D. Hynes Turner W. Hynes & William B. Hynes

Eighth I desire and direct that my three little tracts of land containing in all one hundred & Sixty five acres lying on Fletcher's Creek after my death be sold on a credit of one and two years and the proceeds of said land to be equally divided between my said four children, Susan T. John D. Turner W. & William B Hynes and their Heirs forever.

Ninth I desire and direct that ~~the share~~ all my negroes except Rose, Jacob, Anthony, William which I have given to my four children & their Heirs forever, be divided ~~between my said four children therein named~~ according to my seventh bequest between my said four children therein named to remain with said children Susan T John & Turner W. & William B Hynes for their own use & under their control during their natural lives and after the death of any one or all of said four children I desire and direct that the dividend of each one of them descend to their Heirs forever.

Tenth I desire and direct that the share or portion of my Estate after my death which each of the four children may be entitled to be given to them as they become of lawful age to receive the same and my executors hereinafter appointed are requested and directed to take the negro boy Orange which I have given to my Grandson Micajah Hynes (after my death) & hire him out for the support of sd Micajah

In conclusion I hereby nominate, constitute & appoint Benjamin W Williamson and Lemuel R Brown of Shelby County my said State Executors to this my last will and Testament

(P-126)(Wm. Hynes Contd.) The word my in the 3rd line & the word Grand in my seventh bequest interlined before signed

Signed & Sealed in the presence May 16, 1836

Moses L Alexander Franklin Sanders William Hynes (Seal

State of Tennessee

Shelby County Court

A competent Court present

The last Will and Testament of William Hynes decd. was produced to the Court and Franklin Sanders and Mose L Alexander Subscribing witnesses to the same being sworn say that the said Hynes Executed the said Will in their presence and declared the same to be his act & deed & that the said Hynes was of sound mind & disposing memory. Whereupon it is ordered by the Court that said Will & Testament be fully established and recorded.

Recorded 12 May 1839 John W. Fuller

J.W. Fuller Clk

(P-127) T H O M A S B. O L L I V E R ' S W I L L

I Thomas B Oliver of Shelby County State of Tennessee being of sound mind and memory do make and ordain this my last Will & Testament in manner & form as follows:

Article the 1st. I give unto my three sisters, Elizabeth, Sarah and Ann & M.T.Oliver, Benj. L. Oliver & my son James P. Oliver, the following Negroes, Viz. Dolly and her three children, Eliza, Robert & Louisa Ann,

Article 2nd I leave two Negroes William & Jefferson to my Wife and children for their equal benefit,

Article 3 I wish the ballance of my estate to be disposed of & all my just debts paid & the ballance if ny to be divided between my wife & children

Article 4 I hereby appoint Neill B Holt and Benj. L. Oliver Executors of this my last Will & Testament.

In witness of the above I hereby affirm my hand & Seal this 8th day of March A.D. 1839-

Witness ~~W/Christian~~ Thomas Oliver (Seal)
W Christian
Jno. H Frayser
Robt. V. Oliver Compared March 15/38

State of Tennessee)
April Sessions 1839
Shelby County)

This the last Will & Testament of Thomas Oliver was produced in court & John R. Frayser & Robert V Oliver Witness thereto being sworn say that t the decd. was in his proper senses at the time he executed & declared the same in their presence to be his last Will & Testament which is ordered to be recorded

A coppy of the probate made of the foregoing Will

J.W. Fuller Clk

(P-128) State of Tennessee

Shelby County

In the name of God Amen I Fielding Rennolds of the County & State aforesaid being perfectly in sound mind and memory but weak in body do make this my last Will & Testament.

In the first place. I will my body to the dust from which it came to be decently buried and my Soul to my God who made me. Also my worldly property the Negroes which belong to me, viz. Patsy & her children Joe & Ben, Milly & her children, Louisa & Billy, Mary Ann & her children Nancy, Easter, Riley Martin & Albert, My will is that all these Negroes I loan to my grand children, Catherine M. Thomas & Elizabeth R

(P-128 cont.) F.C. Benjamin, M. Fielding, R. James, C. And Donaldson H. Runnels - untill Fielding Runnels arrives to the age of Fifteen years, at which time all the abovenamed Negroes with their increase, my will is should be divided equally between the above named grandchildren, should either or my grandchildren (Marry) before Fielding becomes fifteen years of age, they may take choice of either of the negroes to wait upon them, until the period arrives that Fielding is fifteen years of age, then the Negroes are to be equally divided among them. All the Negroes My will is that my son Benjamin should keep untill his son Fielding becomes fifteen years of age then have them divided equally as before expressed by me in this instalment

I also give Catherine Runnels one Roan Horse Colt, and I give one Sorrel Horse Colt, to Elizabeth R. Runnels and I say that all instruments of whatever description heretofore made by me Wills or Deeds of any description is declared to be Null & Void & this is my last Will and none other in testimony whereof (P-129) I hereunto set my hand & affix my Seal this 29th of April 1838

Witnesses: Fielding Rennolds (Seal)

Robert B. Daniel

Richard Mason Charles Davis

State of Tennessee)
April Sessions 1839.
Shelby County Court)

This is the last Will & Testament of Fielding Rennolds was produced in open Court and Robert B. Daniel & Richd. Mason witnesses thereto being sworn say that that the said decd. Signed the same in their presence & declared it to be his last Will & Testament & that he was of sound & disposing mind wich is ordered to be recorded.

Recorded May 13 1839 John W. Fuller Clk.

(P-130) LUCY JOHNSON'S WILL

I Lucy Johnson being of sound and discerning mind and memory, make this my last will & testament revoking all former Wills,

First, I will & bequest unto my little Grand Daughter Rosella (daughter of my son Thos G Johnson) My House & lot on which I reside, & numbered on the Town plan 337, fronting second cross street seventy four feet, 3 inches & running back & fronting on 1st ally north of Adams St. one hundred & forty eight feet 6 inches to have & to hold to her & her heirs forever.

Secondly. I will & bequeath to William G Johnson, Marceller Johnson Caroline Johnson & Lawson Johnson, my Grand children (children of my son J G Johnson) to them & their Heirs forever, the one third part of the following negroes, towit, Billy, Bartley, Popmie, James, Malvina and Matilda

(P-130 cont.) and also the one third part of the proceeds of all the remainder of my personall propperty.

Thirdly. I will & bequeath the one third part of all the above named negroes to my Grandchildren (all the children of Dudley G Johnson) together with the one third part of all the proceeds of said personal property forever.

Fourthly. I will & bequeath the one third part of all the above named negroes unto my Grand children (all the children of the body of Devorie G Johnson) to them & their Heirs forever, also the one third part of all the other personal propperty

(P-131)Fifthly. I will & bequeath to my Daughter, Charlotte G Joiner the use control and services of my negro woman Oliva during the lifetime of my Daughter Charlotte & after her death said negro Woman Oliva to be sold & the proceeds of Sale to be equally divided among all of my grandchildren (the children of my three sons Thos. G. Dudley G & Devorix Johnson) to them & their Heirs forever.

Sixly. I decree that my Carriage & Horses & household & Kitchen furniture be sold & all just claims be paid & the residue of said proceeds be divided as above directed

And Lastly It is my Will & desire & do by these presents nominate & appoint my three Sons Dudley G Thomas G. & Devarix G Johnson executors of this my last will & testament

In testimony Whereof I have hereunto set my hand & Seal this Febry 22, 1839.

In presence of P.G. Lucy Johnson (Seal)

Gains Eugene Magevney.

State of Tennessee)
June Sessions 1839
Shelby County)

This the last Will and testament of Lucy Johnson was produced in Court and P G Gains & Eugene Magevney witnesses thereto being sworn, say that the said Lucy executed & declared the same in their presence to be her act & deed & that she was of sound & disposing mind, which is ordered to be recorded ~~A coppy of the probate made of the foregoing Will.~~

Recorded June 13th 1839 J W Fuller Clk.

(P-132) L E W E L L I N G W I L L I A M S ' W I L L

I Lewelling Williams of the County of Shelby and State of Tennessee Planter) do make and publish this my last Will & testament hereby revoking & making void all former Wills by me at any time heretofore made

(P-132 Cont.) And first. That my body be decently interred in said County in a manner suitable to my condition in life & as to such world-estate as it has please God to intrust me with, I dispose of the same as follows:

First I direct that all my just debts & funeral expense be paid as soon after my decease as possible out of any money that I may die possessed of, or may first come into the hands of my Executors.

Secondly I give and bequeath unto my beloved wife during her natural life One Hundred acres of Land taken out of any of my Lands where she may choose. Also the following negroes, to wit. Gilbert, Gabriel, Isaac Eaton, also all of my household & Kitchen Furniture, plantation tools, stock of every description & I request my wife out of the above property to give to my sons, Charles, Benjamin, Markums, & James E Williams each of them one good Feather Bed & bedding. I also give unto my sons Charles Benjamin Markums & James E Williams all of the ballance of my Lands & Tenements to be equally divided among them I also give unto my son Peter William Lewelling Williams, Charles Williams, Benjamin Williams Markums Williams & James E Williams the following negroes to Wit. Warren, Monteal, Jenny, Henry, Ann, Tom Caliph Caty John Jefferson Mary Matilda (P-133) & all of their increase to be equally divided amongst them. I want at the death of my beloved wife for the negroes Gilbert Gabriel Isaac & Eaton to be equally divided between John Williams, Robert Williams, Peter Williams, Lewelling Williams, Charles Williams, Benjamin Williams, Markum Williams & James E Williams & the ballance of the property which I give to my wife during her life, at her death I want divided equally between Peter, Lewelling Charles Benjamin, Markum, & James E Williams. I have given to John Williams one negro Man named Ned.) I have also given unto my Daughter Polly Williams, who married Martin Draper one negro Caly & her increase. I have given Robert Williams One Negro Woman Polly & her increase

I do hereby order & appoint, my beloved Wife Winneford Williams my Executrix & Peter Williams & Lewelling Williams my executors of this my last Will & testament, & I do request my son Lewelling Williams to take charge of my plantation & negroes & work them to the best*advantage for three years for the purpose of paying my just debts And I want my whole estate to be kept together for three years & at the expiration of three years I want a division to take place of all the property which I have not given to my wife. I want my sons, Benjamin, Markum & James E Williams to go to school until they shall have a common English Education & the same to be paid for out of the proceeds ~~###~~ of what is made on the plantation previous to the (P-134) division.

In Witness Whereof I, Lewelling Williams the said Testator have to this my last will & testament written on one sheet of paper set my hand and seal this Twenty eight day of June One Thousand Eight Hundred & Thirty Nine

Lewelling Williams (Seal)

Signed Sealed & published in the presence of the Testator & of each other Isaac Jenkins William T Wesson

P.S. I want Lewelling Williams to be paid for his services during the three years annually for attending to the business which I have before

* possible

(P-134 cont.) requested him to do the day & date before written-

State of Tennessee)
June Sessions 1839
Shelby County)

This the last will & testament of Lewelling Williams was produced in open Court & Isaac Jenkins & William G Wesson subscribing witnesses thereto after being sworn say that the said Lewelling Williams executed & declared the same in their presence to be his act & deed & that he was of sound & disposing mind which is ordered to be recorded

Recorded June 15th 1839 John W Fuller Clk

(P-134) MRS. MARTHA ANN CARR'S WILL

The Noncupative will of Mrs. Martha Ann Carr, who departed this life at the house of Tilman Bettis in Shelby County Tennessee August 7th, 1839-

Item 1st, I give and bequeath unto my Daughter Amanda F Cratton my Negro Man Leo.

Item 2nd- I give & bequeath unto my Daughter Lucy Carr my Negro Girl Hannah,

Item 3rd- I give & bequeath unto my Daughter Mary Hunt my Negro Girl Jane

It is my will & desire that each of said negroes heretofore given to my said Daughters belong to each of them severally for their sole & separate support & benefit to the exclusion of the marital rights of their sd. husbands & to my daughter Lucy to the exclusion of the marital rights of her husband should she ever marry - and it is my will & desire that each of my sd. Daughters have the absolute control & power of disposition over her sd. negro & that they may sell give dispose of or devise the same to their husbands or to any other person or persons they may think proper.

Reduced to writing this 2nd day of September 1839-

The Noncupative Will of Mrs. Martha Ann Carr being produced here into Court for probate & record & it appearing satisfactorily to the Court that the next of kin to the decd. having been regularly notified of this proceeding and that they Hath failed & do not appear to contest the probate of said will and (P-136) thereupon came Tilman Bettis & James F. Lauderdale two disinterested & competent witnesses who depose & say that they were present at the making of said will, that they were expressly required to bear witness thereto by the Testator herself that it was made in her last sickness at the house of Tilman Bettis in Shelby County where she was surprised with sickness from home & that she died without ever re- * to her dwelling that said will was reduced to writing on this day the said Martha Ann having died about three weeks since & was not offered for probate till fourteen days after her death & that they believe she was of sound mind & disposing memory at the time thereof-

* turning

(P-136 cont.) Recorded September 2nd 1839-

J.W. Fuller C.S.C.C.

(P-137) ISAAC RAWLINGS' WILL

In the name of God, Amen, I Isaac Rawlings of the town of Memphis, Shelby County, Tennessee, being in tolerable health and of perfect mind and memory, but considering the uncertainty of this mortal life, do make & publish this my last Will and Testament in manner and form following.

1st. I bequeath my Sister Juliet Rawlings an annuity of Three hundred dollars per Year, if she should live as long for Ten, consecutive Years, making at the end of that time Three Thousand dollars, but should she die before expiration of that time, the annuity will cease at her death, and I require my natural Son, William Isaac Rawlings, of whom I shall speak hereafter to pay her the said annuity out of my property, the day of payment to be on the first of January of Each & Every Year.

2nd. John the son of Clarissa, willed to me by my Sister Susanna Rawlings, deceased, I set free at the age of thirty years or when he shall attain that age until which time I give him to William Issac Rawlings. When free if he cannot enjoy freedom in Tennessee he can go elsewhere-

3rd. To William Isaac Rawlings my natural son, whom I have always considered free & who I have raised and educated in my house & who has now the care of my store and well known to the witnesses to this will, and whose freedom was acknowledged and established by the County Court for Shelby County, Tennessee on my petition to said Court in February 1837 and Baptized 22nd July 1838, by Dr. George Weller of the Protestant Episcopal Church I give & bequeath at my death all my property and Estate not disposed of as above mentioned, that I may die possessed of or be entitled to in Law or Equity of whatsoever Kind, real, personal or mixed and to his heirs forever, which shall be & remain after (P-138) my debts, if there be any unpaid, which I require him forthwith out of my property to pay. At this time I owe my Sister Juliet, he will settle with her liberally. Something will be coming to my Overseer, at Rousby Hall, and I owe Dr. Christian a small Doctor Bill, these are my debts at present, at any time I presume thay will not exceed the Cash I shall leave on hand, and therefore I direct them to be paid at once, if I shall not have paid them, I require & enjoin upon him to take care of Hanah, whom I purchased of Wm. Love of the Chickasaw Nation upwards of Twenty Years ago also of her children and to provide for them reasonably out of the property I leave him and to give them their freedom for me as he can. I further require him to treat & use well the colored Persons I leave him. -

I require him to progress in his studies, as he advances to lawful age to apply himself early & constantly thereafter to business, that his habits may be regularly & correctly fixed, & with the means he will have at his disposal without touching his real estate & the servants therewith, which he had better keep. I suggest to him the propriety of endeavoring to make himself a useful & respectable man of business, a high-minded Honorable man; but to be such he must be virtuous & moral in his habits

(P-138 cont.) & practice, honest & prompt in his engagements, frugal in his expenses so as to keep always within his income, and benevolent in his dispositions, these will protect him against self-reproach and sustain him through life-

4th, I hereby appoint my aforesaid natural son William Isaac Rawlings Executor of this my last Will & Testament and require him to take charge of the Estate I leave at my Death, whether he be of lawful age or not that the debts due me & from me, may be collected, and as there will be no occasion to trouble any Court of Justice about my Will or Estate & as no one can lose by his taking charge of it, I require him to give no Security-

5th, In the event that William Isaac Rawlings aforesaid (P-139) shall die unmarried, before he shall arrive at the age of maturity, the property left him by this Will after deducting therefrom so much as shall be necessary to pay all charges on his account and after Hanah & her children shall be set free and after one hundred & fifty Dollars per annum shall be set apart & secured for Hanah's support during her life, I wish divided among my first cousins by my Mother's side then living, each one having an equal share a majority of whom shall appoint an Executor, whose additional duty it shall be to pay my Sister Juliet her annuity, set John free as provided in this Will set Hanah & her children free & pay her the allowance specified for her per annum-

6th. My property at present but which I am closing up my business, is liable to constant alterations) will consist of Shares in the Farmers & Merchant Bank of GeorgeTown, District of Columbia, Rousby Hall, the land bought of N.C. Dare, my part in "Rawlings Choice," the Negroes & other personal property on R. Hall, Calvert County, Maryland - Land on Big Creek Shelby County & Tipton Counties, Tennessee, supposed to contain 342 acres, Deed recorded, Land on or near Wolf River 500 acres, Shelby County Tennessee Deeds recorded & Houses, Lots in Memphis Deeds recorded, See Ledgers Beginning in A Folio 52, Money on hand in trade & stock on hand See Store & Books, debts outstanding in Notes & open accounts see Ledger D-Negroes, Horses, Cattle, household furniture, Books &c &c at Memphis, Stock in the Farmers & Merchants Bank of Memphis, Stock in the Memphis Marine & Fire Insurance Company, Stock in the Memphis Wharf Company- for these see Ledger D.

7th. I owe on the Stock I hold in the Memphis Marine & Fire Insurance Company to meet the calls on which, when made must not be neglected, as security of the Company (P-140) I have not payed 65 Shares Bank Stock of Farmers & Merchants Bank of Memphis, the certificate of Stock will generally show the account due. My Overseer at Rousby Hall is allowed one hundred & forty dollars a Year paid up to November 1838, he will render an account of everything of mine in his hands.

Reuben Lewis of Albermarle County, Virginia and myself bought in the Year 1819 or 20 four Lots in Cadman Pulaski County, Arkansas, equal & joint owners of which no deed is made, the papers are in the name of R. Lewis. My Books will show how this matter stands, they are worth nothing & mentioned here because a statement of them will be found in the Books.

8th. I do not wish to be buried in the Memphis buring ground, if I have a farm of my own established at my Death, I wish to be buried on it, to be put in two coffins, the outside one to be Tin if convenient.

(P-140 cont.) William will procure two white free stones or marble slabs & place at the ends of my Grave, surrounding it with a Brick Wall & shading the Ground with a Weeping Willow, on one of the Slabs to be inscribed "Here lies the remains of Isaac Rawlings, born in Calvert County County Maryland 13th Aprile 1788, and died _____day of _____in the Year

My burying expenses, I wish paid immediately in cash -

Witness whereof I have hereunto set my hand & Seal this the 7th day of June in the Year of our Lord 1839.

Signed, Sealed, Published & delivered by the abovenamed Isaac Rawlings, to be his last Will & testament in the presence of us W W Tucker, L Hardaway, J. M Moon, J.T. Leath, Jas. Rose

Isaac Rawlings (Seal)

(P-141) State of Tennessee)
October Sessions 1839.
Shelby County)

A paper purporting to be the last Will & Testament of Isaac Rawlings, Deceased, was produced in open Court, thereupon came S.T. Hardaway, J.M. Moon & James Rose, subscribing witnesses thereto, who after being sworn depose & say that he was of sound mind & disposing memory at the time he acknowledged the Same in their presence, and he acknowledged the same to be his last Will & Testament, which is ordered to be recorded-

Recorded November 5th 1839 J.W. Fuller, S.C.C.C

J.W. Fuller, C.S.C.C. By Rudisill D.C.

(P-142) JANE GATEWOOD'S WILL

In the Name of God, "Amen," I Jane Gatewood of the County of Shelby, State of Tennessee and late of the County of Bath and State of Virginia being impressed with the uncertainty of life and feeling that my continuance in this World is drawing to a close, & for the purpose of settling all ~~of~~ my worldly concerns do make this my last Will & testament in manner & form following -

It is my Will and I do hereby direct that all my just debts & funeral expenses be paid as soon as practible after my decease.

I will & bequeath unto the American Bible Society Twenty Dollars. To the General Assembly, Board of Foreign Missions, Ten Dollars.

It is my wish that my Bureau and Bedstead left at my old residence with my son Samuel V. be sold at the discretion of my executor in Va. & the proceeds be transferred for the benefit of the Tract Society of the Presbyterian Church. I will & bequeath unto my son Warrick my Horse colt now in his possession also my old clock, left by me at my old residence also one half dozen of Silver Table & Tea Spoons and a Silver Soup

(P-142 cont.) Ladle and four Tablecloths all of which are in the possession of my Daughter Mary Jane, also one half of all the debt due me by Note or otherwise in the hands of A.W.Cameron also one half of a Three hundred dollar note on Lewis & Shewsbury. If any loss accrue in the collection of any of the abovementioned debts the said loss is to be mutual between said Warrick & my Daughter, Mary Jane. I also give him my Leather Trunk.

I will & bequeath unto my son Samuel Vance my Desk and Book Case now in his possession and to carry out (P-143) the wishes expressed by my late husband in his last Will and Testament. I bequeath unto him & his heirs forever all the Land so registered by my late husband in said Will(leaving only heretofore disposed of my life interest in the same to him.)

I will & bequeath unto my Daughter Mary Jane (who has lately intermarried with Wm. H. Kennedy) my Horse John, with all my Beds, Bedding,furniture &c &c now in her possession except the abovementioned Four Table *Cloths & Leather Trunk. Also my two mahogany Tables now in possession of my Samuel Vance. It is also my wish that my Executor do purchase for her of the best quality of Silver one dozen of Table & one Dozen of Tea Spoons and also a Soup Ladle. I also bequeath unto my sd. Daughter Mary Jane the other half of the abovementioned Notes given to Warrick -

I hereby appoint Cesario Bias for & in the State of Tennessee and A.W. Cameron for & in the State of Virginia to be my executors of this my last Will & Testament hereby revoking all former Wills by me made and declare this to be my last Will and Testament.

In Witness Whereof I have hereunto subscribed my name & affixed my Seal this the twenty sixth day of July, Eighteen hundred & thirty nine.

Published & declared as & for the last Will &
Testament of Jane Gatewood in our presence, who
in the presence of each other witnesseth the same
John R. Parker Cesario Bias J S Kennedy

(P-144) State of Tennessee)
November Sessions 1839
Shelby County)

The last Will & testament of Jane Gatewood was produced in open Court, attested by John R. Parker, Cesario Bias & Jacob L. Kennedy and the said John R. Parker being duly sworn says that the testatrix acknowledged in his presence the said instrument to be her last Will & Testament and that she was of sound mind & disposing memory as he believes, & that the said testatrix was prevented from Signing & Sealing the same by the act of God, and that the said Jacob L. Kennedy being also duly sworn says that he was present & heard the said last Will & Testament of the said Testatrix read to her, who acknowledged it in his presence that it was her last Will & Testament, that he believed her at the time to be of sound mind and disposing memory and that she was prevented from Signing & Sealing the same only by the Act of God, and thereupon the Court ordered the said last Will & Testament to be admitted and Spread on Record.

J W Fuller Clk

Recorded November 4th 1839 By L Rudisill D.C.
J W Fuller Clk

* son

(P-145) THE LAST WILL & TESTAMENT OF JOSEPH KIRK

OF THE TOWN OF MEMPHIS.

In the name of God Amen

First I bequeath my Soul to God. My body to the Earth, rottenness and worms

Second. I bequeath unto my Wife Susanah Kirk all my worldly substance,

Given under my hand in full possession of my sences this 12th Day of March in the year of our Lord One Thousand Eight Hundred and Thirty Nine 1839

Test
Patrick Diwane John Land
Wm Goodman

his
Joseph X Kirk
mark

State of Tennessee)
Shelby County Court) December Sessions 1839

The last Will & Tesament of Joseph Kirk Decd, was produced in open Court and William Goodman & John Land subscribing Witnesses thereto, after being sworn say, that the said Joseph Kirk executed & declared the same in their presence to be his act & deed & that he was of sound mind & disposing memory which is ordered to be recorded

Recorded Dec. 9th 1839 J.W. Fuller C S C C

By Z Rudisill D.C.

(P-146) THE LAST WILL & TESTAMENT OF THOMAS B TAYLOR DECEASED

I Thomas B. Taylor do make & publish this as my last Will & Testament hereby revoking & making void all other Wills by me at any other time made.

First I direct that my funeral expenses & all my just debts be paid as soon after my death as possible out of any monies that I may die possessed of as may first come into the hands of my executors.

Secondly. I give & bequeath to my Brother W.C. Taylor my library

Thirdly I give & bequeath to my Father Lewis Taylor the ballance of what I may be worth

Lastly I hereby nominate and appoint my Uncle Fletcher Taylor & Wm. Z C Alexander my executors to this my last Will & Testament whom I hereby authorize to sell & dispose of all my real as well as personal Estate and transmit the funds to my Father after settling all my just debts

(P-146 cont.) In Witness Whereof I do set my hand and Seal

Thos. B. Taylor (Seal)

Signed Sealed & Published in our presence and we have subscribed our names hereto in the presence of the testator - this 12th day of Jny. 1840.

Test S B Hawkins)
James Davis)

State of Tennessee)
January Sessions A D 1840
Shelby County Court)

The last Will & Testament of Thomas B Taylor was produced in open Court and thereupon came S B Hawkins one of the subscribing witnesses thereto and after being first sworn stated that the said Thomas B Taylor executed & published the same as his last Will & Testament in his presence that he was of sound mind and disposing memory and that in the said S B Hawkins ~~presence~~ subscribed the same as a witness thereto in the presence of the said Testator all of which is ordered to be certified and the said Will filed for further probate

State of Tennessee)
March Sessions A D 1840
Shelby County Court)

The last Will & testament of Thomas B Taylor was produced in open Court for further probate and thereupon came James Davis, one of the subscribing witnesses thereto and after being first sworn stated that the said Thomas B. Taylor (P-147) executed & published the same as his last will & Testament in his presence that he was of sound mind and deposing memory and that the said James David subscribed the same as a witness thereto in the presence of the said Testator all of which is ordered to be certified and said Will established as fully proven which is ordered to be recorded

I John W. Fuller, Clerk of the County Court of Shelby County in complyance with the requisitions of the above order have recorded the said Will in Book 6 page 146-147)

March 25th 1840

THE LAST WILL OF JAMES MASON DECEASED

In the name of God Amen October 8th 1838

I James Mason of the County of Shelby and State of Tennessee being in good health sound mind & memory knowing that it is the lot of liveing to die and cease think proper to make and ordain this my last Will & Testament in manner & form as follows

Item first I wish all my Just & lawful debts paid out of my worldly

(P-147 cont.) Estate.

Secondly I wish to be decently buried at some fit public burying ground.

thirdly I wish my remaining means to be equally divided between my three daughters Martha A Land formerly M A Mason Elizabeth J Mason & Harriett C Knox formerly H C Mason I give the same to them and ~~these~~ heirs of their bodies forever equally in division except that as I have formerly loaned M A Land a negro Girl worth three hundred dollars, I therefore consider it Just that she pay E A Mason and H.C. Knox one hundred & fifty dollars each out of said M A Land's of my Estate I give it them and the heirs of their bodies forever

(P-148) Fourth I give my son John I Mason one dollar I give it to him & his heirs forever -

Fifthly I do hereby constitute and appoint Thomas Dowlin of Tipton County & Owen D Weanes of this County my friends to execute this my last Will & Testament

Witness my hand this day and date above written

James Mason

State of Tennessee)
February Sessions A D 1840
Shelby County)

The last Will & Testament of James Mason Deceased was produced in open Court and Thomas Dowlen Samuel Scott and Washington Bolton after being first sworn depose and say that said Will was found among the valuable papers of James Mason Dcd. and they also believe it to be the handwriting of the said James Mason which is ordered to be recorded

I John W. Fuller, Clerk of the County Court of Shelby County in compliance with the requisitions of the above order have recorded said Will in Book 6 page 147 & 148 this 25th day of March 1840

John W. Fuller.

State of Tennessee)

Shelby County)

THE LAST WILL & TESTAMENT OF WILLIAM GREGORY DECEASED

In the name of God amen Know all persons by these presents.

I do make & publish this as my last Will & Testament hereby revoking ~~all others~~ and making void all other Wills by me made at any other time made

First I will & direct that my funeral expenses allowed and all my just debts be paid as soon after my death as possible out of any money that I may die possessed of or that may first come into the hands of my

(P-148 cont.) executor

Secondly I will & bequeath to my son Tilmon Gregory his heirs and assigns forever - a negro boy named Miles about nine years old also two hundred and fifty dollars

(P-149) Thirdly I will & bequeath to my son Nathaniel Gregory his heirs and assigns forever the tract of land on which I am now residing consisting of two hundred Acres it being the same tract of land I bought of Robert Knox whose bond for a title thereto I hold and who bought the same from James Freeman and took his title Bond which is transferred to me and the entire purchase money for which I have heretofore paid but as there is some doubt about the title to this land if as good and valid title in fee simple cannot be obtained it is my will & desire that my son Nathan shall have whatsoever may be secured from said Knox or Freeman or any other Person as their or either of their Estates in any way of damages for their not making and executing to me a Good & perfect title in fee simple to said land to these Contracts to my son Nathan his heirs and assigns forever

I also will & bequeath to my said son Nathan his heirs and assigns forever a negro boy named Thomas about seven years old

Thirdly I will & bequeath to my Daughter Amanda F Gregory and her heirs and assigns forever a negro Girl named ~~Nancy~~ Patsy about ten years old also one Feather Bed & furniture

Fourthly I Will and bequeath to my Daughter Delia H Gregory an her heirs and assigns forever a negro Girl named Dilsy about Eight years old also one feather Bed & furniture if either of my abovenamed Daughters should die without a Bodily ~~[illegible]~~ Heir I will & desire that her entire estate go to the living one and her heirs forever.

Fifthly I will & bequeath to my beloved wife Mary Gregory during her natural life a negro Girl named Maria about twelve years old and after her death said Girl Mariah and her heirs or increase is to be equally divided between my two daughters Amanda and Adelia also to my wife during her natural life or widowhood the entire possession of the north end of my tract of land on which I am now Residing to the second (P-150) cross fence containing about forty five acres and to her I give my negro Man Miles forever with the following articles (viz) the Ballance of my household & Kitchen furniture my Bay horse Wild my young filly two cows two sows & pigs four head of sheep all my poultry & one horse Cart

Sixthly I will & direct that all the rest & residue of my estate not herein mentioned to be sold after the payment of my debts should there be a remainder I will and direct it to be equally divided between my two Daughters Amanda & Amelia & lastly I hereby nominate and appoint Jared S Edwards my executor in witness whereof I do to this my last will & Testament set my hand and Seal, this 21st day of January 1840

Signed Sealed ~~in the presence~~ and published in his presence ~~of~~ and we have subscribed our names in the presents of the

William his X mark Gregory (Seal)

(P-150 cont.) Testator this the 21st day of January 1840-

Test Nathan Snowden)
S Gregory)

State of Tennessee)
February Sessions A.D. 1840
Shelby County Court)

A paper purporting to be the last Will and testament of Wm. Gregory Deceased was produced in open Court and thereupon came Nathan Snowden and S Gregory subscribing witnesses thereto who being first sworn depose and say that he was of sound mind and disposing memory at the time he acknowledged the same in there presents and that he acknowledged ~~and that he acknowledged~~ the same to be his last Will & Testament which is ordered to be recorded

I John W. Fuller Clerk of the County Court of said County in compliance with the requisition of the above order have recorded said Will in Book C page 148-149 & 150

John W. Fuller Clerk.

(P-151) RICHARD GOLDSBY'S WILL

In the Name of God, Amen. I Richard Goldsby, of the County of Shelby and State of Tennessee, being of sound mind and disposing memory for which I thank God and calling to mind the uncertainty of human life, knowing that it is appointed for all men once to die, do make and publish this my last Will & Testament, That is to say,

First of all. I recommend my soul unto the hand of the Almighty God that gave it, and my Body I recommend to the earth to be buried by decent Christian Burial - and as touching such worldly Estate which it has pleased God to bless me with I give bequeath & dispose of it in the following manner and form-

First. I will that all my just debts be paid.

Second I give and bequeath to my Daughter Feraby Bradley Twenty dollars out of my Estate, she having heretofore received that portion of my Estate that I designed for her,

I Give to my Daughter Eliza Barnett Twenty dollars out of my Estate she having heretofore received that portion of my Estate that I designed for her

I give to my son Thornton B Goolsby Twenty dollars he having heretofore received that portion of my Estate that I designed for him

I Give to my Grand Don Peter R Goolsby Twenty dollars having formerly given to my son Peter R Goolsby the father of my said Grand Son that portion of my Estate, that I designed for him.

I Give all the ballance of my Estate consisting of Land Negroes &

(P-151 cont.) other personal property to my two sons, Miles W. Goolsby & Terril T Goolsby to be equally divided between them.

And I do hereby (P-152) constitute and appoint my two sons Miles W Goolsby and Terril T Goolsby Executors of this my last Will and Testament hereby revoking all other and former wills by me at any time heretofore made.

In Witness Whereof I have hereunto set my hand and and Seal this 14th day of March in the Year of our Lord one thousand eight hundred and thirty nine

Signed Sealed in the presence of Richard Goolsby (Seal)

John Ralston Emanuel Baker William Smith

State of Tennessee)
April Sessions A D 1840
Shelby County)

The last Will & testament of Richard Goolsby decd. was produced in open Court & Hohn Ralston and Emanuel Baker two subscribing witnesses thereto who after being first sworn depose and say that he Richard Goolsby acknowledged the same in their presence to be his last Will & Testament and that he was of sound mind & disposing memory all of which is ordered to be recorded

Recorded April 9th A.D. 1840 John W. Fuller Clk

J.W. Fuller C S C C

By Z Rudisill Depty

(P-153) JAMES FARIS' LAST WILL & TESTAMENT

This is the last and dying request of James Faris on Tuesday morning about 10 o'clock we were called to dying bed of James Faris and he James Faris said in these words. Mathew Bayne and you Dr. Christian I want to take notice I want William Bayne to have all I am worth both of take notice of this for me. Memphis Tennessee December 6th 1839

James Rose J P Mathew Bayne Wyatt Christian

This day came in to Court Mathew Bayne produced a paper purporting to be the last Will & testament of James Faris and the said Mathew Bayne being duly sworn deposeth and states that he was present on the day of the death of the said James Faris who called on himself & Wiatt Christian to witness the verbial dispention he was about to make of his estate in his last illness at the place of his residence he further states that the deceased was in sound mind at the time and capable of making his will that the same was committed to writing on the same day of his death by the deponent and testified thereto within three days before James Rose Esqr, Justice of the peace in Memphis where the Testator died that the deponant signed the paper - as witness with Wiatt Christian and that the

(P-153 cont.) paper here produced is the same and Contains the substance and he believes the verry words used by the deceased in relation of the disposition of his Effects in view of approaching death

This day came into Court Wyatt Christian one of the subscribing witnesses to the last Will & Testament of James Faris Dcd. who after being duly sworn says that he was present on the day of the death of the said James Faris who called on him & Mathew Bayne to witness the virbial dispensation he was about to make of his Estate in his last illness at the place of his ~~at the place of his~~ residence he further states that the deceased was sound in mind at the time and capable of making his (P-154) Will that the same was committed to writing on the same day of his death and testified thereto within three days before James Rose Esqr. Justice of the peace in Memphis where the testator died that the deponent signed the paper as witness with Mathew Bayne and that the paper he produced is the same and contains & he believes the very words used by the deceased in relation of the dispositions of his effects in view of approaching death

Recorded May 12th 184 John W. Fuller, Clerk

J W Fuller

J E S S E C T A T E W I L L

I Jesse C Tate of the State of Tennessee and County of Shelby, being of sound mind & Body do this day make and publish the following as my last Will & testament

1st. I order that all my just debts be paid including decent funeral expenses I give and bequeath to Mary L Bond my negro woman named Ann and her child Ahram I give and bequeath to Uriah M Tate five hundred dollars to be paid in two equal annual installments the first instalment to be paid twelve months after my decease and the second twelve months thereafter

I give & bequeath to B M Tate five hundred dollars to be paid in two instalments as above directed

I give & bequeath to Nicholas Rice Bond my negro girl Louisa.

I give to Sam Bond Int. my negro girl Mary.

I give and bequeath to Minor Bond my negro man Washington and my Girl Matilda & my my horse Saddle & Bridle & whatever else I may die possessed of either in property or money

I do appoint as executors to this my last Will & Testament to Carry its intentions into effect Saml. Bond Dd. & Jesse M. Tate

In testimony Whereof I have hereunto (P-155) signed my name and affixed my Seal this 28th day of December A.D. 1839.

Signed in the presence of Saml. Bond Jes Tate (Seal)
John Griffin

(P-155 cont.) A paper purporting to be the last Will & Testament of Jesse C Tate was produced in open Court for probate and thereupon came Samuel Bond John Griffin subscribing witnesses to the same who being duly sworn depose and say that the said Jesse C. Tate executed & declared the same in their presence to be his act and deed and that he was of sound & disposing memory at the time which is received and ordered to be recorded

RECORDED May 12th 1840 John W. Fuller Clk

J W Fuller Clk.

State of Tennessee)

Shelby County)

I Benjamin Shivers of the County & State aforesaid planter being of sound mind but infirm of body do make & publish this my last will & testament hereby revoking and making void all former wills by me at any time heretofore made. I dispose of the same as follows

First I direct that all my just debts ~~be paid~~ and funeral expences be paid as soon after my decease as possible out of any monies that I may be possessed of or may first come into the hands of my executors from any portion of my Estate real or personal

2nd I give and bequeath unto my wife Nancy Shivers all of my household and Kitchen furniture I furthermore give and bequeath unto my wife Nancy Shivers Eight negroes named as follows - Mary Rilphy Clarisa Hallon John Edwin Vina Jordan furthermore I give unto my wife Nancy Shivers three Chois Horses and also one years' provisions for herself & stock family also fine Chois sows & pigs, fine Chois Cows & Calves also ten Coice ewes & lambs furthermore furthermore give unto my (P-156) Nancy Shivers one choice Cart and Carryall also the hole of the plantation and all farming tools I give the above named articles unto my wife Nancy Shivers during her life for the purpose of supporting and schooling of hur Children and at her death the abovenamed property is to be equally divided between hur children the ballance of my negroes shall be hired out and as my children comes of age they may receive their proportionable part the ballance of my property with the exception of the abovenamed shall be sold and the money ~~and the money~~ shall be equally divided between my Children. I do hereby make ordain and appoint my beloved Brother James Shivers my executor of this my last Will & Testament in Witness whereof I the said Benjamin Shivers have to this will ritten on one sheete of paper set my hand and and seal this the fourth day of August in the year of our Lord one thousand Eight hundred and forty.

Signed Sealed published in the presents Benjamin Shivers (Seal)

of us who ~~have~~ subscribed in the presents

of the Testator and of each other the word Eight

in place of seven interlined between twelfth & thirteenth lines

before Signed. James M. Roach Duncan McCallum William Ross

(P-156 cont.) State of Tennessee)
September Session 1840
Shelby County)

A paper purporting to be the last will & Testament of Benjamin Shivers deceased was produced in open Court James M Roach Duncan McCallum subscribing witnesses thereto after being first sworn depose and say that the said Benjamin Shivers executed and acknowledged the same in there presents to be his act and deed and that he was (P-157) of sound mind and disposing memory at the time of Executing the same.

Recorded September 12th 1840 John W. Fuller Clerk

M U R D O C K M C M E L L A N W I L L

In the name of God amen I Murdock McMellan of the County of Shelby & State of Tennessee do make & publish & declare the following to be my last Will & Testament

I nominate & appoint my beloved wife Jane Dr John Ingram Archibald McRay Alexander G McNutt & Henry L Guin Executors of this my last Will & Testament and I hereby authorize & direct my executors to Collect all debts which are owing to me & to sell so much of my perishable property as they may judge can best be spared by my family to pay my debts should this not be sufficient to pay my debts my will is that my Executors sell so much of the land whereon I now live as may be necessary to pay my debts except three hundred acres including all of the Improvements which I have given to my wife during her natural life. I give & bequeath unto my beloved wife three hundred acres of the land where I now live to include all of the improvements to be hurs during hur natural life. I also give & bequeath to my beloved wife the following negroes Jerry & his wife Hager & Mary, their daughter Billy & Henry all to be hur property absolutely & forever I also give & bequeath to hur my Cariage & the pare of Horses that work cariage the farming utensils household & Kitchen furniture tis my wish & desire that my theological Books be valued & divided amongst my children in equal proportions to each or my entire library divided between my children as my executors may deem equal & Just it is my wish & desire that my executors whenever they may think my estate can with convenience spare this amount that they pay to the Missionary cause three hundred & forty dollars one half say one hundred & twenty dollars in the name of my deceased son John McMellan to the authorized agent of the foreign Missionary (P-158) Society of the Presbyterian Church I have heretofore given Dr. John Ingram one negro boy and girl & four hundred & forty two dollars which I wish to be the basis of the division of my Estate heretofore given & the ballance of my Estate not heretofore bequeathed the same estimated at the time of delivery to nine hundred dollars I hereby authorize my executors to sell the three hundred acres of land bequeathed to my beloved wife if it is her wish to remove from the land in consequence of sickness but not otherwise & to give one fifth of the money received from the sales of the lands to her the ballance to be divided between my children in equal proportions after the death of my wife it is my will & desire that so much of the Estate as may not be hereby given to hur absolutely & forever which may be in her possession at her death shall be di -

(P-158 cont.) vided between my Eight daughters It is my wish & desire that my Executors pay to the American board of foreign Missions or the Commissioners thereof whatever may due either to the board in Boston or to the Editors of the Missionary herald prior to the agency Established at Sinsinnatti I do hereby ratify & confirm this to be my last Will & Testament hereby revoking all wills heretofore made by me

WITNESS my hand & Seal this 14th day of September 1840

his
Signed Sealed published in the presents of Murdock X McMellan
mark (Seal)

James Meriwether L Henderson

A paper purporting to be the last Will & Testament of Murdock Mc Millan deceased was produced in open Court & James Merriwether & L Henderson subscribing witnesses thereto after being sworn depose & say (P-159) That they were present at the execution of said will and that the said deceased acknowledged the same in their presents to be his act and deed that he was of sound mind memory at the time of acknowledging the same & ordered to be recorded.

Recorded in C Page 158 & 9 John W. Fuller Clerk
November 26th 1840
John W. Fuller Clk

ARCHIBALD M McLEAN DECEASED, WILL

Being about to undertake a journey to Europe in a few days and intending to be absent several months I deem it a matter of duty and necessity on my part in case of axident or death to leave in writing some document by which it might be understood in what manner I wihhed my property to be disposed of and for whose benefit I desire that it should be applied. Therefore it is my Will that after my death M.B. Winchester Merchant & James T. Leath lawyers both of Memphis in the State of Tennessee & William J Furgason of the town of Washington Near Natchez in the State of Mississippi should act or any two of as my Trustees in the event of my death and use the proper legal means for the purpose hereinafter described Viz)

First my Books & papers which I have deposited in the hands of M. B. Winchester should be examined and the amounts of my debits & Credits thereon properly ascertained and a fare & Correct ballance taken after including the stock of Merchandise stored with M.B. Winchester amounting per Invoice subjoined to my day Book according to the selling ~~pro~~ rates marked on each article to about Twelve thousand Dollars-

Second. that a favorable opportunity be taken to sell said goods immediately after my death is clearly ascertained and the proceds applied to the payment of my Just & lawful debts both in this County & in Scotland all of which may be ascertained with some small exceptions from my Books

Third that the ballance which my remain after payment of my debts as above Stated (P-160) be placed in the hands of the State Bank of Tennessee in Memphis in Such a way as my dearly beloved wife Lucy Lenore may be placed in full possession of the Same whatever it may be and use the amount as she may think proper for her own sole benefit and use.

(P-160 cont.) Fourth That my said Trustees for the trouble to which they may have been put in the fulfilment of the duties hereby imposed upon them be entitled to retain from my estate whatever they or a majority of them may consider a sufficient remuneration.

Fifth In order that my will may not be misunderstood I repeat that my wife Lucy Lenora is the sole executor to my Estate whatever the same may be after the payment of my just and legal debts-

In testimony of which I have subscribed this my last Will at Baltimore in the State of Maryland in the United States of America, waiving all legal objections which may be had after my death to the form thereof by any person or persons who may wish to defeat the same the 8th day of July in the year One thousand Eight hundred and forty.

Arch McLean

State of Tennessee

Shelby County

A paper purporting to be the last Will and Testament of Arch McLean Deceased was produced in open Court this day and thereupon came into Court Joseph D Davis, Jacob N. Moon, Calvin Goodman, Charles D McLean John Ross who being first duly sworn ~~that they~~ depose and say That they are acquainted with the handwriting of the deceased and that they have examined the instrument produced as the last will and testament of the said deceased and that they believe it to be his own proper handwriting in every part thereof. Whereupon it is ordered that the same be recorded

Recorded December 22nd 1840 John W. Fuller Clerk.

J W Fuller Clk

(P-161) JAMES REMBERT DECEASED LAST WILL

In the name of God Amen

I James Rembert of the County of Shelby & State of Tennessee being of sound & disposing mind & memory do make ordain constitute & publish this my last Will & Testament in manner & form following to Wit

first I give & bequeath my wife my Children & my soul & body to God whose they are leaveing to the discretion of my dear wife the temporary disposition of my body

Item I give & bequeath unto my beloved wife Sarah Rebecca Rembert her heirs & assigns upon Conditions hereinafter expressed the following property to Wit the tract of land whereon I now live & the negroes Bot Vilot his wife July & Milly his wife Harriet & Nero their Children Ned & Tamer his wife & little Ned their Child Betty & Stephen Jack Alec Charles & Madison hur Children York & Matilda and his wife Qually & henry their Children Juay Littleton & Martha his wife & Mary Abraham & Lucy their Children Gabriel & Cinder his wife Julian & Clarisa & Sarah hur Children Saly Polidon

(P-161 cont.) Tom Daniel Winney & Madison together with the increase of their Bodies all & Singular said property both real & personal hur hur heirs & assigns forever

Item. I give & bequeath my son Lewellen Cassels Rembert one Negro girl Sally together with the increase of her body to him his heirs & assigns forever

Item I give & bequeath to my beloved Daughter Louisa Rebecca Rembert one Negro girl Rhoda together with the increase of her body to hur hur heirs & assigns forever.

Item I give & bequeath to my beloved son James Andrew Rembert one Negro Girl Rose together with the increase of hur body to him his heirs & assigns forever

Item Should another heir be born unto me of my wife, it is my will & desire that the Girl Mary allready (P-162) bestowed upon my wife be set apart as the legacy of him or hur so born

Item as to all the rest residue & remainder of my Estate both real & personal whether equitable or legal in possession or reversion I give & bequeath to my beloved wife to her heirs & assigns forever with full power to give sell & dispose of any & all the property by this will herein unto hur devised (under conditions above alluded to) and other investments to make at pleasure & without the responsibility to any person & tribunal whatever

Item I do hereby ordain my beloved wife Sarah R. sole executrix of this my last Will & Testament hereby revoking all former wills by me made nevertheless this my executrix shall not as such be held in any manner bound to the Court either in Bond or by oath

Lastly should my affectionate wife at any time during the lifetime of my above named Children or either of them or during the lifetime of any other Child of hers born & by me begotten forget hur first love & marry a second time then in that event it is my will & request & my last will & request that all the property herein devised to her & at such time in possession both real & personal together with prophets & rents debts & damages & accruing as from thenceforth revert to the surviving heir or heirs of her body by me begotten to be divided share & share alike according to the Statute of distribution in such case made & provided and in that event I furthermore do hereby appoint ordain & constitute my affectionate brotherinlaw George L Hines sole & only Guardian of such my Children & their property which said Guardian shall in no wise be required to give bond & security in any Court for the performance of his duties as such unless upon charge ~~upon~~ & prove of waste but shall under this my last Will & Testament (P-163) have full ample & complete control of the same until these my Children shall respectively by law be entitled each to his distributive share nevertheless nothing herein contained shall be so construed as to prevent this my brotherinlaw & friend from reserving as much the shear or moiety of each Child & will constitute such an aggregate sum as he may deem sufficient for the decent & proper support and maintenance of their mother

In witness whereof I have hereunto set my hand & Seal this the 5th

(P-163 cont.) of May A D 1838

Acknowledged by the Testator in ~~presence~~ to be his last Will & Testament in presence of us this the 8th day of May A D 1838.

James Rembert (Seal)

Witnesses Samuel Rembert George L Hines Turney T Lindsey

The last Will & Testament of James Rembert Deceased was produced in open Court George L Hines & Turner T Linsey subscribing witnesses thereto after being duly sworn depose & say that the testator acknowledged the same in their presence to be his last Will & Testament & that he was of sound mind & disposing memory at the time of acknowledging the same which is ordered to be recorded

Recorded April 22nd 1841. John W Fuller Clerk

John W Fuller Clerk

(P-164) JOHN N. LEWIS WILL

I John N. Lewis of the County of Shelby & State of Tennessee, do make this my last Will & Testament revoking all others made of a previous date

1st. It is my wish that all my just debts be paid out of the moneys due me I gave to my beloved wife Frances C Lewis all of my property to enjoy as long as she remains my widow and if she marries she shall have one fourth of my Estate both real & personal to enjoy so long as she may live and thereto dispose of it as she pleases

3rd It is my wish that my Children Sarah Frances and Gilly M. Lewis and the Infant yet unborn should be well educated and in the event one should not arrive to years of maturity his or her portion of the Estate shall revert to the other Children and be equally divided between them

4th. It is my wish that my Children should be educated out of my estate before the Estate is divided or in the event that Frances C. Lewis should marry & Claim the one fourth part of my Estate my Administrators shall reserve property enough to educate my Children & she shall then have the one fourth of the remainder to this my last Will & Testament I appoint my Brother Charles W. Lewis & my Friend Bennet Bagby my Executors as witness my hand & seal in the year of our Lord one thousand Eight hundred & forty one Feby. 26th

John N Lewis

Signed Sealed & delivered in the presence of

Andrew Shane William Puryear

(P-164 cont.) State of Tennessee)
May Term A D 1841
Shelby County)

A paper purporting to be the last Will & Testament of John N. Lewis, Deceased was produced in open Court and Andrew Shane & William Puryear subscribing witnesses thereto after being duly sworn depose & say that the testator signed and acknowledged the same in their presence to be his act and deed that he was of sound mind & disposing memory (P-165) at the time of signing and acknowledging the same which is ordered to be recorded

Recorded May 18th 1841 John W Fuller Clerk

John W Fuller Clerk

THOMAS ABERNATHY WILL

I Thomas Abernathy of the County of Shelby and State of Tennessee do hereby make this my last Will & Testament revoking all other whatsoever

It is my desire that my Executors which I shall hereafter name in the first place pay all of my Just debts

2nd it is my desire that four negroes namely Sarah Eliza Lavina & Sam be sold & the money laid out in other negroes such as they may think best and most suitable for their use & benefit

3rd It is my desire that my wife Martha Abernathy shall holdthe land ~~for~~ as a home for her during her widowhood or natural life also three negroes namely Ben Claburn and Dosey with all the perishable property belonging to me except my tools which I wish sold and one of the negroes that may be bought with the money arising from sale of the aforesaid Negroes.

4th I desire that my daughter Nancy should have a negro Girl Emerline which she is now in possession of to belong to hur & hur bodily heirs forever

5th I give to my son John S Abernathy one of the negroes that may be bought with the money arising from the sale of the aforesaid negroes

6th I give unto Martha H Abernathy my daughter a negro girl named Vilet

(P-166) 7th I give unto my son James R. Abernathy a negro that may be purchased with the money arising from the sale of the aforesaid negroes which I have directed should be sold

8th It is my further desire that my wife should give unto my aforementioned Children any property that she may have at any time that she can spare without injury to herself and at her death it is my desire that all the property be equally divided between my Children & furthermore I appoint my son John S Abernathy & my soninlaw Richard H. Crouch my executors to this my last Will & testament

(P-166 Cont.) Given under my hand & Seal this the 24th day of March 1841

Witness Reuben Massey Thos. Abernathy (Seal)

Henry G Jones

State of Tennessee)
May Sessions A D 1841
Shelby County)

A paper purporting to be the last Will & Testament of Thomas Abernathy was produced in open Court & Reuben Massey & Henry G Jones witnesses thereto after being Sworn depose & say that the Testator signed & acknowledged the same in their presence to be his last Will & Testament & that he was of sound mind and disposing memory at the time which is Ordered to be recorded

Recorded May 22nd 1841 John W Fuller Clk.

John W Fuller Clk

(P-167) JOSEPH CARR DECEASED WILL

Know all ye whom it may concern that I Joseph Carr, son of the late Thomas D. Carr of the County of Shelby and State of Tennessee being feeble in body but sound in mind in case of my death do make and declare this to be my last will & testament and the disposition ~~and the disposition~~ which I require shall be made of whatever Estate I may die possessed of

Item 1st I desire that my doctor's Bill and all other just debts be ~~paid~~ fully ~~paid~~ and promptly paid & discharged.

Item 2nd. It is my will & desire that my Executor hereinafter appointed shall dispose of a portion of my real & personal Estate to an amount not exceeding one thousand dollars and to pay the same over to the following trustees (VIZ) Anderson B Carr Tilman Bettis & M.B. Winchester and himself whom I desire shall purchase a site & erect a Tomb sufficiently large ~~sufficiently large~~ for the ~~bodies~~ reception of the Bodies of the different members of my Father's family who have departed this life and in which I desire also that my Body may be deposited leaving it discretionary with my said Trustees and the survivors of them either to take & retain the title to the said site & Tomb in trust to themselves & their heirs or to convey it in trust for the purposes aforesaid to any other individual or to any coperation if they deem it best to do so

Item 3rd I do hereby particularly enjoin upon my Devisee and Executors the Execution and Complyance with two several Contracts bearing date the 3rd day of June 1838 and the 15th day of April 1840 which I executed and entered into with Robertson Topp Esqr. to secure the emancipation of Negroes George Maris and their Children Francis Alfred Martha Leny Emily and Jane

(P-167 cont.) Item 4th all the rest & residue of my Estate both real personal and mixed Consisting of lands town lots Slaves Chattels or Improvements of whatsoever kind and ~~disposition~~ description I do hereby devise in fee and absolute property to my Brother John Carr

Item 5th for the execution of the foregoing Will I do hereby appoint my said Brother John Carr my (P-168) Executor with full power and authority to Carry out the intentions of my will.

In ~~testimony~~ witness of the foregoing I have signed my name and affixed my my seal June 11th 1841

Witnesses present   Joseph Carr (Seal)

M. B. Winchester W W Whitsett Neil McCoul

State of Tennessee)
August Sessions A D 1841
Shelby County)

A paper purporting to be the last Will & Testament of Joseph Carr Deceased was produced in open Court & W W Whitsett & Neil McCoul subscribing witnesses thereto after being duly sworn depose & say they were acquainted with the said Testator and that he acknowledged the same in their presence to be his last Will & Testament and that he was of sound mind & Disposing memory at the time he executed the same which is ordered to be recorded.

Recorded August 13th 1841   John W Fuller Clerk

John W Fuller Clerk

(P-169) JAMES P. TAYLOR WILL

I James P. Taylor being Sick of Body but of sound mind and memory do make & ordain this my last will & testament I desire that my Executors have me buried in Christian like manner along side of my Children and that my Eliza be removed from where she is now buried & reinterred along side of me

I will that all my Just debts be paid as soon as possible by my Executors and that the debts due me be forthwith Collected & Constitute a fund for that purpose. My will is that my Executors sell all my house property which may not be needed by the family and any an all of my negroes if they become unruly & unmanageable if said Executors if said Executors it an that as any other accounts advisable when I settled as Executer of my Father with the Commissioners of the County Court each heir fell in debt to me upwards of six hundred dollars which ballance then shown will be smartly enhanced by a variety of payments in taxes Lawyers' fees & the like I sold Roans Creek Iron works some years ago to David Waggoner and my Bond is out for the title when all my Father's heirs are of age my nephew Landon & Alfred, sons of my sister Betsy must make the title for their mother and on on that Condition I release them of the debt they in right of their mother's heretofore mentioned are due me which is a bequest to them I think of upwards of two hun-

(P-169 cont.) dred dollars they haveing been in the stead of of their mother entitled to five hundred dollars her portion of of the price of the Iron works &c in trade & Money one half each.

It is my will that my wife Mary C Taylor have my dwelling and such lands Connected with it as she needs for farming purposes during hur life then to decend to my Children To Wit) Emilina E Taylor, Nathaniel G Taylor Alfred M C Taylor & Mary P Taylor I also give and bequeath unto my wife Mary C Taylor all my houshold & Kitchen furniture except my Forte-piano which I give to my daughter Emilina and hereby direct my Executors should my daughter Mary ned one to purchase her one at the proper time,

(P-170) I give & bequeath unto my wife all the grain endhand and growing also my Bacon & also all my farming utensils wagons and as and as many of my horses Hogs Cattle &C as she may wish also my New Carriage my old Carriage I give & bequeath unto my Mother Mary Taylor.

I give & bequeath unto my wife Mary C Taylor all my negroes until my oldes Child comes of age or marries then it is my will that my wife have absolutely two fifths of my negroes & that the Ballance be allotted out equally among my Children as they may come of age or marry my Gold watch I present to my son Nathaniel and hereby direct - that my Executor in due season purchase one for my son Alfred my Books I direct my Executors to sell or retain for the benefit of my sons as they may think proper the library Called my wife's I give unto hur I do hereby direct my Executor to give my Children a good education if they will receive it out of any funds belong to my Estate. I hereby authorize my executors to sell any of my lands should they think the interest of my estate would be promoted by it, except my home farm, and the lands thereunto adjoining, the proceeds to be applied if necessary to the support and education of my children the balance if any to be paid over to them, with all the interest thereon as they may come of age or marry. The balance of my land which may remain unsold together with that portion of the roatangred lands not in the possion of my with, I give unto my children to be allotted to them as they may come of age or marry the land not allotted to my wife I do hereby direct my executors to rent out when they may think the interest of my estate requires it and apply the rent to the support of my family, and the balance if any toward the education of my children after the payment of my debts it is my will that the money arising from the sale of my stock and the debts due me be (P-180) (Editor's Note: Page 180 of O.MS should be page 171 - Discrepancy of ten pages) equally divided between my wife and children the portion, of the children not used in their education to be paid out to them as they may come of age or marry. I give and bequeath unto my wife the tract of land lying in Giles County Tennessee which decreed to her from her father's estate and which was conveyed to me by the heirs of Landon Carter. I give unto my nephews James P.T. Love, James P Taylor Son of A.W. Taylor, James P.T. Carter, son of A.W. Carter, James T. Carter, son of Wm. B. Carter, Fifty Dollars each, Also to James P. Taylor son of Leroy Taylor Twenty-five Dollars and to James T.P. Gifford a horse with twenty five Dollars, the horse to be paid over to the parents for the benefit of the child when my executors may think best The harness belonging to the carriage heretofore devised to go with them Should any lawsuit be brought against my executors or any difficulties occur in the settlement of my business my executors are hereby authorized to adjust the same any manner they may think will promote the interest of my estate in as full and ample a manner as I myself

(P-180 cont.) could do. I do hereby direct my executors to pay one third of the redemption money necessary to procure a title to some lots in the town of Covington sold as the property of Thomas Taylor and to see that a title is made to said lots to the children of my sister Betsy. I do hereby appoint my brother Alfred W Taylor my executor and my wife Mary C Taylor my executrix of this my last will and testament Also my son Nathaniel to one of my executors on his coming of age and do not wish security to be required of them. It is my Will that my wife be my executrix while she continues single and no longer.

In Testimony Whereof I have hereunto set my hand and (Editor's Note: A Discrepancy of Ten pages in O.MS.) (P-190 and Seal this 6th of January 1833

Signed Sealed and acknowledged in presence J.P. Taylor (Seal)

of us Wm. B. Carter Wm. R. Dulaney Saml. W.Williams.

State of Tennessee

Carter County

I James L. Bradley Clerk of the County Court for said County do certify that the within is a true copy of the original Will now on file in my office Given under my hand at office at Elizabethtown this 21st day November 1840

Recorded August the 14th 1841 James L. Bradley Clerk

John W. Fuller Clerk By C.W. Neilson D.C.

Count Court of Shelby County

(P-191) JOSEPH WHITE WILL

I Joseph White do make and publish this my last will and testament hereby revoking and making void all other wills by me at any time made

1st I give and bequeath to James Cutler all my real Estate in the town of Memphis consisting of one undivided half of three Houses and Lots on the north side and fronting on Winchester Street they being a part, and the Eastern Portion of Lot No. / One hundred and Forty Seven on the original plan of the said Town and described in deed recorded in the Register's office of Shelby County To Feeney & White to the same

In Testimony Whereof I do to this my Will set my hand and seal this 10th day of March 1841

Signed Sealed & Published in our presence and we have subscribed our names hereto in the presence of the testator this day and year above written Joseph White (Seal)

Test Robert A. Feeney P G Gaines J B Feeny

(P-191 cont.) State of Tennessee)
September Sessions A D 1841
Shelby County)

A paper purporting to be the will of Joseph White was produced in open Court Robert A Feeney J B Feeney subscribing witnesses thereto after being duly sworn depose & say that the aforesaid Joseph White acknowledged the same in their presence to be his last will and testament and that he was of sound mind and disposing memory at the time he acknowledged the same (P-192) it is therefore ordered to be recorded

Recorded September 10th 1841 John W Fuller Clk

State of Tennessee)
February Session A D 1843
Shelby County Court)

A Competent Court Present

On motion of Joseph White it ordered by the last Will and Testament of said White which was produced in open Court at a former Term ~~of~~ and proven by Robert A. Feeney and J.B. Feeney and ordered to be recorded be and the same is hereby made void in all things appertaining thereto

A true copy from the same

John W Fuller Clerk.

(P-193) JAMES TREZEVANT WILL

I James Trezevant formerly of County of South Hampton and commonwealth of Va. and now of the County of Shelby and State of Tennessee do hereby make and ordain this my last will & Testament revoking & disannulling all other and former wills by me heretofore made

I direct that my body after death shall lie three days before it be intered and that it shall be placed in a Coffin lined with tin and that Coffin be placed within another made in a plain & substantial manner and that it be placed in the vault by the side of the remains of my beloved son James Edmund I furthermore direct that my Executors do in some convenient time cause a grave to be sunk at the South end of the said vault sufficiently capacious to contain the two Coffins with my own and the remains of my said son and to be lined with a well built brick wall and that the said Coffins with their contents be deposited in it and covered over with brick and surmounted by a small mound and that at the west end of the said mound a stone be fixed with an inscription showing the object of the mound

It is my will that my negroes by Kept on the plantation where I now live under the care and management of my Executrix hereinafter named until my son Nath'l, Macon shall arrive to the age of twenty one years or shall marry and that the annual nett procedes arising from their labour be applyed to the payment of any debts which may be unpaid at the time

(P-193 cont.) of my death and to the support and maintenance of my wife and support and education of my said Son Nath'l. Macon

I give to my said son Nath'l. Macon whenever he shall marry or arrive at the age of twenty one years the plantation whereon I now live the Stock of horses, Mules, Cattle, Sheep & Hogs the plantation utensils and impliments household & Kitchen furniture and ~~all~~ the crops of all kinds then on hands or growing whenever my said son shall marry or arrive to the age of twenty one years I direct that my negroes be then divided into three equal parts one of which I give to my said son one to my daughter Catherine Cocke Tucker wife of Dr. W W. Tucker (P-194) & in case she should be then dead to such child or children as she may have left and that may be then liveing and the other I give to my wife but in case my wife should again marry I give it to hur only for & during her natural life and at hur death to be equally divided between my said son & daughter and in case my said daughter be then dead between my said son and such child or children as she may have left and that may then be liveing said son taking one half

In case my said wife should be dead when my said son should arrive ~~arrive~~ to the age of twenty one years or should marry then I direct that my negroes shall be ~~equally~~ divided equally between my said son & daughter and in case my said daughter should be then dead one half of my ~~said~~ negroes I give to my said son and the other half I give to such child or children as my daughter may have left and that may then be liveing

In case my daughter should be dead when my son arrives to the age of twenty one years or should marry and should leave no child then liveing then I give to ~~to~~ my Said son what hereinbefore was designed for hur & hur child or children

In case my son ~~son~~ should die before he arrives to the age of twenty one years or marries then the plantation Stock of every kind plantation utensils household & Kitchen furniture and crop then on hand and growing I give to my wife during her natural life and at hur death I give the same to my said daughter and in case she should ~~then~~ be then dead to such child or children as she may have left and that may then be liveing

In case my son should die ~~before~~ he arrives to the age of twenty one years or marries and my daughter should be also dead and leaving no child then I give the whole of my estate to my wife during her natural life and at her death ~~and at her death~~ to be equally divided between my Nephews Jno. P. Trezevant Lewis Edmond Trezevant James Hamilton Trezevant and James H. Harrison, James Edmond T Wyatt son of my Nephew George H. Wyatt.

(P-195) All the lots in Memphis and pieces of land near to Memphis which were held by Dr. Wm. W. Tucker and myself as joint owners, I give to the said Dr. Wm. W. Tucker, one lot in Memphis which I own lying on the railroad depot and all the lots I own in Pickering I give to my wife absolutely and I also give hur a carriage and horses and hur choice of the beds & furniture Bureaus &C Chambers furniture I give to my son Nath'l, a pattent lever gold watch presented to me by my friend the late Dr. Andrew Bailey of Turney County Virginia.

that portion of my estate which may remain in money after paying

(P-195 cont.) all debts and above what may be necessary to carry this will in to effect in relation to my son & wife I give in the same manner to the same persons in the same proportions as I have given my negroes. I desire that my Executrix or Executors will so order that my negroes shall be treated with humanity be comfortably clad and cloathed be bountifully fed taken care of specially when sick or aged and infirm and that as in my life a portion of the fruits of their labour be annually bestowed upon them to enable them to purchase articles that may contribute to their comfort

It is not only my wish but my positive instruction that my son Nath'l. M shall render during his manority in a non slave holding State and this injunction in the most explicit terms I impress upon his Guardian it is also my wish that he should receive a classical and collegiate education and that he should study some one of the liberal professions It is also my desire that my wife should spend her time in the vicinity of the place where my son may be educated for the purpose of extending to him hur parental care and advise

I hereby appoint my wife Mary Blunt Executrix to this my will and Guardian to my son Nath'l. Macon and in case of hur death or marriage during the minority of my said son I appoint my soninlaw, Dr. Wm W Tucker my brother Lewis C Trezevant and my nephew John P Trezevant to succeed hur in both offices

In testimony of the above I hereby declare that the whole of this writing was done by my own hand and no other and that I have affixed my name & seal to the same as my last will and Testament this the 6th day of March A D 1841

James Trezevant (Seal)

(P-196) State of Tennessee)
November Session A D 1841
Shelby County)

A Competent Court present

This day was produced in open Court a paper writing perporting to be the last Will & Testament of James Trezevant deceased thereupon came into Court Lewis C. Trezevant after being duly sworn depose & say that said paper writin was found among the valuable papers of the said Trezevant and thereupon came into Court Lewis C. Trezevant Jeptha Fowlks & Joseph Leno Creable witnesses who after being duly sworn depose & say that they are acquainted with the handwriting of the said Jas. Trezevant deceased they believe said paper writing and every part thereof to be in the handwriting of the said Jas. Trezevant deceased which is ordered to be recorded

Recorded November the 8th 1841 J W Fuller Clerk

J W Fuller Clk

(P-197 S H E D E R I C K C R O S S' W I L L

In the name of God Amen

I Shederick Cross do hereby make & publish this my last will & testa-

(P-197) ment revoking & making void all other wills made at any time before by me-

Item first it is my wish *that my personal expences & all my just debts be paid out of whatever money I may be posesed of when I die or that may first come into the hands of my Executors

Item Second It is my wish & desire that my wife Elizabeth Cross shall have the following described property of which she is to have the benefit during her natural life subject However to the following limitations & restrictions & at her death it shall revert to my son Coleman, that is to say, one negro woman named Mahaily with her youngest child america & all her future increase, all my poltry, one iron gray Horse ten year old, five head of Sheep the best of my flock, one cow named Suky & her calf one feather bed bed stead & bed furniture & chest one Spinning wheel & reel, one pot which is hooped one small oven & Skillit to be furnished by my Executors, one large pail & piggin, one pair of pot hooks, one pair of Andirons, one set of cups & saucers one set of plates, one dish, two chairs, one table & table cloth, one set of knives & forks and one sad iron all of which property shall be given to my son Henry S Cross in trust for the benefit of my wife Elizabeth during her natural life And it is my wish & desire that Henry C Cross, whom I appoint as Trustee shall provide my wife Elizabeth with a comfortable House & support her comfortably and he shall have as a remuneration the increase of the said stock & the service of the negroes which he hold in trust-

(P-198)(Continued) Item third- I give & bequeath to my son Francis M Cross the tract of land on which he now lives containing one hundred acres more or less, also one Negro Boy named Mack & one negro boy named James and also all the personal property I have heretofore given him on condition that he pays to my Executors one hundred and ninety two dollars-

Item fourth - I give & bequeath to my son Micajah Cross one hundred acres of land of the tract I purchased of Joseph Logan, the division line to be run North and South so as to include the house where he now lives- I also give to him one Negro Girl Barthenia & also one negro Girl Nancy provided he pays R.A. Miller fifty dollars & all personal property I may heretofore given him

Item fifth - I give and bequeath to my son Benjamin F Cross - one hundred acres of land, part of the tract I purchased of Joseph Logan, the division line to run North & South so as to given him the west end of said tract of Land I also give him one Negro Girl Harriet one cow & calf - which are now in his possession, one hundred & fifty eight dollars in money to be paid to him by my Executors & also one set of old carriage wheels -

Item Sixth - I give & bequeath to my son Andrew J Cross one hundred acres of land part of the tract of land I now live on, the division line to commence on Schulyler Roberts' East boundary line running thence East to the turn in the land, thence North & East for compliment, so as to divide the whole tract according to quality & so as to give him the northern divisions I also give to him one negro woman (P-199) and her two Children Allen & John, two steers worth fifteen dollars one feather bed & furniture, one set of wagon wheels & all the personal property I have heretofore given him, on condition that he pays to my Executors ninety two dollars

*& desire

(P-199 cont.) Item Seventh I give & bequeath to my son Henry C. Cross the south half of the tract I now live on, one Negro Boy Samuel, one Negro man Emanuel, one Negro woman Polly, one Roan horse one yoke of oxen Mose & Tom, two cows & calves Stately & Dosey three sows & pigs, two Known by the name of the Aken sows & the other by the name of the young Ferry sow five hundred pounds of pork one feather bed & furniture & my best wagon, on condition he pays to my Executors one hundred & thirty three dollars

Item Eighth I give and bequeath to my son Coleman H Cross thirty two & one half acres of land lying in Giles County & State of Tennessee it being a part of my wife Elizabeth's estate & one Negro Boy Jesse to be given into the hands of Henry C. Cross as Trustee, all of which property shall be held by said Henry C Cross as Trustee, until said Coleman H. Cross becomes of age for his maintenance & education and in case of the death Coleman H the property shall then be given into the hands of my Executors, and I also wish my son Coleman H to have six hundred dollars in money which is to be obtained out of that portion of my estate not heretofore appropriated if this be be that amount and if there is not I wish the deficit made good by all the Legatees(Editor's Note:page torn off) their proportional part equally (P-200) And the Executors shall loan the money on interest taking bonds & renewing the same until he is of age or dies

Item Ninth It is my wish that my Executors pay to the heirs of Benjamin Ishmail two hundred twenty three dollars when they call for it

Item Tenth- It is my wish that the residue of my property if any & the balance of my estate be equally divided between all my children

I nominate & appoint my two sons Frances M. Cross & Micajah Cross my Executors, who are authorized to carry out the intentions of this my last will & testament

Witness my hand & seal this 18th day of August A.D. 1841-

Test. Wm. M. Perkins
Richardson Whitby Edwin Phillips-

Shederick his X mark Cross (Seal)

State of Tennessee)
SS October Sessions 1841
Shelby County)

A Competent Court present

A paper purporting to be the last will and testament of Shederick Cross was produced in open court and William Perkins & Edwin Phillips subscribing witnesses thereto after being duly sworn depose & say that the Testator acknowledged the same in their presence to be his last will and Testament & that he was of sound mind and disposing memory at the time he acknowledged the same which is ordered to be recorded

Recorded 16th November 1841 John W Fuller Clk

John W Fuller Clk

(P-201) NANCY TOSERS WILL

I Nancy Toser of the County of Prince George do make and ordain this my last will & Testament in manner & form as follows

Item 1st I give and bequeath unto my Daughter Georgianna C Johnson one Negro woman Named Levinea and Girl Sally as her propotion of her brother's estate

Item 2nd After paying my just debts I lend the whole of my property to my daughter Georgianna C, Johnson to manage as she may think best for her benefit her natural life then to go to the lawful begotten heir or heirs of her body but if she should die without such heir or heirs I wish it to be divided between my two daughters Eliza M B. Simmons & Martha C. Hall their natural life and then to their lawful begotten heirs of their body and if either of them should die without such heir or heirs my wish is it should go to the remainder of my grandchildren to them and their heirs forever

I do nominate my daughter Georgianna C, Johnson Executrix of this my last will and Testament I desire no security be required

Signed in the presence of Elizabeth Epps Martha L Jones February 22nd 1833 — Nancy Tosers (Seal)

State of Virginia

Sussex County Towit

We John Winfield & William Chambliss Justices of the peace for the county & State aforesaid do hereby certify that Elizabeth Epps a subscribing witness to the within will of Nancy Toser personally appeared before us in our said county & made oath the Testatrix in her presence signed and (P-202)(Nancy Tosers Will) acknowledged it to be her will & that she was of sound mind & disposing memory at that time

Given under our hands this 8th day of June 1839

John Winfield, J.P.

Wm. O Chambliss, J.P.

Virginia Sussex County SS

I Littleton Lanier Clerk of the County Court of Sussex ~~County~~ in the State of Virginia aforesaid do hereby certify that John Winfield & William O Chambliss who have given the proceeding certificate are now and were at the time of signing the same acting Justices of the peace in and for the county aforesaid duly commissioned and qualified & that full faith and credit are due to all their original acts as such

Given under my hand and seal of Office this 11th Day of June A D 1839

L Lanier

(P-202 cont.) State of Virginia

Town of Petersburg Towit

I David Meade Bernard Clerk of the Hastings Court of the town of Petersburg in the State of Virginia do hereby certify that John Pollard & Luke White whose names are subscribed to the certificate at the foot of this page are justices of the peace in & for the said town duly appointed & qualified as such & that full faith & credit are due & ought to be given to all their official acts

In Testimony Whereof I hereto set my hand & affix the seal of the said court this 29th day of June in the year 1839

D M Bernard (Seal)

Virginia Town of Petersburg To wit

We Luke White & John Pollard Justices of the peace for the Town aforesaid do hereby certify that Martha L formerly M L Jones a subscribing Witness to the within will of Nancy Toser personally appeared (P-203) before us in our said Town & made oath that the Testatrix in her presence signed ~~sealed~~ and acknowledged the same to be her will & testament & at the time of making it was of sound mind and disposing memory

Given under our hands this 29th day of June 1839

John Pollard, Seal

L White, Seal

State of Tennessee)
October Session 1841
Shelby County)

A Competent Court present A paper purporting to be the last will & testament of Nancy Toser Deceased was produced in open Court which was received & ordered to be recorded

Recorded 16th November 1841 John W. Fuller Clerk

John Fuller Clk

(P-204) SAMUEL MAKEY WILL

In the name of God Amen I Samuel Mackey of Shelby County & State of Tennessee being of sound and disposing mind memory & understanding knowing the uncertainty of this life do make this my last Will & Testament give & devise as follows

Item it is my wish & desire after all my Just debts and necessary expenses are paid that my Brother Philemon Mackey who now lives in Baltimore Maryland have all my real & person Estate & lastly I do appoint William H Chaplain Executor of my Estate to settle all my unsettled business and after all expences are paid to pay over to my Brother Philamon Mackey

(P-204 cont.) all that is left.

Saml Mackey (Seal

Signed & sealed in the presence of us who at the same time see him subscribe his name hereunto this 26th day of August A D 1841 Interlined before signed

E.F. Ruth J L Kennedy F Newhall

State of Tennessee)
October Session A D 1841
Shelby County)

A Competent Court present

A paper perporting to be the last Will & Testament of Samuel Mackey deceased was produced in open Court E F Ruth & J L Kennedy Subscribing witnesses ~~to~~ there to after being duly sworn depose & say that the testator acknowledged the same in their presence to be his last Will & Testament & that he was of sound mind & disposing at the time he acknowledged the same which is ordered to be recorded.

Recorded November 21st 1841 John W Fuller Clk

(P-205) E L D R I D G E W J O N E S W I L L

I Eldridge W. Jones of the County of Shelby & State of Tennessee do make & publish this as my last Will & Testament hereby revoking & making void all other wills by me at any time made.

first I direct that my funeral expenses and all my debts be paid as soon after my death as convenient out of any moneys that my first come into the hands of my Executor

Secondly I give & bequeath to my beloved wife Charlotte Jones the following property during her lifetime or or widowhood Viz the tract of land on which I now reside being the same purchased of Benjamin Robins Esqr. hur choice of the two negro girls Mary and Malinda two Feather Beds & Bedsteads & furniture as many other things about the house & Kitchen as she may think proper to Keep five head of Cattle of any sort or Kind that she may chose out of my Stock of Cattle two sows & pigs Stock hogs enough to make hur a sufficiency of meat the first year after my death exclusive of the sows & pigs a sufficiency of corn for her support for twelve months fifty pounds of Coffee & fifty pounds of Sugar one Barrel flour two hoes one axe Cotton enough to furnish hur for one year and money enough to buy a good serviceable family horse when my executor shall think it necessary to purchase one for the use of the family

thirdly I direct that provided my wife Charlotte Jones shall marry again after my death that she shall be dispossessed of all that I have bequeathed forthwith and the executor of my estate to rent out the land till the youngest child becomes of age and dispose of the ballance of the things as may seem to him best

(P-205 cont.) Fourthly I direct my Executor to sell a certain tract or parcel of land in Pitt County (P-206) North Carolina now in possession of William Galloway the proceeds to be applied to the payments of my debts and all monies that may remain after my debts are paid I want to be put to interest and that Interest to be applied to the Education & support of my children

Fifthly I request my Executor to have a small dwelling house built on some part of the land and rent out a part of my land and have moore cleared if in the opinion of my wife and himself that it will be an advantage to hur & to the Estate

Sixthly I request my executor to have a sale of all the property belonging to me that has not been bequeathed to my wife Charlotte Jones as soon as convenient after my death upon a twelve month Credit except the Negro Girl & her I want Sold upon a credit of Eighteen months

Sevently I direct my executor provided there is money enough to pay all my debts without selling the negro not sell hur but direct giveing my wife the money to buy a horse and I give hur the negro girl for the same length of time and on the same terms that I have given hur the other things.

lastly I do hereby nominate and appoint Elijah Amonet my Executor In witness whereof I do to this my will set my hand & seal this 30th day of July in the year of our Lord 1841

his
Eldridge X W. Jones (Seal)
mark

Signed sealed and published in our presence and we have subscribed our names hereto in the presence of the Testator this 30th day of July 1841

H. F. Hamner Wm. J Robins
Joshua Ecklin

(P-207) State of Tennessee)
October Session A.D. 1841
Shelby County)

A Competent Court present

A paper perporting to be the last Will & Testament of Eldridge W Jones deceased was produced in open Court and Wm. J Robins & Joshua Ecklin subscribing witnesses thereto after being duly sworn depose and say that the Testator acknowledged the same in their presence to be his last will & Testament and that he was of sound mind & disposing memory at the time he acknowledged the same which is ordered to be recorded.

Recorded November 21st 1841 John W Fuller Clerk

J W Fuller Clerk

A C H E L E S J O N E S W I L L

In the name of God Amen I Achelles Jones of the County of Shelby

(P-207 cont.) & State of Tennessee do make this my last Will & Testament

Article 1st I will & bequeath to my sister Mary Indianna Boyd in her own right my negro woman Rebecca and Child

Article 2nd I will & bequeath to my Brother Cesar A Jones two thousand dollars to be paid by my Executor herein named

Article 3rd I will & bequeath to my Brother Chamberlayne Jones (whom I appoint my executor with requiring of him to give security) all the ballance of my estate both real & personal not named above

Article 4th my desire is that my executor shall keep my property under his management until all my Just debts are paid and then the net proceeds of it applied to the to the payment of the two thousand dollars left to my Brother Carsar A Jones until it is paid

Article 5th I will & bequeath in addition to the two thousand dollars my negroes Charles & Lolly to to my (P-208) (Continued) Brother Carsar A Jones.

In testimony whereof I affix my hand and seal this the 2nd day of September 1841

Witnesses Catherine Greenhill Joshua Starkey

Achelles Jones (Seal)

State of Tennessee)
October Session A.D. 1841
Shelby County)

A Competent Court present

A paper perporting to be the last Will & Testament of Achelles Jones was produced in open court & Joshua Starkey one of the subscribing witnesses thereto after being duly sworn depose & say that the testator acknowledged the same in his presence to be his last Will & Testament and that he was of sound & disposing memory at the time of acknowledging the same which is ordered to be filed for further probate

John W Fuller Clerk

State of Tennessee)
~~October~~ December Session
Shelby County) A D 1841

A Competent Court present

The last Will & Testament of Achelles Jones decd. was produced in open court and Catherine Greenhill a subscribing witness thereto after being duly sworn deposeth & Sayeth that Achelles Jones acknowledged the same in hur presence to be his last Will & Testament and that he was of sound mind & disposing memory at the time of acknowledging the same which is ordered to be recorded

John W Fuller Clerk

Recorded December 20th 1841

John W. Fuller Clerk

(P-209) MOSES HORN WILL & TESTAMENT

State of Louisiana

Parish of West Feliciana

I Moses Horn at present residing in the County of Shelby and State of Tennessee revoking all others do make and declare this to be my only last Will & Testament

First It is my will & desire that my house woman Ann Higdon should be ~~be~~ free at and after my death

Second It is my will & desire that my negro man Guy should be free at and after my death

Third I give & bequeath to my Servant girl Ann Higdon Five hundred dollars to be paid to her by my Executors in cash

Fourth I give & bequeath to my Nephew Benjamin Whitwell Cotton my land lying and being in the County of Halifax and State of North Carolina being the same Willed and bequeathed to me by my Sister Dolly Hawkins to him & his heirs forever

Fifth I give & bequeath to my Niece Mary C Cotton the plantation whereon I at present reside lying and being in the County of Shelby & State of Tennessee to her and her heirs forever

Sixth It is my will & desire that my colored boy should remain with Drewry T Mitchel until March 1845 and then to be free

(P-210) (Continued) Seventh I give & bequeath unto my hereinafter named Executor R Mumford Esqr one thousand dollars

Eighth It is my will & desire that the ballance of my Estate after paying all my Just debts be equally divided between my Nephew Benjamin W Cotton Emily Dickson and Mary C Cotton Share and Share alike

Ninth I do hereby nominate constitute and appoint my friend Robinson Mymford to be the executor of this my last Will & Testament hereby giveing to my said Executor the Leisure and possession of my entire Estate with power to continue from year to year until my entire Estate is Settled enjoining it on my said Executor to see this my last Will & Testament faithfully executed according to the intent expressed therein and with the least expense the law will permit.

this my last will & testament is written by my Self and completed & Signed with my own proper Signature at the house of Robinson Mumford in St. Francisville Louisianna this 1st day of Febry 1841

Moses Horn

State of Tennessee)
January Sessions A D 1842
Shelby County)

A competent Court present

(P-210 cont.) A paper perporting to be the last Will & Testament of Moses Horn deceased was produced in open court thereupon came into court John Pope and after being sworn (P-211) depose & Say that said Will & Testament was found among the valuable papers of the said Moses Horn ded. thereupon came into court C.D. McLean W Christian and John Pope who after being duly sworn depose & say that they are acquainted with the handwriting of Moses Horn and that they believe said Will & Testament and every part thereof to be in the handwriting of said Moses Horn which is ordered to be recorded.

Recorded Feby 24th 1842 John W. Fuller Clerk

John W Fuller Clerk

Codicil to the last Will & Testament of Moses Horn dcd.

I Moses Horn of the County of Shelby & State of Tennessee lately of the State of ~~the State~~ Louisianna haveing heretofore made & executed a will a copy of which will be found among my papers and also a copy of which is left in the possession of Robinson Mumford of the town of St. Francisville Louisianna, do make and ordain thereto this paper as a codicil and direct that the same may be executed and fully carried out and administered by my executor as part of the same

Item It is my will and devise that my Sister Mary Cotton of Halifax County of North Carolina should have the use occupation and possession of the farm or Homestead on which I now live together with the use and benefit of all the live Stock farming utensils household furniture and fixtures of every Sort Kind & description which may be found on the said farm or homestead place during her natural life also of my three Servants Isaac Henry and Mary & ther increase

Item 2nd To my Niece Mary C Cotton after the death of my said Sister I do hereby give grant and devise forever all the aforesaid live Stock farming utensils household furniture & fixtures of every sort Kind (P-212) and description upon the said farm or homestead to have and possess to herself and heirs forever

In witness of which I have hereto set my hand and Seal December the 29th 1841

Witness present Moses Horn (Seal)
M.B. Winchester

State of Tennessee)
Febry Session A D 1842
Shelby County)

A Competent Court present

A Codicil to the last Will & Testament of Moses Horn deceased was produced in open Court and M. B. Winchester a subscribing witness to the same after being duly Sworn deposeth & Sayeth that the said Moses Horn acknowledged the same in his presence to be his codicil to his last Will and Testament and that he was of sound mind & disposing memory at the time of said acknowledgment which is ordered to be recorded

John W Fuller Clerk

(P-212 cont.) Recorded Febry 24th 1842

John W. Fuller Clerk

(P-213) J O S E P H C O T T O N D E C E A S E D W I L L

In the name of God Amen. I Joseph Cotten of the State of Tennessee & County of Shelby being feeble in body but ~~but~~ of sound and disposing mind do make and publish this the following to be my last Will & Testament hereby revoking and annulling all others before made by me

It is my desire that all my property personal & real shall be Kept together and worked undividually untill all my debts are paid except my Goodward plantation which I order to be sold as the expiration of Twelve Months.

Should my Estate be pressed for means to discharge my debts in that case I empower my executors hereinafter appointed to sell forty Such negroes as they may Select or to make any other arrangement for the purpose of liquidating my debts as I myself might properly do if liveing

Item It is my desire that all my landed property remaining after the payment of my debts be Equally divided among my Sons.

It is my desire that all my personal property except what is here after bequeathed to my beloved wife Elizabeth H Cotton be equally divided among my Children except ~~except~~ my dear daughter Mary Ann Mayes who is hereinafter provided for

I give to my beloved wife Elizabeth H Cotton my Carriage and Carriage horses together with a child's part of my personal estate in fee simple forever

I give unto my Son Jas. A. Cotton in trust not for his benefit but for the benefit of my beloved daughter Mary Ann Mayes and the heirs of her body an equal dividen with my other children in all my negro property that may belong to my estate after the final settlement of all my debts should my dear daughter Mary Ann Mayes die leaving no heirs of her body ~~then in that case~~ the property herein bequeathed to Jas. A Cotton for her benefit and the benefit of the heirs of her body to revert to my Estate and be equally divided among my Sons

(P-214) I give unto my son Jas. A. Cotton the gold watch which I now ware and ~~and~~ order that my executor whenever my estate is released from debt give unto each of my younger sons a good Gold watch should a further sale of property become absolutely necessary besides wat is heretofore ordered I direct a further sale of as many and no moore than may be requisite to liquidate remaining Claims-

I appoint my friend M D Cooper of ~~New Orleans~~ New Orleans La and my two Sons James N Cotton & Jospph A Cotton Executors to carry into fect the purposes and intentions of this my last Will & Testament it is my desire that no security shall be required of them either Jointly or individually.

(P-214 cont.) It is my desire that this will be properly aranged and prepared for probate and registration in West Felicianna Paris La wherein my lands newly purchased of James C Leake lie

In testimony whereof I have hereunto set my hand & affixed my seal this 23rd Jany. A D 1842

W Christian Washington Bond   Joseph Cotton (Seal)

Samuel Bond

State of Tennessee)
                                   Feby. Session A D 1842
Shelby County Court)

A Competent Court present

A paper perporting to be the last will and testament of Joseph Cotton deceased was produced in open Court Washington Bond and Samuel Bond Subscribing witnesses thereto after being duly sworn depose & Say that the testator acknowledged the same in their presence to be his last Will & Testament and that he was of sound mind and disposing memory at the time of acknowledging the same which is order to be recorded

Recorded Feby. 24th 1842   John W. Fuller Clk

John W. Fuller Clk

(P-215) J O H N S N O W D C D. W I L L

I John Snow being of sound & perfect mind and memory do make & publish this my last Will and Testament in manner & form following.

First I give and bequeath unto my beloved Grand son Green Summerfield Snow my Negro Slave Sam

Secondly I give and bequeath unto my beloved Daughter Marth Halley my negro boy Wesley

Thirdly. I give and bequeath unto my beloved daughter Sarah Snow my negro girl Mary also one horse bridle and Saddle and one Bed and furniture

Fourthly I give and bequeath unto my beloved son John Snow Jr. his heirs and assigns all my right title claim and Interest in and to one hundred and forty five acres of land with all the Improvements &c thereunto belonging lying and being in the County of Shelby and State of Tenhessee on the waters of Wolf River being the place whereon I now live

I also give and bequeath unto him the said John Snow Jr. further my negro woman Loucinda and her two children Henry and Tom I give him further all my Stock of Horses Cattle Hogs and Sheep the foregoing bequests are without reserve and uncoditional

I now given and bequeath unto my beloved son Jon Snow Jr. my two

(P-215 cont.) negro men Anthony & Jack on conditions following

First that he takes good care of myself and his mother during our lifetime and also takes good care of his Sister Sarah free of charge during her lifetime or while she remains Single and secondly on the condition further that he payes to my eldest son William Snow the sum of three hundred dollars within two years after my death and also payes unto my beloved Daughter Polly two hundred dollars (P-216) (Continued) within three years after my death and that he payes to my beloved daughter Sarah Snow one hundred dollars and to my beloved son Edmond Snow two hundred dollars within five years from the time he takes possession of the property herein specified

It is my will that provided the said John Snow Jr. does not comply with the conditions above specified that at the end of five years from my death the above negro men Anthony and Jack shall be sold and the amount specified in the conditions above Specified paid over to the persons therein named out of the procedes of such Sale and the ballance of the procedes of the sale to be equally divided between the Legatees named in this will provided however - that the said negro man Anthony* are not to be sold during the lifetime of my well beloved wife Sarah Snow if she survives me moore than five years, but after her death they are to be sold and the and the procedes of such Sale applied as before stated If the said John Snow Jr. should fail to fulfil the conditions on which I give them to him

I hereby constitute and appoint John Snow Jr and Paschal C Halley Executors of this my last Will & testament

Signed sealed & published this the 4th day of November in the year of our Lord 1840

In presence of T A Young
Thos M Ross

John Snow (Seal)

State of Tennessee)
October Session A D 1841
Shelby County)

A Competent Court present

(P-217) A paper perporting to be the last will & Testament of John Snow deceased was produced Court and Thomas M Ross one of the subscribing witnesses thereto after being duly sworn depose & Say that the Testator acknowledged the same in his presence to be his last Will & Testament and that he was of sound mind and disposing memory which is ordered to be filed for further probate

John W Fuller Clerk

State of Tennessee)
January Session A D 1842
Shelby County)

A Competent Court present

A paper perporting to be the last will & Testament of John Snow deceased which was proven in open Court at the October term of said Court and proven by Thomas M Ross one of the subscribing witnesses thereto was this day produced in open court and T A Young the other subscribing witness there-

* and Jack

(P-217 cont.) to after being duly sworn deposeth and saith that the Testator acknowledged the same in his presence to be his last Will & Testament and that he was of sound mind and disposing memory at the time of acknowledging the same which is ordered to be recorded

Recorded March 1st 1842 John W Fuller Clerk

John W Fuller Clerk

(P-218) EDMOND H VAUGHN WILL

State of Tennessee)
Feby 20th 1842
Shelby County)

In the name of God Amen

I Edmon Vaun ~~of the~~ being in a low state of health but in sound and disposing mind I do make this my last Will & Testament.

Item 1st. I give unto my beloved wife Lory Vaun all of my property consisting of household & Kitchen furniture and all of my bonds & notes and all monies that may hereafter belong to

I do not will any of my property to any of my children as they heretofore received that portion of my Estate that allotted for them

It is my will & desire that John Ralston esqr. should attend to the settling of my business and I leave him as my Executor

Given under my hand and seal this the 20th of Febry 1842.

Test Emanuel Baker E H Vaughn (Seal)
John J Medlock

State of Tennessee)
April Session A D 1842
Shelby County Court)

A Competent Court present

A paper perporting to be the last Will & Testament of of E. H. Vaughn dcd. was produced in open court thereupon came into court E Baker one of the subscribing witnesses thereto who after being duly sworn depose and say that said testator acknowledged the same in his presence to be his last Will & testament and that his mind was sufficiently sound to make his last Will & Testament ordered that said Will be recorded

Recorded May 28th 1842 John W Fuller Clk

(P-219) R O B E R T W A R E W I L L

I Robert Ware being perfectly in my senses and haveing a desire to regulate my temporal concerns I hereby ordain this my last Will & Testament by which I give unto my beloved wife Lolly Watson property real & personal for her own use during her widowhood except such part thereof as may be necessary to give to each of my children as may marry or otherwise wish to go to themselves that is each of ~~them~~ such one horse, one cow & calf one Bed & furniture and should my wife Lolly Watson marry after my dc. I hereby ordain and appoint that all my property personal or real shall be equally divided between all my children encluding what amount each one may have received previously to such division & I do hereby further appoint John Ralston & Wm. Shelby to Execute This my last Will & Testament

Signed in the presence of Robert Ware
John C Johnson Richard C Wyatt this 10th day of Jany 1841

State of Tennessee)
May Session A D 1842
Shelby County Court)

A Competent Court present

A paper perporting to be the last Will & Testament of Robert Ware dcd. was produced in open court thereupon came into court Richard C Wiatt one of the subscribing witnesses thereto who after being duly sworn depose & say & say that said Testator acknowledged the same in his presence to be his his last Will & Testament and that he was of sound mind and disposing memory at the time he acknowledged the same ordered that said Will be recorded

Recorded May 28th 1842 John W Fuller Clerk

John W.Fuller Clk.

(P-220) J O H N P W A G N O N W I L L

In the name of God Amen

I John P Wagnon of the State of Tennessee and county of Shelby being of sound mind but weak in body conscious that I must sooner or later be called off from this life do now make this my last Will & Testament Viz)

First- It is my will that after the tract of land formerly owned by Mrs. Lockey Sanders is sold to meet first the debts due the heirs of Thomas Sanders & Ann Martin they being entitled to their respective shares in the above named land as the heirs of Thomas Sanders the above named Ann Martin is in her right entitled to a portion of the Estate abovenamed

Secondly that my Just debts be paid out of the ballance of the

(P-220 cont.) proceeds as far as it will go and should that not be sufficient the remainder must be met by any assets belonging to my Estate

Secondly it is my will that after my Just debts ate paid my beloved wife Mary should have the controll of my estate during her lifetime for the purpose of keeping it together and supporting and educating my children should my wife find that she cannot conveniently manage for all my children at home it is my will that she should lend out some of the younger boys for a period not exceeding three years also that my wife have a sufficient support during her lifetime out of my estate apart of the assets above mentioned is a note for Eighteen hundred dollars which will be due me by November next It is my will that my son Edward L Wagnon should retain the negro Boy Bundy now in his possession also a cow & calf and pigs now in his possession

It is also my will that as my Daughters come of age or should marry that they each have a negro girl and as my sons come of age that they have a negro boy or negro man save my son Edward to whom I have already willed the boy Bundy (P-221) (Continued) It is my wish that James T Lamaster and Thomas Holeman should serve as my Executors and that my wife should act as Executrix

In testimony whereof I have this day set my hand and this ~~the~~ 10th day of March in the year of our Lord one thousand Eight hundred and forty two

In the presence of W. T. Sanders Henry McAllen W J Wagnon (Seal)

State of Tennessee)
April Session A D 1842
Shelby County)

A Competent Court present

A paper perporting to be the last Will & Testament of John P. Wagnon dcd. was produced in open court & Wm. T. Sanders and Henry McAllen subscribing witness thereto who after being duly sworn depose and say that the testator acknowledged the same in their presence to be his last Will & Testament and that he was of sound mind and deposing memory at the time he acknowledged the same which is ordered to be recorded.

Recorded May 30th 1842 John W Fuller Clerk

John W Fuller Clerk

(P-222) Z E N A S M E L O N S W I L L

I Zenas Melon of the county of Shelby and State of Tennessee being of sound mind and memory do make this my last Will and Testament revoking all others, in manner & form following viz-

I give and bequeath to the Cumberland Presbyterian Church to which I belong three acres of Land to be laid off in a square to include the pre-

(P-222 cont.) sent church of which the church is now to have the benefit I also give and bequeath to the abovementioned church after the death of my beloved wife Marinda forty acres more adjoining and off the South end of my land-

I give and bequeath to John T. Henderson and his wife Cynthia fifteen acres of land to include where he now resides the field surrounding the house to be enlarged so as to make the fifteen abovenamed This I give to the abovenamed John T. Henderson and his wife Cynthia during their lifetime on residence on said land

I give and bequeath to my negro girl Frances commonly called Frank Sixty acres of land off the North end of my Tract for her to live on should it be her choice or to be sold for the purpose of sending her to some free state or Island but this not until the death of my wife Marinda unless it should be her pleasure to set her free during her lifetime. I further bequeath to said Frances her freedom after the death of my wife.

I give and bequeath to William Perry Soward son of James Soward my half Brother and to his heirs Sixty acres of Land and at the death of my wife Marinda it is my Will and desire that the said William Perry Soward and his heirs after him shall have the remaining Sixty acres of my land to include my present residence

It is my will and desire that my beloved wife Marinda shall have during her lifetime the exclusive use and benefit of my landed Estate with the exception (P-223) (Continued) of the acres above bequeathed to the Cumberland Presbyterian Church and the fifteen acres above bequeathed to John T. Henderson and wife Cynthia and should the above named John T. Henderson and ~~his~~ wife Cynthia see proper to remove from said land it is my will and desire that it shall also be subject to the control of my wife Marinda the same as my other lands It is my will and desire that my wife Marinda shall sell* such of my stock of horses cattle and hogs and household furniture as can be most conveniently spared for the purpose of paying my just debts and providing her with family necessaries

All my other property of whatever description I give and bequeath to my beloved wife, Marinda for her use & benefit Whenever the fifteen acres bequeathed to John T. Henderson and wife Cynthia reverts to my estate it is my will & desire that it also after the death of my wife Marinda shall go to William Perry Souard above named in manner and form as his other bequests. I give and bequeath ~~to said church~~ for the benefit of the abovenamed church and lands bequeathed to said church the timber on five acres of Land on the ridge line West and adjoining a field now owned by George Clark said field is the North part to the occupant owned by Arther Callis

I give and bequeath to John T. Henderson and wife Cynthia as much timber as may be necessary for keeping up the enclosures and other necessary uses

It is my will and desire that there be no more timber cut on my lands than may be necessary for keeping up the present enclosures with those abovenamed.

* at public sale

(P-223 cont.) In Testimony of the above I annex my hand and seal this 14th day of July 1842

Zenas Melon (seal)

In presence of G. Clark D McFadyn,
Thos. J Coghill

(P-224) (Z Mellons Will Continued)

State of Tennessee)
August Session 1842
Shelby County)

A Competent Court being present.

A paper purporting to be the last Will & Testament of Zenas Mellon Deceased, was produced in open court and thereupon came D McFadyn & Thos. J Coghill Subscribing witnesses thereto who being duly sworn according to law depose and say that the Testator Signed the same in their presence & acknowledged it to be his act & deed for the purposes therein named. And that he was of sound mind and disposing memory at the time of making said acknowledgment which is ordered to be so certified

Recorded August 12th 1842 John W Fuller Clk

John W Fuller Clerk

(P-225) A N N T I N S L E Y S W I L L

In the name of God Amen

I Ann Tinsley of the County of Goochland & State of Virginia, for the convenient disposition of any estate after my death do hereby make ordain & declare & utter and publish this as & for my last Will & testament.

Imprimis I will & desire that all just debts be paid

Item, I give and bequeath to my Executors hereinafter named and to the survivor of them & to the heirs & Executors of the Survivor of them in trust from my daughter Marie F. Brown during her life three thousand dollrs the interest of which I direct them to pay to her quarterly during her life, and at her death I give the said sum of three thousand dollars to the children of my grandson Henry P Richardson & my great granddaughter Mary Ann Walker to be equally divided between such of the children of my said grand son Henry P Richardson & my said granddaughter Mary Ann Walker as shall be alive at the death of my said daughter Marie F Brown.

Item, I give & bequeath to my grandson Henry P Richardson the choice of two work steers & five hundred dolls to be paid by my Executors.

Item, I give and bequeath to my executors hereinafter named in trust for Martha Richardson the wife of my grandson H P Richardson during her life for her exclusive use the following slaves to wit Gilbert & his wife Betsy & her three children Robert Jane & Jackson & Harry & Amy Timberlake & the future increase of the females. And at the death of the said

(P-225 cont.) Martha I give the abovementioned slaves and their increase to be generally divided among the children of my said Grandson Henry P Richardson & the decendants of such of them as may then be dead having left children, as shall be alive at the death of said Martha,

Item I release to Doctor Edwin F Watkins his bond due to me for one thousand dollars

Item - I give and bequeath to Frederick Perkins in trust (P-226) (Ann Tinsleys Will Continued, for my granddaughter Mildred Watkins during her life my girl Elizabeth and her future increase to her exclusive use, and after her death I give the said slave & increase to the children of the said Mildred & to their heirs.

I give my boy Henry to my great grandson Washington Watkins & his heirs but in case my said great grandson shall die before he attains the age of twenty one years I then give the said boy to Frederick Perkins in trust for his mother the said Mildred Watkins during her life and at her death to her children & their heirs.

Item I give bequeath to my Grand daughter Ann Perkins and her heirs my carriage and carriage horses and my servant Jim

Item,- I give and bequeath to my granddaughter Elizabeth Johnson & her heirs the sum of five hundred dolls -

Item - To my granddaughter Harriet Johnson & her heirs, I give & bequeath the sum of five hundred dollars and my gold watch,

Item - I give & bequeath to my granddaughter Sarah Ann Tinsley & her heirs the sum of one thousand dollars and the following slaves "towit" Mariah & all her children & their future increase & William the brother of Mariah and also my Book case & Library & a bed & bedstead and furniture for the same,

Item - I give and bequeath to my daughter Eliza P Royster & her heirs the sum of two thousand dollars Also all my household furniture & stocks of horses, cattle, sheep, hogs & oxen & farming utensils of every description not heretofore disposed of. I also desire & bequeath to my said daughter Eliza during her life all my real estate and the following slaves towit, Amy Holland, Cary, Robert & Edmond & Charles & Money to be taken care of and if my granddaughter Sarah Ann Tinsley shall survive her mother the said Eliza P (P-227) (Ann Tinsleys Will Continued) Royster, I then desire the said real estate & the said Slaves and their future increase after the death of my said daughter to her the said Sarah Ann & her heirs but in case my said granddaughter Sarah Ann shall die before her said mother & then to my said daughter Eliza the power of disposing of the said real estate and Slaves as she may choose by deed or Will.

Item - I direct my executors to give to my servants Milly & Moses twenty five dollars each

Item - I direct my executors to give to my Servant Lucy fifty dollars & give my said servant Lucy to Eliza P Royster with this request & a confidence in her that she will allow her all the liberty & freedom which

(P-227 cont.) the laws of Virginia will permit

Item All the balance of my estate I give to Doctor Frederick Perkins Henry P Richardson & Mareweather Johnson & their heirs to be equally divided between them

Item - I hereby appoint, ordain & constitute my friends Frederick Perkins, Arthur Brice, James Fife & Edwin Porter Executors of this my last will & testament hereby revoking & annulling all former wills heretofore made by me

In Witness Whereof I have hereunto set my hand & affixed my seal this 23rd day of March 1836.

Signed Sealed & published in our presence Ann Tinsley (Seal)

as ~~the~~ & for the last Will & Testament of

Ann Tinsley Thomas Binford James Galt, Mary

French

At a court held for Goochland County 15th August 1836

This writing was produced in court and proved by the oaths of Thomas Binford and James Galt to be the last Will and testament of Ann Tinsley dcd. and ordered to be recorded (P-228) (Ann Tinsleys Will Continued) Then on motion of Frederick Perkins & Archibald Bryce two of the Executors therein named who made oath according to law and the said Frederick Perkins together with Thomas Johnson and Elisha Melton his securities entered into and acknowledged a bond in penalty of forty thousand dollars conditioned as the law directs and the said Archibald Bryce together with ~~John~~ John B Pemberton & Thomas Curd his securities Also entered into and acknowledged a bond with like penalty and condition. Certificate was granted them for attaining a probate of said Will in due form

Test

Nar W Miller D C C C

State of Virginia Goochland County S C

I William Miller Clerk of the court of said county of Goochland do certify that the foregoing is a true copy of the Will of Ann Tinsley decd. as the same now exists along the records of the said county court

(L S of Court) In attestation of which I have hereto set my hand and annexed the seal of said county & court this 14th day of February in the year of our Lord 1840 and in the 64th year of the Commonwealth

Wm. Miller C C C.

State of Virginia Goochland County S S

I William Bolling presiding Magistrate of & in said County of Goochland do hereby certify that the foregoing certificate & attestation

(P-228 cont.) of William Miller who is clerk of the court of said county are in due form certified under my hand and seal this 17th day of February 1840

Recorded in my office the 7 day of March A D 1840 in Book B pages 390-91-92 Will Bolling (Seal)

Wm. Miller Clerk

(P-229) (Ann Tinsleys Will Continued)

State of Tennessee)
July Sessions 1842
Shelby County)

A Competent Court being present

The Last Will & Testament of Ann Tinsley deceased was produced in open court properly authenticated. It is ordered ~~that~~ by the court that said Will be recorded

John W. Fuller Clerk.

Recorded August 12th

(P-230) RICHARD J (Editor's Note: Page torn but body of document shows name)

I Richard J Person (Editor'd Note: piece gone out of page) make and publish this my last Will and Testament hereby revoking and making void all other Wills by me made at any time

First. I direct that all my debts be paid as soon after my death as possible out of my moneys I may die possessed of or may first come into the hands of my Executors

Secondly it is my wish that all my personal estate be equally divided between my wife and my two Sons William & John and the one or more She is now enscient with

It is further my wish that maylanded estate in North Carolina be Sold by my Executors when they think the interest of the Estate would be promoted by it and it is my wish that the proceeds arising from the Sale of those lands be invested in Some Stock or to be expended in some ways so as to promote the interest of my wife Mary L Person and my children.

It is my ~~desire~~ devise that my wife Mary L Person have the tract of Land on which I live during her natural life with the exception of the mill which I wish to give to my son William The balance of my real estate I wish to be equally divided amongst my children which I now possess or may hereafter possess

I do hereby nominate & appoint William Person Sr. of the State of North Carolina and(Editor's Note) part of page gone) Brothers Wm. Person & Benjamin E Person my Executors

In Witness Whereof I do to this my Will set my hand and seal this

((P-230 cont.) the 11th day of May A.D. 18 (Editor's Note: Rest of date torn off)

Witnesses Thos. Holeman   Richd. J Person (Seal)

William Walker

(P-231) State of Tennessee)
September Sessions A D 1842
Shelby County)

A Competent Court present

A paper writing perporting to be the last Will & Testament of Richard J Person decd. late of a resident of the county of Shelby State of Tennessee was produced in open court and thereupon came into court Thomas Holeman and William Walker the Subscribing Witnesses to the same who are not interested in any way in the devisees- therein contained & who being joint duly sworn depose and say that the said last Will & Testament was (Editor's Note: page torn off here) in the said Richard J Person's life & was Signed Sealed & published by him in their presence on the day it bears date as his last Will & Testament that he was of sound mind & memory that they the said Witnesses Subscribed Signed & attested the Same as Subscribing witnesses thereto at the same time in the presence of the said Testator & at his request and that said Will was then layed in the the hands of the said Holeman for safekeeping.

They further depose & say that the said Richard J Person has since departed this life To wit - on the day of July 1842 & that he was at the time of his death and for some considerable time previous thereto a resident citizen of said county of Shelby. It is therefor ordered by the said court here that said last Will & Testament be received & fully proven and that the same be admitted to record as Such. Let it be recorded.

It is also further ordered by the said cout that letters testamentary be issued to William Person on of the Executors (Editor's Note: Page torn off here) in said last Will & Testament he having entered into bond and security & qualified as the law directs

Recorded September 7th 1842   John W Fuller Clk

(P-232) LEONARD BOSHER WILL

Know all men by these presents that I Leonard Bosher of the county of Shelby and State of Tennessee being in the decline of life but of sound and disposing mind and understanding do make and publish this my last Will and Testament hereby revoking and making void all other wills made by me at any time

Article 1st. I direct that all my personal property be sold on a credit of six or twelve months except my negroes and all my real property be sold on a credit of two and three years I also direct that all my debts be paid as soon after my death as possible out of any moneys that I may

(P-232 cont.) die possessed of or may first come into the hands of my Executors,

Article 2nd. I give and bequeath unto Mrs. Mary Smith the grandmother of my children the sum of one hundred dollars annually during her ////// natural life provided she shall live with me as long as I live, the same to be paid her - regularly by my Executors at the end of each year commencing at my death

Article 3rd. I give and bequeath one hundred dollars annually to be applied to the support and maintenance of my Brother Charles Bosher during his natural life but should this sum be found insufficient to maintain my said Brother Charles then and in that event I direct my Executors to appropriate fifty dollars addition to his support

Article 4th I give and bequeath unto my yellow man called Billy Diggs aged about 20 years his freedom for life provided he will remove to the State of Ohio or some other free State and provided nevertheless that he shall be under the Guardianship of my Executors and shall be subject to be hired out two years after my decease or until he shall have made money to defray the expence of his passage to a free State and furnish him one years allowance and I do direct that the whol procedes of his hire be applied to this purpose by my Executors deducting the cost of his cloathing if the same should not be paid by the said man but should he be unwilling to (P-233) remove to a free State and be free then in that event I place him under the guardianship of my Executors to keep and manage so as not to be an expense to my Estate unless he afflicted but it is my will /// wish and desire that the whole procedes of his labors shall be applied by my Executors to his own use at the discretion of my Executors A B Taylor and Alex Dowel whom I have nominated and appointed his Guardians

Article 5th I give and bequeath unto my daughter Nancy Price Bosher two Negro girls (viz) Eliza about 14 years ////// old and Martha about 16 months old to be kept by her guardian to wait on her them and their increase to be valued to her at my decease by three disinterested persons I also give and bequeath to my daughter Nancy one half of all the ballance of the Negroes that I may die possessed of all the above Negroes property and their increase I give to my only daughter Nancy Price Bosher nevertheless upon this condition that if she should die without any bodily heir then in that case I give them to my son Wm. M Bosher or his heirs I also give and bequeath to my said daughter half the procedes of the sale of my real property except the value of the two negroes Eliza & Martha which I have given above to my daughter the amount of the value of the said negroes I wish first set apart for my son Wm, M. Bosher out of the sale of my real property and the ballance to be equally divided between my daughter Nancy Price and William M. Bosher

Article 6th I give and bequeath unto my dearly beloved son William M Bosher one half of all my personal property except that which is otherwise disposed of and bequeathed in the 2nd 3rd and 4th article in this my last Will & Testament and the proceds of the sale of one half of all my real property and so much money as the value of the two negroes which I have given to my daughter Nancy Price Bosher so as to make them equal for it is my will / wish and desire that both of my children shall have equal //////// proportions-

(P-234) Article 7th I do hereby nominate and appoint A.B. Taylor and Alex Dowel my Executors and Guardians for my children requesting them immediately after my death to take charge of them and carefully superintend their education.

In testimony whereof I do hereunto set my hand and seal this day of September one thousand Eight hundred and forty two

Test E M Bell John L Mason Richard Mason

Leonard his X mark Bosher (Seal)

State of Tennessee)
January Session A D 1843
Shelby County Court)

A Competent Court present

A paper writing purporting to be the last Will & Testament of Leonard Bosher deceased was produced in open court thereupon came into court E M Bell & John L Mason subscribing witnesses thereto who being first duly sworn depose and say that the testator acknowledged the same in their presence to be his last Will and testament and that he was of sound mind and disposing memory Ordered that the same be so certified and recorded

Recorded January 9th 1843 JohnWW Fuller Clerk

John W. Fuller Clerk

(P-235) ROBERT SCRUGGS WILL

I Robert Scruggs of the county of Shelby and State of Tennessee do make and publish this my last Will and Testament hereby revoking and making void all other will by me at any time made

First I direct that my personal expences be paid and all my Just debts be paid as soon after my death as possible out of any moneys that I may die possessed of or may first come into the hands of my Executors.

Secondly I give and bequeath to my daughter Amanda M. Ford one negro Slave Amanda

Thirdly I give and bequeath to my daughter Ann Elizabeth one negro slave Amelia

Fourthly I give and bequeath to my son Richard L Scruggs two negroes Slaves Peter and Melissa

Fifthly I give and bequeath to my son Robert L Scruggs all the property both real and personal that I may be possessed of at my death in the State of Mississippi

Sixthly I give and bequeath to my much beloved wife Maria all the balance of my Estate both real and personal to have and hold during her

(P-235 cont.) natural life and at her death to be equally divided between my six children (viz) Robert L Scruggs Richard P Scruggs Mary W Key Linton B Ford Amanda M. Ford and Ann Eliza Woodward

Lastly I do hereby nominate and appoint my sons Robert L Scruggs Richard S Scruggs and my wife Maria my Executors.

In Witness whereof I do this my will set my hand and seal this 26th day of September A D 1842

Robert Scruggs (Seal)

Signed sealed and published in our presence and we have subscribed our names hereto in the presence of the Testator this 26th day of September A D 1842

Harvey Drew S W Ledbetter J A Lewis

(P-236) State of Tennessee)
December Sessions A D 1842
Shelby County Court)

A Competent court present

A paper writing purporting to be the last will and testament of Robert Scruggs deceased was produced in open court and thereupon came into S.W. Ledbetter a subscribing witness thereto who after being duly sworn according to law deposeth and saith that the said Robert Scruggs deceased acknowledged the same in his presence to be his last Will and Testament upon the date it bares date and that he was of sound mind and disposing memory at the time of acknowledging the same, which is ordered to be certified and recorded.

Recorded January 10th 1843 John W. Fuller Clerk

John W Fuller Clk

F O U N T A I N M c G E H E E W I L L

State of Tennessee)
August 30th 1842
Shelby County)

Know all men that I Fountain McGehee of the County and State aforesaid being of good intelect and of proper disposing capacity but weak in body indicating a probable departure of this life do make and ordain this my last Will & Testament

First - I do by these presents request nominate and appoint my beloved wife Cynthia McGehee Executrix to this my last Will & Testament and after paying my just debts she shall hold and enjoy the remainder of my Estate (viz) lands and Tenements negroes household & kitchen furniture horses & mules Cattle hogs - goods & chattels of every description moneys Notes and dues of every description to have to hold and enjoy the same in

(P-236 cont.) right of herself during her natural life or widowhood and after her death my whole Estate to be inherited by my infant son William Livingston McGehee (P-237) and it is my wish and desire that if my Executors should think it to the interest of the Estate at any time to dispose of the whole or any part of the landed property she hereby has full power to make sale either privately or publicly of the same and convey titles and I do further request that my Brother John C McGehee of DeSoto County, Mississippi and William Thompson of Fayett County Tenn. shall aid my Executrix in the Administration and I do hereby make null and void all other Wills heretofore made by me.

In testimony of the soundness of my intentions in the ~~above~~ devise made above I have hereunto set my hand and affixed my seal the day and date above written in presents of subscribing Witnesses

James M Brooks — Fountain McGehee (Seal)

Alfred P. Brooks

State of Tennessee)
December Session A D 1842
Shelby County Court)

A Competent Court present

A paper writing purporting to be the last Will & Testament of Fountain McGehee which was filed in this court on yesterday from probate was this day taken up for further proceedings thereon and thereupon came into court James M Brooks and Alfred P Brooks subscribing witnesses thereto who after being duly sworn according to law depose and say depose and say that the said Fountain McGehee signed and acknowledged said Will in their presence to be his last Will & Testament for the purposes therein contained and upon the day it bares date and that he was of sound mind and memory at the time of signing the same which is ordered to be certified and recorded

Recorded January 11th 1843

John W Fuller Clerk

John W Fuller Clk.

(P-238) WILLIAM H KENNEDY WILL

In the name of God Amen I Wm. H. Kennedy of sound mind good bodily health and disposing memory knowing the uncertainty of this life do make this my last Will and testament for the purpose of settling my worldly affairs haveing made no other Will before this

I will & bequeath unto my most affectionate and dear wife Mary Jane all the property of which I am now possessed and which may hereafter come into my possession both real and personal during her natural life with the understanding that she is to take two of my four sisters (viz) Elizabeth Catherine Mary & Ellin to live with her and support should either or any one of them liveing with her become disrespectful as they are yet but children she is always at liberty to exchange such one for another and should the support of two consume all the proffit of the farm thereby pre-

(P-238 cont.) venting my wife to lay up any proceeds for herself at her own discretion she may take but one to live with her-

Should my wife marry again after my death and have Issue then at her death my property shall revert to such issue in connection with my four sisters abovenamed equally but should she die without issue then my property is to be divided when the youngest becomes 20 years of age equally between my brother Jacob L and my four sisters named above. In any event should my sisters heir any part of my estate it is to be understood I will it to them and their children only

I will to my brother Jacob L my Gold watch my shot Gun and any of my cloaths that he can wear requesting him earnestly that he will conduct himself uprightly before God and man as to give him a good character and an approving conscience and that he will extend a brotherly supervision and affection over his sisters and Sisterinlaw, as should be expected of him

I will & bequeath unto my dear friend Cesario Bias my Gold Pencil case as a small memento of my respect for him, ~~It is my wish~~ It is my wish should my partner be willing that my farming should be continued with said Bias for at least ten years or moore should my wife wish it

I will and bequeath unto my brother Jacob L (P-239) my section of Land in Arks. known as Sec ten in town Ten South Range Nine west

I hold note on my father for two hundred dollars dated the 1st day of April 1832 on demand which I will and bequeath unto him thanking him most heartily for the good advice and examples set me from my childhood to the day of my leaveing his roof to launch into the world on my own exertions and should he wish to ~~ever~~ remove to the country it is my will that he should have the privilege of clearing and using as much of my land till his death as he can use provided it does not diminish the quantity my wife may wish to cultivate

I hereby appoint as my Executors of this my last Will and Testament my respective friends John Timothy Trezevant Wiley B Miller and Jacob N Moon one only being necessary and in the event of the death of the first then the second

In testimony whereof I have hereunto set my hand and affixed my seal this 10th day of December one thousand eight hundred and thirty nine

Wm. H. Kennedy (L S)

The foregoing will as acknowledged by Wm. H Kennedy to us to be his and in his own handwriting

John Pollard Trezevant J N. Moon
Lewis Shanks Jeptha Harrison

State of Tennessee)
January Sessions A D 1843
Shelby County)

A Competent Court present

(P-239 cont.) A paper purporting to be the last Will & Testament of Wm. H. Kennedy dcd. was produced in open Court whereupon came into court John Pollard Trezevant and Jeptha Harrison subscribing witnesses thereto who being first sworn depose and say that the testator acknowledged the same in their presence to be his last Will & Testament and that he was of sound mind and disposing memory which is ordered to be certified and recorded.

Recorded January 11th 1843

John W. Fuller Clerk

John W Fuller Clk.

(P-240) S A R A H J S M I T H W I L L

October 21st in the year of our Lord one thousand Eight Hundred forty two

I do will & bequeath all and every thing I own to my dear mother Elizabeth McNobb all the property that I possess in this world signed sealed in the presence of us

Test J.B. Hodges A Dowell Sarah J Smith

State of Tennessee)
February Sessions A D 1843
Shelby County Court)

A Competent Court present

A paper writing purporting to be the last Will and testament of Sarah J Smith was produced in open court and thereupon came into court A. Dowell and J B Hodges subscribing witnesses thereto who being duly sworn depose and say that the said Sarah J Smith acknowledged the same in their presence to be her last Will and Testament and that she was of sound mind and disposing memory at the time of signing the same which is ordered to be certified and recorded

Recorded May 9th 1843 John W. Fuller Clerk

John W Fuller Clk

(P-241) B E N J A M I N E P E R S O N W I L L

I Benjamin Person of the County of Shelby & State of Tennessee being of sound mind and disposing memory do make and publish this my last will and testament hereby revoking and making void all former wills by me at any time heretofore made

And first I direct that my body be decently interred and that my funeral be conducted in a manner corresponding with my Estate and situation in life

And as to such worldly estate as it has pleased God to entrust me

(P-241 cont.) with I dispose of the same as follows

First I direct that all my just debts an funeral expences be paid as soon after my decease as possible out of the first money that shall come into the hands of my Executors from any portion of my Estate real or personal

Second I give ~~and~~ bequeath and devise unto my brother William Person of the said County and State all my estate whether real personal or mixed of every kind and description either in the State of Tennessee North Carolina or elsewhere to have and to hold the same to the said William Person and his heirs or assigns forever to his and their only proper use and behoof.

And thirdly I do hereby make & ordain my said Brother Wm. Person my sole Executor as well as heir of this my last Will & Testament and request that no security be required of him by the probate Court for the Execution of the same

In ~~testimony~~ witness whereof I the said Benajmin Person the testator have to this my will written on sheet of paper set my hand and affixed my Seal this 1st day of November in the year of our Lord 1842

Signed Sealed and published in the presence of us who have subscribed in the presence of each other and of the said Testator

George W Smith Sylvester Bailey B.E. Person (Seal)

Thos H Turley

(P-242) State of Tennessee)
Febry Session A D 1843
Shelby County Court)

A Competent Court present

A paper writing purporting to be the last Will and Testament of Benjamin E Person deceased late a resident of Shelby County & State of Tennessee was produced in open court thereupon came here in open court G W Smith Sylvester Bailey and Thomas J   the subscribing witnesses to the same who are not interested in any way in the devisees therein contained who being first joint & duly sworn depose and say that the said last Will and Testament was written in the said Benjaming E Person life and was signed sealed and published by him in their presence on the day it bares date as his last will and Testament that he was of sound mind and memory at that time and that they the said witnesses subscribed signed ~~signed~~ and attested the same as subscribing witnesses thereto at the same time in the presence of the said Testator and at his request and the said will was then lodged in the hands of said (Editor's Note: (blank) for safekeeping they further depose and say that the said Benjamin E Person has since departed this life to Wit on the ____ day of ________ 1842 and that he was at the time of his death and for some considerable time previous thereto a resident of the said county of Shelby. It is therefore ordered by the Court here that said last Will & testament be admitted as fully proved and that the same be admitted to record as such. It is also further ordered by the said court that Letters Testamentary be Issued to William Person Executor

(P-242 cont.) named therein

Recorded May 9th 1842 John W Fuller Clerk

(P-243) J O E L H E R I N G W I L L

In the name of God Amen.

I Joel Herring Senr. of the County of Sampson and State of North Carolina being in perfect sound mind and memory but knowing that it is appointed for all men to do make and declare this to be my last Will and Testament in manner & form following (to Wit)

Item first - It is my will that all my just debts and funeral charges be paid by my executors hereafter named

I give & Bequeath to my beloved son Lewis Herring Seventy five acres of land joining his own land the one half and upper part of the tract I purchased from Sampson Lee for one hundred and fifty acres near Burnt-Perquason also two Negroes by the names of Lotty & Jerry and their increase hereafter with one set of Blacksmith tools one feather bed stea cord ~~cord~~ and a sufficiency of furniture and one small chest the two lots of articles now in his possession to him & his heirs forever

Item I give and bequeathto my beloved son Joel Herring reserving my lifetime in said Gift three hundred acres of Land including the plantation and Grist Mill where I now live together with fifty acres I purchased of Enoch Herring and Seventy four acres I purchased of Sampson Lee the one half of a one hundred and fifty tract near Burnt Perquason also nine negroes viz.) Penny C Wallis Dinah Ally Handy Calvin Mary Isaac & Alfred and their increase also the two cows and calves one feather bed stead cord and sufficiency of furniture with all the crops of every description at this time on the plantation reserving a sufficiency for my bodily support to him and his heirs forever

Item, I give and bequeath to my beloved daughter Ann Wetherington two negroes by the names of Rhedick and fanny forever and their future increase

Item, I give and bequeath to my Four grandchildren Eliza Mary Moritta Benajah, (viz) (P-244) Four Negroes by the names of Eadith Boyet Kinian and Mariah to be equally divided when as they come of age or should marry if one or more of the children should die then the survivor to share and share alike to them & their heirs forever

Further My will & desire is that my beloved son Joel Herring & my worthy friend Moses Cox be my Executors

I the aforesaid Joel Herring Sr. do revoke and disannul all other Will or Wills by me made.

In ~~testimony~~ Witness whereof I the said Joel Herring Snr. have to this my last Will and Testament set my hand and affixed my Seal this 9th day of April A D 1828

Joel Herring (Seal)

(P-244 cont.) Signed Sealed*& declared by the Testator in his lifetime to be his last Will & Testament in the presence of witnesses

R.R. Lee William House

North Carolina)
Court of Pleas and Quarter Sessions
Sampson County) November Term 1832

Then was the foregoing Will proven in open court by the oath of Wm. House and ordered to be recorded.

Recorded in Book A pages 139 & 140 Thomas J Harison Clk.

Thos. J Harrison Clk.

State of North Carolina

I Thomas Harison Clerk of the Court of Pleas and Quarter Sessions in & for the County of Sampson do hereby certify the foregoing to be a true copy from the original on file in my office and endorsement of probate entered thereon

(P-245) (S E A L) In testimony whereof I have hereunto set my hand and affixed the Seal of Office this 24th day of October A D 1842 and the 67th Year of Independence-

Thomas J Harison Clerk

State of Tennessee)
Shelby County) Feby. Session A D 1840

A Competent Court Present

A paper writing purporting to be the last Will and Testament of Joel Herring decd. was produced in open court and it appearing to the satisfaction of the court that the same had been legally proven it is ordered to be recorded

Recorded May 9th 1843 John W Fuller Clk

John W. Fuller Clk

- JOSEPH SCALES DCD WILL RECORDED DEC. 2ND 1883

In the name of God Amen. I Joseph Scales do make & declare this my last will and testament in the manner & form following.

First my will and desire is that all my just debts be paid. Also I give & devise unto my daughter Sally P Rhea wife of John S Rhea all that tract of land upon which I lately resided lying in the County of Davidson in the State of Tennessee distant about three and half miles from the town of Nashville, adjoining to the lands of Jesse Wharton John C McLemore & others containing about two hundred & eighty acres. To have and to hold the said tract of land with all it appurtenances unto the said Sally P. Rhea her heirs & assigns forever. But I do hereby declare that the foregoing

*published

(P-245 cont.) described tract of land is intended to be given to my said Daughter Sally upon the following condition (P-246) (Joseph Scales Will) namely that the said John S Rhea & Sally P his wife shall within twelve months from the time of my decease sell a certain tract of land heretofore conveyed by me to the said Sally P Rhea lying in the County of Franklin in the State of Alabama designated & known as Section Seventeen in Township four range Elven west containing about six hundred and forty acres. The said land to be sold to be sold in such manner as the judge of the County Court of said County shall order and also said Rhea shall execute his bond to said judge in such penalty & with such security as said judge may prescribe conditioned to apply the proceeds of such sale to the payment of the legacies hereinafter given, and in case said Rhea shall fail to comply with the foregoing condition my will is that the said tract of land described as lying in Davidson County Tennessee shall be sold by my executor & the proceeds thereof applied to the payment to the payment of legacies hereinafter mentioned. I also give & bequeath unto my said daughter Sally P. Rhea, the sum of five thousand Dollars in money, to be paid out of the first moneys collected by my executors after the payment of my debts. Also I give and bequeath unto my said daughter Sally P. a negro man by the name of Nathan & his wife Becky. Also all the stock of horses cattle, hogs farming utensils & household & Kitchen furniture which may belong to or be upon the said tract of land in Davidson County at the time of my decease. Also I give and bequeath unto my daughter Martha T. Conner, the sum of Five Thousand dollars in money to be and remain to her sole & separate use during her natural life & after her death to be equally divided between her children share & share alike, & my intention is that the husband of the said Martha T Conner shall in no event (P-247)(Joseph Scales Will) have the control of said money, & my executors are required to pay the same to the said Martha T or to the guardian of her children in case of her death, & her or their receipt shall be a complete discharge for said Legacy, the same to be paid out of the first monies realized out of my estate after satisfying the legacy hereby given to my daughter Sally P. Rhea. Also I give and bequeath to my son James Scalles two thousand Dollars in Money. Also I give and bequeath unto my son Jeremiah Scales the sum of two thousand Dollars in money Also I give & bequeath unto my daughter - Betsy Bosley the sum of four Dollars. Also I give & bequeath unto my daughter Lucy Robertson the sum of Four Dollars Also I give and Bequeath unto my soninlaw Joel Waller the sum of four Dollars. Also I give and bequeath unto my soninlaw Obediah Waller the sum of four Dollars. Also I will & ordain that the executors of this my last Will & Testament on their or either of their executors for & toward the performance of my said testament Shall with all convenient speed after my decease bargain sell & alien in fee simple all that my quarter section of land lying in the County of Lawrence State of Alabama, Known as the Southwest corner of Section 19 in Township 4 Range 8 West, for the doing executing & perfect finishing whereof I do by these presents give to my said executors and their executors full power & authority to grant alien bargain sell & convey the said land to any person or persons in fee simple by all & every such lawful ways & means in the law as to my said executors or their executors or to their counsellors in the law as shall seem fit or necessary-

Also I do hereby appoint my trust friend John S Rhea & Micajah Tarver, executors of this my last (P-248) Will & Testament, and finally all the rest residue & remainder of all my estate & effects real & personal whatsoever not hereinbefore ~~mentioned~~ effectually & especially disposed of, I do give devise & bequeath unto my daughter Sally P. Rhea & Martha T Conner & my sons James Scales & Jeremiah Scales to be equally divided between them the said

(P-248 cont.) Sally P. Martha T. James & Jeremiah, share & share alike

In Witness Whereof I have hereunto set my hand & affixed my Seal this eighteenth day of January in the year of our Lord One thousand eight hundred & thirty.

Joseph Scales (Seal)

Signed Sealed published & delivered by the said Joseph Scales as & for his last will & testament in the presence of us who at his request & in his presence have subscribed our names as witnesses thereto.

R. Hatch Joshua Prout David Dishler

State of Alabama)
Orphans Court April Sessions 1830
Franklin County)

This day appeared in open Court Ralph Hatch & Joshua Prout who being duly sworn maketh oath & say that they saw Joseph Scales whose name is subscribed to the foregoing will (hereunto attached) sign & seal the same on the day therein mentioned and that the said Joseph Scales published & declared the same to be his last will and testament in their presence of these affiants & in the presence of David Dishler the other subscribing witness thereto and that these affiants & the said David Dashler subscribed their names as witnesses to said will in the presence of said Scales in the presence of each other Sworn to in open court

R Hatch Joshua Prout

Test Michael Dickson C C C

(P-249) (Joseph Scales Will - cont.)

State of Alabama)

Franklin County)

I Michael Dickson Clerk of the County Court for the County aforesaid do hereby certify that the foregoing transcript contains a true copy of the last Will & testament of Joseph Scales deceased as proven on the application of John S Rhea & Micajah Tarver executors of said last will & testament & ordered to be recorded by the judge of the County Court of Franklin County.

Witness my hand & seal of office this 12th day of July 1832

(Seal) Test Michael Dickson C.C.C.

State of Alabama)

Franklin County)

I G.D. Stone sole judge of the Orphans Court of said County of Franklin do hereby certify that Michael Dickson whose name appears to the foregoing certificate is Clerk of the County & Orphans Court of said County and as such register of will thereof, that full faith & credit should be given to all his official as such & that his said certificate and attestation are

(P-249 cont.) in due form of law.

In Testimony whereof I have hereunto set my hand & seal this 12th day of July 1832.

G.D. Stone (Seal)

Judge of the Orphans Court

County Court of Franklin

County

State of Tennessee)
October Session 1832
Davidson County)
Court

No. 165 Joseph Scales Extrs Plffs)

v.) Contested Will

John M Robertson)

This day came the parties by their attornies & thereon came a jury &c viz Henry Bateman, Moses Wright, Aaron Wright, Neal Hopkins Jefferson Page Bardal M Ewing Anderson Tucker, John Thomas P Adams James Wilson John Adams & James Thomas, who being elected (P-250) tried & sworn the truth to speak upon the issue joined & to say or not a paper writing here produced in Court duly certified from the Orphans Court of Franklin County in the State of Alabama & purporting to be the last will & testament of Joseph Scales, dcd. bearing date January 18th 1830, is such will of the said Joseph Decd. Upon their oaths do say that said paper writing is such will of the said Joseph deceased and thereupon it is ordered by the Court that said paper writing be admitted to record as such last will & testament of said deceased & that the defendant pay costs of this proceeding &c and that execution issue &c. From which judgment the defendants prayed an appeal to the honorable Circuit Court of Davidson County & to them it was granted provided bond & Security is given to the Clerk within thirty days from the rise of this Court.

Test. Henry Ewing Clerk of said Court.

State of Tennessee)

Davidson County)

I Robert B. Castleman Clerk of the County Court of said County do hereby certify that the foregoing writing is a true copy of record of the last will & testament of Joseph Scales deceased & probate thereof

In testimony whereof I Robt B Castleman Clerk as aforesaid have hereunto set my hand & caused the seal of said Court to be affixed at office in Nashville this 21st day of June 1843

Robt. Castleman

Clerk of said Court

(P-250 Cont.) State of Tennessee)
July Sessions A D 1843
Shelby County)

A Competent Court present

A paper writing purporting to be a copy of the last Will and Testament of Joseph Scales deceased was produced in open Court, and it appearing to the satisfaction of the Court, that the same had been regularly proven in Franklin County, Alabama ordered that the same be recorded-

Recorded Sept. 26th 1843 John W. Fuller Clerk

(P-251) D A V I D R O Y S T E R ' S W I L L

I David Royster of the County of Shelby and State of Tennessee (Planter) do make and publish as my last will and Testament, hereby revoking and making void all former wills by me at any time heretofore made

And first I direct that my body be decently interred at my present residence in said County, in a manner suitable to my condition in life, and as to such worldly estate as it hath pleased God to entrust me with, I dispose of the same as follows:

First, I direct that all my just debts and funeral expenses be paid as soon after my decease as possible, out of any monies I may die possessed of or may first come into the hands of my Executors from any portion of my estate real or personal

Secondly I lend to my Daughter Ann C. Thurman wife of Fendal C Thurman for and during her natural life the negroes Kitty Eliza Preston and Jim, which she has had in possession the last fifteen or twenty years with the increase heretofore and hereafter of the females and at her death the said negroes Kitty, Eliza, Preston and Jim and the increase of the females shall inure and belong to the children of my said daughter Ann C. Thurman, and the said lot of negroes including their increase shall be valued at the sum of Eight hundred Dollars and no more, without interest the Eight hundred Dollars to be brought into the division of my Estate.

Thirdly. I advanced to my son Joel W. Royster some years ago five hundred and eighty one Dollars which I now give to him and his heirs forever, but to be brought in upon a division of my estate without interest

Fourthly, I loaned to my son Richard W Royster ~~some years ago~~ in 1833 six hundred and fifty Dollars which has since been reduced by payments to five hundred and thirty four Dollars I give to him and his heirs forever but to be brought in upon a division of my estate without interest(P-252)

Fifthly, I advanced some years ago to my son Stephen S Royster six hundred & fifty Dollars to be laid out in land in Tennessee which I now give to him and his heirs forever, to be brought in upon a division of my estate without interest

Sixthly I have advanced at different times to my son Francis W. Roy-

(P-252 cont.) ster One thousand Dollars which I now give to him and his heirs forever, but to be brought in with the rest of my estate upon a division without interest.

Seventhly. I give to my Daughter Jane Donelson the sum of five hundred Dollars over and above her equal portion of my estate in consideration of her not having the same advantages of education which my other children have had, to be paid to her before a division of my estate. I have loaned to my said daughter Jane Donelson a negro girl by the name of Delpha about fourteen years old value Five Hundred Dollars which said negro girl Delpha and her future increase if any I now lend to my*daughter Jane Donelson for and during her natural life and at her death to inure and belong to her heirs, the said five hundred Dollars without interest to be charged to her in the division of my estate.

Eightly, I have loaned to my daughter Mary E Nelson a negro girl by the name of Mary about sixteen years old value at five hundred dollars, which said negro girl Mary and her future increase if any I now lend to my said daughter Mary E. Nelson for and during her natural life and at her death to inure and belong to her heirs, the value of five hundred dollars abovementioned to be charged to her without interest in the division of my estate.

Ninthly I have loaned to my daughter Sarah C Donelson a negro girl by the name of Edney about twelve years old valued at three hundred and fifty dollars I now lend to my said daughter Sarah C. Donelson for and during her natural life the said negro Girl Edney and her future increase if any, and at her death to inure and belong to her heirs the said three hundred and fifty without interest to be charged to her in the division of my estate

Tenthly. I lend to my granddaughter Mary Heth Royster daughter of my son Joel W. Royster, a negro girl by the name of Nancy between ten and twelve years old valued at three hundred (P-253) & fifty dollars the said girl Nancy and her future increase if any to inure and belong at the death of ~~said~~ my said granddaughter Mary Heth Royster to her heirs the value of three hundred and fifty dollars, without interest to be charged to my son Joel W Royster her father in the division of my estate

eleventh I lend to my son Stephen S Royster for and during his natural life and at his death to inure and belong to his heirs, a negro girl by the name of Laura about nine years and her future increase if any valued at three hundred dollars, the said sum of three hundred dollars without interest to be charged to him in the division of my estate.

Twelfth. It may be proper to state that the value of the negroes conveyed in the ninth and tenth articles above have been changed & from four hundred dollars each to three hundred & fifty each and in doing so there are two erasures in each of those articles

Lastly, now it is my will and desire that after the payment of my just debts, and the bequest of five hundred dollars to my daughter Jane Donelson that my estate be equally divided between all my children Joel W Royster Richard W Royster Stephen Sampson Royster Francis W Royster Mary E Nelson Jane Donelson, Sarah Catherine Donelson, and Ann Curd Thurman,

* said

(P-253 cont.) each one however accounting in the division for the values as specified against them in the foregoing articles except the bequest to my daughter Jane abovementioned of five hundred dollars -the land and negroes allotted to each in the division to be a loan to each of my sons and daughters for and during their natural lives and at their death respectively to inure and belong to their lawful heirs and if either of my children die without surviving issue of his or her body then that portion of my estate which they have inherited shall revert inure and belong to my surviving children and their heirs.

I do hereby constitute and appoint my four sons Joel W Royster Richard W Royster Stephen S Royster and Francis W Royster executors of this my last will (P-254) and testament.

In Witness Whereof I David Royster the said testator have to this my will written on one sheet of paper set my hand and seal this 4th day of July in the year of our Lord One thousand and eight hundred and forty two

David Royster (Seal)

Signed Sealed & published in the presence of us who have subscribed in the presence of the testator and of each other.

C.J. Pleasants Carns Watkins John Donelson

State of Tennessee)
June Session A D 1843
Shelby County Court)

A Competent Court present

A paper ~~writing~~ purporting to be the last will & testament of David Royster deceased was produced in open court and thereupon came into court C.J. Pleasants and John Donelson subscribing witnesses thereto who being first sworn depose and say that the said testator acknowledged the same in their presence to be his last will and testament and that he was of sound mind and deposing memory at the time of acknowledging the same which is ordered to be recorded.

Recorded Septr. 26 1843 John W Fuller Clk

(P-255) N I C H O L A S M C K E O N ' S W I L L

In the name of God, Amen. I Nicholas McKeon of the town of Memphis, Tennessee being in ill health and weak in body, but of sound and deposing mind memory and understanding, considering the uncertainty of life and therefore desirous to settle my worldly affairs do make and publish this my last will and testament in manner and form following that is to say.

First committing my soul into the hands of Almighty and my body to the earth, I give and bequeath unto my beloved borther Thomas McKeon, all my stock in trade goods wares and merchandise of whatsoever kind or description which, now are or at the time of my death may be in store on Front Row at the railroad Depot leased by me from E.L. Conant, and all fixtures therein

(P-255 Cont.) which I have the right to remove, all counter drawers and whatsoever besides belong or appertain to the trade or business of the said store, and should the plan of business be changed to any other store hereafter then I give and bequeath all and singular the stock in trade &c before mentioned in like manner.

Item. I give and bequeath to my said brother Thomas all monies or cash on hand at the time of my decease whether deposited in Bank or otherwise howsoever and Bills notes & accounts to me due or owing, he paying any debts or expences out of the same which I may have left unpaid or which to my Estate may be Justly chargeable and finally after my debts & funeral expences are paid I give & bequeath to him all my goods & chattels and personal Estate of whatsoever description

And I do hereby constitute and appoint my said beloved brother Thomas to be the sole Executor of this my last Will & Testament and it is my will that he may execute the same without entering into any Bond or security which the law might otherwise require of him

In testimony whereof I have hereunto set my (P-256) hand and affixed my Seal the 20th day of May A D 1843

Nicholas McKeon (Seal)

Signed Sealed and published in the presence of us who have subscribed our names in the presence of the Testator and of each other.

John Farrell

Rufus T Joiner John McKeon

State of Tennessee)
July Sessions A D 1843
Shelby County Court)

A Competent Court present

A paper writing purporting to be the last Will & Testament of Nicholas McKeon was produced in open court and thereupon came into Court Rufus T Joiner a subscribing Witness thereto and after being duly sworn deposeth and saith that the said Testator acknowledged the same in his presence to be his last Will and Testament and that he was of sound and that he was of sound and deposing memory at the time of acknowledging the same and that both of the other subscribing witnesses are now beyond the limits of this state and that Both of said Subscribing witnesses subscribed their names to said Will in his presence

Ordered that said Will be recorded

Recorded September 27th 1843 John W. Fuller Clerk

J W Fuller Clk.

(P-257) ~~October 21st in the year of our Lord one thousand and and Eight hundred forty two I do will and bequeath all & every thing I own~~

(P-257 cont.) G A B R I E L G R E E N H A W W I L L

In the name of God Amen. I Gabriel Greenhaw of the County of Shelby and State of Tennessee being of Strong Mind but low in body doth ~~do~~ ordain and acknowledge this my last Will & Testament

Item first. I will to God my Soul with all he may be pleased to take.

Item 2nd My Will & desire is that my land be equally divided be it sold or not leaveing them to be their own Judges

Namely my wife Jemima Greenhaw and my five youngest sons Namely Job Jasper Newton Franklin and James Greehaw

Item 3 My will is that all my perishable property property both here and in Arkansas be to pay my debts if a nuff if not I can say no more only that the Six Named Legitees above must make out the ballance

Item 4th My Will is that My son William Greenhaw keep all that I have heretofore given him also that my Daughter Nancy Boring keep all I have heretofore given her and that my son Jackson return my young horse to the Estate and my will is that he keep all the ballance I have heretofore given to him

This is my last Will & Testament. Given from under my hand and Seal this the 21st day of December in the year of our Lord Eighteen hundred and forty two

G Greenhaw (Seal)

Test Robert C Ledbetter
John A Gregory

(P-258) State of Tennessee)
June Session A D 1843
Shelby County Court)

A Competent Court Present

A paper purporting to be the last Will & Testament of Gabriel Greenhaw was produced in open court and thereupon came into court Robert C Ledbetter and John A Gregory subscribing witnesses thereto who being first sworn depose and say that the Testator acknowledged the same in their presence to be his last Will & Testament, and that he was of sound mind and disposing memory at the time of acknowledging the same which is ordered to be recorded recorded

Recorded September 27th 1843 John W Fuller

John W Fuller Clk

T H O M A S N U T T ' S W I L L

I Thomas Nutt do make this my last will and testament, hereby revoking all other will by me made at any other time.

First I direct that my debts be paid out of my personal property.

(P-258 cont.) Second I give the balance together with my land to my two daughters Penelope and Mary Jane Nutt and my wife Sally Nutt I also provide that the unborn infant with which my wife Sally is great shall shear equal with the two girls and my wife all of which property my wife Sally Nutt is to have the management of also of the children till they come of age then she is to give off to the children their shears dividing equal between themselves

In witness whereof I this 3rd day of August 1842 have set my hand and seal.

Sampson Nutt W H McNeely Thomas Nutt (Seal)

Denis Speer John McNeely

(P-259) (August 4th 1842)

I give my part of a tract of land, if obtained lying on the Catawba River North Carolina to my wife and children to be divided between them as the property mentioned in my above will my part of said claim being two thirds one third of which I have promised to Lawyer Smith for to attend to the recovering of said land

(Seal)

State of Tennessee)
June Sessions A D 1843
Shelby County Court)

A Competent Court present

A paper purporting to be the last will and testament of Thomas Nutt deceased was produced in open court and thereupon came Sampson Nutt and John Mc Neely subscribing witnesses thereto, who being first sworn depose and say that the said Testator acknowledged the same in their presence to be his last will and testament and that he was of sound mind and disposing Memory at the time of acknowledging the same which is ordered to be recorded

Recorded Sept 27th 1843 John W Fuller Clk

John W Fuller Clk

(P-260) JAMES L. EDMONDS LAST WILL & TESTAMENT

Shelby County Tennessee May 1843

It is my request that If I should never recover from my Illness that what property I have shall be equally divided amongst my two Brothers namely Zachariah and Samuel Edmonds and Sister Sally Gandy the property which I mean in the following Negroes (Viz) Nicey and her son Coleman Biddy and her three Children namely Amanda Sarah and Ann and if the above named persons cannot peaceably divide the same, It is my wish that they shall all be set free the above is the substance of the request of James L Edmonds who died May last made while he lay sick at the residence of William Turnage made in our presents

his
Zachariah X Turnage
mark

(P-260 cont.) State of Tennessee)
October Sessions A D 1843
Shelby County Court)

A Competent Court present

This day came into Court Zachariah Turnage the subscribing witness to the last will & Testament of James L. Edmonds dcd. who after being duly sworn says that he was Present at the Illness which resulted in the death of James L. Edmonds who called on him to witness the verbal disposition he then made of his property in his last Illness at the house of Wm. Turnage he further states that the deceased was sound in mind at the time and capable of making his will and the said witness signed the paper which he produced and contains the substance of what deceased said in relation to the disposition of his effects in view of approaching death said will is ordered to be recorded. It appearing to the court that he died within the last six months

Test John W Fuller Clk

Recorded November 17th 1843

John W Fuller Clk

(P-261) LAFAYETTE JONES' WILL

In the name of God I La Fayette Jones of the County of Shelby Tennessee being of sound mind and memory do make and ordain this my last will and Testament as follows

Item 1st. that all my just debts be paid by my Executors

Item 2nd I give and bequeath unto my wife Susan A Jones one half of all my property both real and personal and of every description whatever that I may die possessed of

Item 3rd I give and bequeath to my son Chamberlayne Jones the other half of all my property both real and personal and of every description whatever I may die possessed of

Item 4th I appoint my brothers Chamberlayne Jones and Caesar A Jones Executors of this my last will & Testament of whom no security shall be required

Item 5th I direct my Executors to keep my Negroes together upon a farm untill a division is called for by my wife Susan A Jones or my son becomes of age

Item 6th. I do hereby empower my Executors to sell and dispose of my land in Shelby County Tennessee by sale or otherwise also the Stock and the appurtenances thereunto belonging and buy land anywhere else they may think proper in the State of Tennessee or out of it to remove my Negroes to the same and give the same power and authority out of the State of Tennessee as in it

Item 7th If my son Chamberlayne should die before he becomes of age

(P-261 cont.) then all of my Estate that may belong to him at his death shall go to my brothers Chamberlayne Jones and Caesar A Jones to be equally divided between them

Item 8th If my wife Susan A Jones should die Childless and without will then my desire is that all the portion of my Estate that may belong to her at ~~her death shall be equally~~ the time of her death shall be equally divided between her Brother Dudley Dunn and Sister Camilla Dubose ~~having all the right and title to it at her death~~ the heirs of the body of Camilla Dubose haveing all the right and title to her portion of it at her death

(P-262)Item 9th It is hereby declared that my wife Susan A Jones Shall have a life Estate in that portion of my Estate bequeathed to my Brothers Chamberlayne and Carsar A Jones in the event of the death of My son Chamberlayne according to Item 8th

In testimony whereof I affix My hand and (Seal) this the 10th of September 1843

Lafayette Jones (Seal)

Witness David McClanahan Isham J Boyce

State of Tennessee)
October Sessions A D 1843
Shelby County Court)

A Competent Court present

A paper writing purporting to be the last will and Testament of La Fayette Jones deceased was produced in open Court and thereupon came into court I J Boyce and David McClanahan subscribing witnesses thereto ~~who~~ after being duly sworn depose and say that the said Testator acknowledged the same in their presence to be his last Will and Testament and that he was of sound mind and disposing memory which is ordered to be recorded

A Copy Test John W Fuller Clk

Recorded November 17th 1843

John W Fuller Clk

(P-263) SION PARHAM'S WILL

Desoto County State of Mississippi In the year of our Lord one thousand Eight hundred and forty three on fifth of November

I Sion Parham being in my right mind do make this my last Will and Testament that is to say that after my just debts are all paid I give to my Eldest Sister Aby Wordrough all my Estate consisting of two Negroes women Namely Fanny & Rachel together with my stock of horses and Cattle to her & her heirs forever. It is my wish that my stock of Horses & Cattle May be sold and the money arising from the sale be sent to my above named Sister

(P-263 cont.) In witness whereof I have hereunto set my hand and seal the date and year above written

Jas. T Wilcox James W Alston Sion his X mark Parham (Seal

State of Tennessee)
December Session A D 1843
Shelby County Court)

A Competent Court present

A paper writing purporting to be the last Will and Testament of Sion Parham was produced in open court and thereupon came into court Jas. T. Wilcox a subscribing witness thereto who being first duly sworn deposeth and ~~saith~~ saieth that the said Testator acknowledged the same in his presents to be his last Will & Testament and that he was of sound mind and disposing memory at the time of acknowledging the same which he ordered to be recorded

John W Fuller Clerk

Recorded Jany 19th 1844.

John W Fuller Clk

(P-264) WILLIAM WENDEL'S WILL

I William Wendel being of sound mind, do make this my last will and testament

First I desire that all my just debts be paid, out of my property and that my executor dispose of it to the best advantage for that purpose, and I do hereby fully authorize and empower, my executor to sell and convey, any or all of the real property, of which I may die, seized or possessed. The surplus of my property after the payment of my debts, I wish disposed of as follows If the excess should not exceed one hundred dollars will and direct the same to be paid over to Granville D Searcy, and all the surplus after paying my debts and said one hundred dollars, to G.D. Searcy, I give and bequeath to my nephew William Searcy. I appoint my friend James May my executor and request that he be not ruled to security as I have the utmost confidence in his honesty and integrity-

I own the lots in Barnes Grove in Nashville No. 55 - 56.
I owe Jas. F. May one hundred dollars Mrs Barry about sixty dollars and the daughter of an old free negro man, who died ar Capt. William Black, on Mill Creek, one hundred dollars which debts I am desirous should be paid, and I wish Jas. May either to take Said lots and Satisfy Said debts or sell the same, as he may think best. If my property will pay my debts, without the sale of my watch, I will and bequeath Said watch, to my nephew William Searcy, with a request, that if he should ever have a son, he will give to him in remembrance of me.

Given under my hand and seal this 20th day of August 1843

Test - G.D. McLean Saml. Gilbert Wm. Wendel (Seal)

(P-265) State of Tennessee)
Feby. Term A.D. 1844
Shelby County)

A Competent Court present

A paper writing purporting to be the last Will & Testament of William Wendel dcd. was produced in open court and thereupon came into court C? D. McLean and Samuel Gilbert subscribing witnesses thereto who being first duly sworn depose and say that they are well acquainted with Wm. Wendel the testator and that he acknowledged the same in their presence to be his last Will & Testament and that he was of sound mind and disposing memory at the time of acknowledging the same which is ordered to be recorded.

Recorded Feby 7th 1844 John W Fuller Clk

SUSANNA SMITH LAST WILL & TESTAMENT

In the name of God amen. I Susanna Smith widow of Macon Smith late of Fayette County deceased weak and sick in body but of sound and disposing mind and memory do hereby make and declare this my last Will and Testament in the following manner that is to say

It is my will that in the first place that my just debts and incident expences and charges be paid by my Executor hereinafter appointed the residue of my property of every description which I now have in possession or to which I have just claim, I give and bequeath as follows to my beloved Niece Eliza G Reid a Daughter of Thomas Reid late of Shelby County deceased the said Eliza G being raised and brought up by me from her father's death, viz.

I give to the said Eliza G Reid all my share as widow ~~of~~ being the one half of my late husband's personal property of which Darling Long of Fayett County is the Administrator (P-266) whether consisting in money notes & securities or other goods and chattels, and my share and Interest in one woman negro slave named Matilda and her increase to be settled and accounted for by the said Administrator

Item I give to the said Eliza G Reid two horses and household furniture and the growing crop on the farm or plantation rented by me in Fayett County from Jesse Barnes.

Item I give to the said Eliza G Reid two cows & two Calves & the residue of my household & kitchen furniture which I have in the town of Memphis and County of Shelby and all other property not hereinnamed to which I have Just claim and title

And it is my will, that should the abovenamed Eliza G Reid die before she is of lawful agre or unmarried and without issue, that the property above bequeathed to her shll go to her sister Zerilda A T Reid and in the event of her death also before lawful agre or unmarried and without issue then to her mother Rachel Wells formerly Rachel Reid

In witness whereof I hereunto set my hand & Seal this third day of

(P-266 cont.) July A D 1842

Susanna Smith (Seal)

Signed Sealed and published by the abovenamed Susanna Smith as her last Will and Testament before us, who, at her request in her presence and the presence of each other do hereunto sign our names as witnesses thereto

P C Gallahar John Smoot

I the above named Susanna Smith (now) of Memphis Shelby County do make this present codicil which I order and direct shall be taken as a and far part of my above written last Will & Testament which will I do hereby (P-267) ratify and confirm with the following addition that is to say haveing full trust and confidence in the honesty and trustworthiness of my friend Alexander Wells whom I have constituted and appointed Executor of my foregoing will it is my further will that the said Alexander Execute my aforesaid Will and all the powers and & trusts therein contained without being obligated to give Bond and security according to the laws of this state

In witness whereof I hereto have set my hand and seal this day of July 1842

her
Susan X Smith
mark

Signed sealed and published by the said Susan Smith as a codicil to her last Will & Testament in presence of us who at her request and her her presence sign our names as witnesses thereto

John L Sweeney Littleton Benthal

State of Tennessee)
Feby. Session A D 1844
Shelby County Court)

~~A Competent Court present~~

A Competent Court present

A paper writing purporting to be the last Will and Testament of Susan Smith dcd. with a codicil thereto attached was produced in open court and thereupon came into court John L Sweeney a subscribing witness to said codicil who after being duly sworn deposeth and saith that he was acquainted with Susan Smith and that she acknowledged the abovementioned codicil to be her act and deed and that she was of sound mind and disposing memory at the time of acknowledging the same. Ordered that said Will be filed for further probate

John D Fuller Clk

State of Tennessee)
March Session A D 1844
Shelby County Court)

A Competent Court present (P-268)

(P-268) A paper writing purporting to be the last Will and Testament of Susan Smith dcd. was produced in open court and thereupon came into Court P C Gallaher a subscribing witness thereto who being first sworn deposeth and saith that the said Susanna Smith Acknowledged the same in his presence to be her last Will and Testament and that she was of sound mind and disposing memory at the time of acknowledging the same & that he believes John Smoot the other witness to said Will is not at this time a resident of this State. It is ordered by the Court that said Will be recorded

Recorded March 26th 1844 John W Fuller Clk

John W. Fuller Clk

(P-269) JACOB ISH'S WILL

I Jacob Ish of the County of Loudown and State of Virginia labouring under bodily infirmities, but of sound mind and memory, do make my last Will & testament in the following Manner, viz.

1st It is my will that all my just debts & funeral expences be paid as soon as convenient after my decease

2nd It is my will that as soon after my departure as may be practible that all my property both real & personal of every description & kind (except such property as I shall herein or hereafter price myself or otherwise especially order) be apraised and sold at public Auction and the proceeds applied as herein directed.

3rd. It is my Will and desire that Susanah my Wife Wife shall have one third part of my Estate during her Natural life, and if she chooses may select from among my servants such as she pleases to take at the valuation and the ballance or all in case she does not choose to take any servants to be paid to her in bonds by my Executors as soon as practible. It is my desire that she shall be entitled to a home in my mansion house during her life, or as long as she may choose to reside with my son Robert Alexander Ish in said house. I also will her my clock during her natural life.

4th I will & bequeath to my daughter Margaret Prosser one equal Tenth part of my Estate (Except such parts as shall be otherwise disposed of) to her to her heirs or assigns forever.

5th I will and bequeath to my daughter Mary one Negro Girl named Isabella for which I have heretofore made her a deed of gift & for which she shall not be charged anything in the settlement of my Estate. I also will to her one Bed & Bedstead & various articles of Bedding which she made herself, all that she may claim in that way, & also sundry articles on the Side Board which she bought herself. To have & to hold without charge all the above (P-270) named things. I in addition to the above will & bequeath to her the said Mary one Equal Tenth part of my Estate(not otherwise disposed of) to be paid to her as soon as practable by my Executors.

6th I will & bequeath to my son William King Ish one tenth part of my Estate (not otherwise disposed of)

7th I give & bequeath to Elizabeth Simpson One tenth part of my Estate

(P-270 cont.) (Not otherwise disposed of) to enclude a tract of land which I bought of Samuel Simpson, Containing One hundred & five acres be the same more or less for which she shall be charged Ten dollars per acre. To my daughter Elizabeth Simpson and her heirs to have & to hold for their own proper use & benefit forever.

8th I will and bequeath to my hereafter named Executors, one tenth part of my whole estate (except such as may be otherwise disposed of) in trust for the only use & benefit of my daughter Lucinda and her ~~only use & benefit~~ her children to be enjoyed by her & children during her life, and after her death I desire that it shall be equally divided among her children. And to enclude a tract of land which I purchased in Shelby County State of tennessee containing five hundred and five acres be the same more or less, with which they(My Executors) in consideration of her the said Lucinda's portion designed for her entire use & benefit during her life are charged as Trustees on my Book Accounts.

9th I give and bequeath one equal tenth part of my whole este (except such parts as may be otherwise disposed of) to My daughter Naomi Carnes

10th. To Thomas Humphrey & Pheba his wife I will and bequeath One Equal tenth part of my whole Estate (Except such parts as may be otherwise disposed of) to include a house & Lot purchased of William Vickers for which they shall be charged three hundred & fifty dollars. Also one hundred & thirty seven acres of land adjoining the land of Nathaniel Skinner be the same more or less for which they shall be charged Ten dollars per Acre (it being the land I bought of Blaker) (P-271) (Jacob Ish's Will Continued)

11th To my son John Ish, I give & bequeath One equal tenth part of my Estate (except such parts as may be otherwise disposed of) to him & his heirs forever.

12th To my son Robert Alexander Ish I give & bequeath one equal tenth part of my whole Estate (except such parts as may be otherwise disposed of) to him & his heirs or assigns forever, his portion shall consist of the Tan Yard & Mansion House lot containing Seven Acres more or less with all the buildings & improvements thereto belonging and also all the tanyard comprising all the bark, all the hides, in tan & out of tan, all leather all the oil, tools & all other things belonging or appertaining to the tanery or taning business, for all of which the above named property he shall be charged ten thousand dollars. Also a tract of land which I bought of Sally Russell containing one hundred acres be the same more or less for which he shall be charged Eighteen dollars per acre, also a tract of land on the East Side of the Bull run Mountain which I bought of Ephraim Garrison containing one hundred & Seventy two acres and a half, for which he shall pay six hundred & thirty two dollars & fifty cents for the whole of it, as it is the precise amount which I paid for said land. It is my will that Robert Alexander's portion (one tenth part of my whole Estate not otherwise disposed of) be taken from the amount of property that I have willed him. And that the ballance (if any) he shall have four years credit on, then to be paid in without interest, say at four years after my decease.

13th To my son George Henry Ish I give & bequeath One equal tenth part of my whole Estate (Except such parts as may be otherwise disposed of) to him & his heirs or assigns forever. Also I will my Clock to him after his Mother's death without charge

(P-271 cont.) 14th It is my will and desire that all my land (P-272) not otherwise disposed of (if any there be) be equally divided among those of my children who have not had any allotted to them at fair valuation.

15th It is my will and desire that those of my children who have had the least, shall first have to make them equal with those who have had the grestest portion given them.

16th It is my will & desire that my Account which I have Kept against each of my children which will be presented ~~against~~ by my Executors and in the Handwriting of one or more of them for certain advances either in money or property in a Book Kept for the special purpose be deducted out of each one's portion that I have willed to unless wherein I may or shall have otherwise directed. I expect in case I should live Several years to make advances to some of my children in future, which will be entered in the Same Book as above described and which I desire to be Kept secure & executed as above Ordered,

17th My will and desire is that if either or any of my children aforesaid deny or dispute their accounts against them as aforesaid, so as to cause confusion & trouble in settling the affairs of my estate according to the true intent & meaning of these presents they or either of them of offending shall forfeit their claim or claims respectfully to an equal division of my Estate as abovementioned & shall be cast off with One dollar each

18th And lastly I do hereby Nominate, constitute & appoint my sons, John Ish, & Robert A Ish to be the only true and lawful Executors of this my last will & Testament. And it is my Will that they shall sell at Public Auction all my property not herein bequeathed and disposed of of the proceeds thereof to the benefit of my Estate dividing the Sale bonds among the legatees for (P-273) (Jacob Ish's Will Continued) each to collect his or her own dividend or share of bonds

I do publish & declare this to be my last Will & testament hereby revoking & annulling all other wills by Me heretofore made.

In Witness whereof I have hereunto set my hand and affixed my Seal this the fourteenth day of January in the Year of our Lord One Thousand Eight hundred and thirty Nine

His
Jacob X Ish (Seal)
mark

Signed Sealed & published in the presence of us the Subscribers

Dean James
Nathl. Skinner
Francis Adams

At a court held for Louden Cty August 10th 1840. This paper purporting to be the last will & testament of Jacob Ish dcd. was this day presented to the court, proved by the oaths of Nathaniel Skinner & Francis Adams, two of the subscribing Witnesses thereto, and ordered to be Recorded. And on the Motion of Robert A Ish one of the Executors therein Named who qualified as such and with French Simpson John Ish Thomas G Humphrey and Nathaniel Skinner his Securities entered into & acknowledged a bond in the penalty of forty

(P-273)(Jacob Ish's Will continued) thousand dollars conditioned as the law directs, Certificate is Granted him for obtaining a probate thereof in due form

Test Chas. G Eskridge Clk

Virginia ToWit

I Charles H Eskridge clerk of the county court of Loudown in the State aforesaid do hereby certify that the foregoing is a true Transcript from the Record.

In testimony I have (P-274) hereunto Subscribed my name and affixed the (S E A L) seal of said Court at Leesburg this 22nd day of February 1841. And in the 65th year of the Commonwealth

Test Chas. G Eskridge Clk

Loudown County, Towit.

I John Rose Presiding Trustee of the County of Loudown in the State of Virginia do hereby Certify that Charles G Eskridge who hath given the proceeding certificate is the Clerk of the County Court of Loudown duly commissioned and qualified & that his said attestation is in due form.

In testimony whereof I have hereunto subscribed my name & affixed My seal this 25th day of February 1841.

John Rose (Seal)

State of Tennessee)
July Sessions A D 1844
Shelby County)

A copy of the Last Will & Testament of Jacob Ish was produced in open court & it appearing to the satisfaction of the Court that the same had been leagally proven in Loudown County in the State of Virginia. It is ordered that the same be recorded.

Recorded July the 9th 1844. John W. Fuller C.S.C.

John W Fuller C.S.C.

(P-275) WILLIAM Q. JOHNSON'S WILL

Know all men by these presents that I William Quarles Johnson being of sound mind do make this my last Will & Testament as follows Towit.

1st I give to my brother David T Johnson a Note of hand which I hold from him for three hundred dollars on condition that the said D T Johnson Shall pay or cause to be paid to my sister Thomaline Johnson one hundred & twenty five dollars which sum it is my wish she shall spend in a Watch or ot other jewelry she may select

(P-275 cont.) 2nd I give my Watch to my Nephew Thomas H Perkins and wish him to wear it as a token of Me.

3rd I give all else of whatever description that I may be possessed of at the time of my death in trust to Dr. E.F. Watkins on the following conditions. He shall first pay all my just debts & whatever may remain over & above the amount requisite for this he shall invest in such property as he may in his judgment seem expedient, the profits arising from which amount he shall pay to my sister Mildred B. Watkins during her life & at her death the said property shall rest absolutely in all of the children of the sd. Mildred as may be living at the detirmmination of said life estate.

4th I Appoint Dr. E.F. Watkins the Executor of this my last Will & testament, having the utmost confidence in the honor & Honesty of said E.F. Watkins it is my will & desire that no security shall be required of him, either as my Executor or as trustee as appointed above -

In testimony that the above is my own Act and deed I have hereunto Affixed my hand at Memphis this the Ninth day of June 1844.

William Q. Johnson

(P-276) We do hereby certify that William Q Johnson whose name is signed to the Will on the other Side written did on the eight day of June 1844, while of sound Mind and Memory did acknowledge the Same to be his last Will & testament and that the signature attached thereto was in his own proper handWriting, erasiers from the word death to the 4th Item haveing been made in our presence & by his request, and the word " the said property shall rest absolutely in such of the children of said Mildred as may be living at the detirmmination of Said life Estate," entered in lieu thereof, such Acknowledgment was made in our presence each being at the time in the presence of the testator & of each other,

A R Herron W J Tuck J J More Jos R Williams

State of Tennessee)
July Sessions 1844
Shelby County)

A Paper purporting to be the Last Will & testament of Wm. Quarles Johnson was produced in open court, and thereupon came into court W J Tuck, J J Moore and Joseph R Williams Subscribing Witnesses thereto who being first duly sworn depose & say that the said Testator acknowledged the same in their presence to be his last Will & testament & that he was of sound Mind and disposing Memory at the time of acknowledging the Same Which is ordered to be recorded -

Recorded July the 9th 1844 John W. Fuller C.S.C.
in Book C, page 275 & 6

John W. Fuller C S C

(P-277) F. C. THURMON'S WILL

Know all yea whom it may concern to know anything of my affairs that I Fendal C Thurmon of the County of Shelby and State of Tennessee being in feeble health but of sound mind and in the exercise of liberal judgment and being also on the eve of undertaking a journey to distant Countries with the hope of recovering my health, in the presence of my old and valued friends Tilmon Bettis Anderson B Carr and Marcus B Winchester do make and declare the following to be the disposition which I desire and require should be made of my affairs in case of my death

Item 1st I desire that all my just debts shall be paid as soon as they conveniently may be without prejudice to my Estate.

Item 2nd To my beloved wife Ann, I give and bequeath during her widowhood the use possession and control of all my property both reall and personal and mixed to be applied to her own support and that of the family and to the education comfort and protection of my children and at the end and expiration of her widowhood as aforesaid to be divided in accordance with the laws of the State. It is not intended herein however to prevent my said wife Ann from dividing off any reasonable and due proportion of my property to any of my children as they may come of age or marry provided she choses to do so thereby settling upon them at once a good and perfect title to any property so divided and given in severalty and provided always that they be held accountable to my Estate for the valuation put on the property at the time of such division until there is a final ~~division~~ Settlement and partition of the whole Estate

Item 3rd Should any of my sons desire to be educated for a profession It is my desire that an account be Kept against them for extraordinary expenditures and deducted from <u>their</u> proportion of the Estate

Item 4 It is my will & desire that my old and faithful servant Peter should remain with my wife during her widowhood but at the termination of the same (P-278) that he should be free to go where he choses and to employ himself as he likes and I do hereby enjoin on them who at any time may have the Administration of my Estate to defray the necessary expence of support and protecting my said servant

Item 5th I do hereby appoint my beloved wife Ann Sole Administratrix of this my last Will & Testament and during her widowhood I desire that the Courts of my Country shall require neither Bonds nor security for the faithful Administration of the same

In testimony of which I have hereunto set my name at the town of Fort Pickering June 9th 1844

Witnesses present F.C Thurmon (SEAL)

his
Tilmon X Bettis A B Carr M B Winchester
mark

State of Tennessee
September Session A D 1844
Shelby County)

(P-278 cont.) A Competent Court present

A paper writing perporting to be the last Will and Testament of F C Thurmon dcd. was produced in open court Tilmon Bettis one of the subscribing witnesses thereto who being duly sworn depose and say that the testator acknowledged the same in his presence to be his last Will and Testament and that he was of sound mind and disposing memory at the time of acknowledging the same which is ordered to be recorded

Recorded September 26th 1844 John W Fuller Clk

(P-279) Memphis May 30th 1844

The undersigned being perfectly sound of both body and mind and knowing the uncertainty of Human life and being desirous that his friends should know his wishes as to the disposition of his little Estate makes this his last Will and Testament

First. It is my desire that the business of F. & R.E. Titus be closed as soon as practicable and that G Buntyn act as my Executor in settling the same after it is settled and the debts all paid off I wish my wife Indiana Titus to have the amount be it much or little for her individual use arising from said Business.

Second I give to my wife Indiana Titus my household and Kitchen furniture my horse & buggy and all things belonging to me about my premises also my Negro Boy Jim in the possession of my Bros. A J & Thos. F Titus in Red River County Texas also, my entire undivided interest in the Est. of my Father James Titus who demised in Red River County Texas consisting of land Negroes &C also all monies due me by note or otherwise after my just debts are paid it is my wish that E Titus and G Buntyn act as my Executors to the above Will without being required to give security I wish Indiana to mary again if she thinks best but should she marry contrary to the wishes of her father then I wish the amount of property comeing to me from Texas to be applied to the Education of Nieces and Nephew Ebinezer B Titus Louisa M & H H Kimbrough and A.J. Titus take possession of it for that purpose.

Witness R E Titus

A M Wood James H Epps

State of Tennessee)
September Session A D 1844
Shelby County Court)

A Competent Court present

A paper writing perporting to be the last Will & Testament of R E Titus was produced in open Court A M Wood & James H Epps subscribing witnesses thereto who being first duly sworn depose and say that the Testator (P-280) acknowledging the same in their presence to be his last Will and Testament and that he was of sound mind and disposing memory at the time of acknowledging which is ordered to be recorded

Recorded September 26th 1844 John W Fuller Clk

(P-280 cont.) MISS JULIET RAWLINGS LAST WILL & TESTAMENT

State of Tennessee Shelby County

I Juliet Rawlings of the County of Shelby and State aforesaid do make and publish this to be my last Will & Testament hereby revoking and making void all other wills by me at any time heretofore made being of feeble health but of sound mind and disposing memory, I will and dispose of my worldly Estate as follows

Item 1st I will and bequeath to my cousin John James Rawlings of Calvert County Maryland one Negroman a Slave now being in the said County of Calvert by the name of James Somerville and whatever sum of money if any there may be due me for the hire of said slave after satisfying Doctor Sedgwich for his trouble with said slave and pay all my just debts in said County I also will and bequeath unto said John James Rawlings all my interest or title in a certain tract or parcel of land in the said County of Calvert known as Rawlings choice, together with the sum of two hundred dollars to be paid to him by my Executors when said legitee arrives at the age of twenty one years and likewise for the legal interest on said sum of two hundred dollars from the time of my death to the age of twenty one years of said legatee my Executor must be accountable and pay over to him for the use of said sum of two hundred dollars

Item 2nd I will & bequeath to John Lewis Rawlings son of Thomas J Rawlings of Shelby County aforesaid one Negro boy slave by the name of James I also will and bequeath to said John Lewis Rawlings my Negro Girl slave named Mary Ann and her child being the only child said slave Mary Ann now has together with her further increase if any to him the said John Lewis and his heirs

(P-281) Item 3rd I will & bequeath to Vergil Rawlings as son of Doctor Thomas Rawlings and his heirs my Negrowoman a slave named Betsy and two of her children by the name of owen & William Henry. I wish Betsy to remain in Memphis and work for the benefit of Virgil so long as the laws of this State will permit and when she is old I wish Virgil and John Lewis Rawlings to see that she is well taken care of

Item 4th I will and bequeath to Olivia Ann Daughter to Joseph J Rawlings one Negro Girl slave by the name of Clarisa(daughter of Negrowoman Betsy) I also will & bequeath to said Olivia Ann one feather Bed marked S N one pillow and bolster two pair sheets two pair pillow cases one pair blankets and quilt with lining to it which is unquilted and two plain finger rings

Item 5th. I will and bequeath to Ruth Wallace Rawlings (sister to Olivia Ann above mentioned one feather bed marked J R bolster & pillow one blanket one white counterpane two sheets two pair pillow cases one quilt already quilted together with my breast pin and set ring

Item 6th I wish to be decently buried a tombstone to be placed over my grave with my name marked or engraved on it I desire my funeral to be preached by an Episcopal Minister

Item 7th I wish J J Rawling to satisfy himself for any trouble I

(P-281 cont.) may have caused him out of any money of ~~mine~~ mine in his hands to pay my Doctors bills funeral expences and all my just debts all monies then owing to me whether by Bill Bond note or otherwise and all other property that I may have I wish to be equally divided between my two Cousins Joseph J Rawlings and Doctor Thomas J Rawlings should any money money be comeing to me out of my brother Isaac Rawlings Estate I wish in dividing it between said J J & T J Rawlings for Thomas to have the largest portion by one hundred dollars-

(P-282) Item 8th I wish Negro Girl Mary Ann to have my small red quilt which has netting around it

Item 9th. Lastly I wish Joseph J Rawlings to act as Executor to this my last Will & Testament Signed sealed and published as my last Will & Testament this 14th day of November A D 1844

Juliet Rawlings (Seal)

Signed sealed and published in our presence who have subscribed our names hereto in the presence of the Testator this 14th November A D 1844

L M Daniel Thos Ethridge

State of Tennessee)
December Session A D 1844
Shelby County Court)

A Competent Court present

A paper writing purporting to be the last Will and Testament of Juliet Rawlings dcd. was produced in open court and thereupon came into Court Lewis M Daniel and Thomas Ethridge subscribing witnesses thereto who after being duly sworn depose and say that the said Testator acknowledged the same in their presence to be her last Will and Testament and that she was of sound mind and disposing memory at the time of acknowledging the same which is ordered to be recorded

Recorded Jany. 28th 1845 John W Fuller Clk

(P-283) In the name of God Amen

I William Wallace Bruce of the County of Shelby & State of Tennessee though of sound mind & bodily Strength being fully persuaded that the days of man are butfew at best and being particularly desirous that my Estate both real & personal should be disposed of as now to me seemeth best Hath influenced me to make this my last Will & Testament

Item the Ist It is my wish and desire that my body be disposed of in a plain yet genteel manner

Item 2nd It is my desire that all just claims that may be against me at the time of my death be paid

Item 3rd it is my desire that Adolphus B and William M Ellis receive from my Estate five hundred dollars each to be paid unto them so

(P-283 cont.) soon as may be deemed practicable by my Administrator or Executor

Item 4th It is my wish and desire that my mother Nancy G Buster shall have the remain of my Estate both real and personal to hold and use during her natural life or widowhood after which it is my desire that the whole of which be fairly and equally divided between Samuel Nancy Walter L John D and James C Buster to keep & hold to them and their heirs forever

Item 5th Reposeing special confidence in my esteemed and valued friend Stephen M Rutland I desire that he and by these presence appoint him to act as my legal executor to this my last Will and Testament

In testimony whereof I have hereunto set my name and caused my seal to be affixed done this the 10th of March 1844

Test B B Buchanan William Wallace Bruce (Seal)
J L Harrison

(P-284) State of Tennessee)
December Session A D 1845
Shelby County Court)

A Competent Court present

A paper writing purporting to be the last Will and Testament of William Wallace Bruce was produced in open court & thereupon came into court B B Buchanan and J L Harrison subscribing witnesses thereto who after being duly sworn depose and say that the said Testator acknowledged the same in their presence to be his last Will and Testament and that he was of sound mind and disposing memory at the time of acknowledging the same which is ordered to be record-

Recorded January Jany. 28th 1845

John W Fuller Clk

(P-285) JOHN WOODS LAST WILL & TESTAMENT

State of Tennessee)

Shelby County)

In the name of God Amen I John Woods Merchant of the City of Memphis in the county and State aforesaid know that it is appointed for all men to die and being at this time in weak and dellicate health of body but of perfectly sound and disposing mind memory and understanding do hereby make publish & declare the following as my last Will & Testament hereby revoking and declareing to be null and void all other or former wills by me at any time ~~made~~ or supposed to be made

And Imprimis I bequeath immortal Soul to God by whom it was given to me and my body to the dust whence it comes and as to the goods and chattels rights and credit property & Estate of all sorts and kinds real personal

(P-285 cont.) & mixed which I have or hold am ~~seized~~ sized and possessed of or have or claim right and title to in this world I hereby devise and bequeath & dispose of in the manner following to wit

Item first I require and direct my Executor hereinafter named immediately after my death to pay all the debts by me justly due and owing to citizens of the town of Memphis out of the money that may be on hand, or if anough money ~~may not~~ for the purpose may not be on hand out of the first money comeing into the hands of my Executors out of my Estate by sales of property collections or otherwise

Item Second I require and direct that my Executor shall ~~next~~ pay all my debts due either to banks or individuals upon or for which my Executor or any other of my friends are bound or liable as security or endorsed for me.

Item third I require and direct that my store shall be kept open and my stock of goods on hands sold out by retail or wholesale as the said business is now going on until the Stock of goods on hand shall be so fare reduced or sold off as to render it best and most advantageous for my Estate for the remnant of the Stock to be sold at auction or otherwise closed my Executor being hereby required and directed to close said business by Auction or otherwise when in his judgment it may be best for the interest of my Estate to do so

Item Fourth After all my debts are fully paid and satisfied I give and bequeath the entire balance of my property constituting my whole Estate to my brother James Woods who who is (P286)hereinafter appointed my Executor & hereby require and direct him to give the one half thereof to my be loved wife Lettitia Maria Woods and to retain the other half thereof in his hands as trustee for the sole & separate use & benefit of my only child Josephine Harrison Woods until she marries or become of the age of twenty one years at which time the same shall be delivered and paid over to her should my said child die before she marries or becomes twenty one years ~~of age~~ old then in that ~~case~~ event I give and bequeath to my wife the half of my estate herein & hereby given to my child. At the death of my ~~wife~~ beloved wife I give and bequeath to my said child all that portion of half of my Estate that is given to my wife, which may remain unexpended or undisposed of at the time of the death of my wife I hereby require & direct my Executor to invest the half of my Estate given to my child in stock or real Estate or such other property as he may deem best for her interest out of the annual proceeds or income of which my child is to be supported & educated, if sufficient for that purpose, if not then my estate hereby given to my child to be used for that purpose or so much thereof annually as may be required for object - I also require and direct my executor to render unto my wife all the counsel, aid and assistance &C she may require in revesting the half of my estate given to her in the best & most judicious & profitable manner for her interest-

Item Fifth and Last - I hereby nominate constitute and appoint my brother James Woods of Memphis Tennessee the sole executor of this my last will & testament and direct & require that he take have and hold the sole and exclusive execution of this my will, & the sole & exclusive set(P-287) tlement & management & management of my affairs and business until the same is fully and completely settled up and closed and I also hereby appoint

(P-287 cont.) my said brother James Woods the guardian of my said child Josephine Harrison Woods so far as the management investment control &c of the property is concerned herein & hereby given to my said child.

And I require & direct that my said executor shall not be required to give any bond or security either as my executor or as the guardian of my said child-

In testimony whereof I have hereunto subscribed my name & affixed my seal this 27th November 1844-

John Woods (Seal)

Signed sealed & published in the presence of us

Seth Wheatly Nath. Anderson

State of Tennessee)
January Sessions A.D. 1844
Shelby County)

A Competent Court present

A paper writing purporting to be the last will and testament of John Woods deceased was produced in open Court and thereupon came in to Court Nathaniel Anderson and Seth Wheatley subscribing witnesses thereto who being first sworn depose and say that they were acquainted with the said testator and that he acknowledged the same in in their presence to be his last will and testament and that he was of sound mind and disposing memory at the time of acknowledging the same (P-288) ordered that said will be recorded

Recorded Jan 28 1845 John W Fuller Clerk

John W Fuller clerk

Ny B G Dowell D C

(P-289) E L I J A H G R I F F I N W I L L

In the name of God Amen! I Elijah Griffin at present of the County of Shelby & State of Tennessee being aged and infirm, though of sound Mind & Memory well knowing the uncertainty of Human Life, think it a duty to make a distribution of my worldly Substance,

Item 1st I Commit my Soul to God the Giver & My Body decently to the earth from whence it came,

Item 2nd I Bequest all my Estate to my beloved Wife Mary Griffin to say, My Nine Negroes Namely, John Clarry, Sam, Cillor Cirene, Mary, Lucy, Ann & Jordon, during her Natural life & and at her decease the aforesaid property to be equally divided Among My Children Agreeable to a Schedule hereinAfter Made that their shares May be equal of my Estate from the beginning Except Kesiah Numby Faulkner & her Sister Mary Gold Faulkner who

(P-289 cont.) are to have the whole of their Mother Sarah Faulkners Estate in Virginia & their Sister Sarah Jane Faulkner is to come in as a full Heir at the decease of My Wife Mary with my other children Hereinafter named, except the advance of Fifty Nine dollars to her Mother.

I have advanced to My Children as a part of their portion of My Estate to be charged to Each of them in a division ToWit,

To Margaret Stone One hundred & thirty three dollars 33cts
To Susan Greggory One hundred & Twenty Nine dollars 33 cts
To Elizabeth Stone One hundred & Sixty three dollars 18 cts.
To William Griffin One hundred & Eight dollars
To Sarah Faulkner fifty Nine Dollars 8 cts
To Gold Griffin Two hundred & forty dollars
To Mary Wortham Seventy dollars Ten cents
To Lucy Estis forty one dollars, Twelve Cents
To Nancy Jones Fifty dollars Ten Cents

Item 3rd It is my will and desire that My Daughter Jane havea a bed and furniture with a Horse, Saddle (P-290) and Bridle at her Marriage & be an equal Heir in all My Estate with the foregoing Children.

Item 4th I do hereby Nominate and Appoint My Son William Griffin & My SonsinLaw Thos. Wortham & Stephen Jones Executors to this my last Will & Testament hereby revoking all former Wills -

Given under My hand and Seal County & State first within written this 28th February 1837

In presence of R M D J Elliott Elijah his X mark Griffin (Seal)
Thos. C. Horn

State of Tennessee)
February Sessions 1845
Shelby County)

A paper writing purporting to be the last Will & Testament of Elijah Griffin dcd. was produced in open court & thereupon came into court Thos. G. Horn subscribing Witness thereto who being first duly sworn deposeth & saith that he was acquainted with the Testator & that he acknowledged the same in his presence to be his last Will & Testament & that he was of sound mind & disposing Memory at the time of Acknowledging the same Also Appeared in open Court Thomas Wortham who being first sworn deposeth that although he was not a subscribing Witness he was present at the time the Said Testator acknowledged the same & that he was of Sound Mind & disposing Memory which is Ordered to be Recorded

Recorded April 1st 1845 John W. Fuller Clk

John W Fuller Clk

(P-291) I S A A C A H E R R O N W I L L

I Isaac A. H. being under apprehension of approaching dissolution

(P-291 cont.) & being of sound Mind & Memory do make & publish this my last Will & Testament

I give & bequeath to my four Nieces Sarah, Mary, Eugenia & Elizabeth Herron daughters of Thos. R Herron dcd. My Negro Man Joe, his wife Caroline & their five children to be settled upon my said Nieces in such Manner as that in case of their Marriage, their husbands shall not be Able to dispose of said property but that the Same Shall decend to their heirs. Said property to be divided equally Among the said four Nieces-

I give & bequeath my four Negro fellows, Nelson Doctor Anthony & Jim to my Brothers Abram R Herron Jas. M. Herron & Andrew H Herron to be divided equally ~~among~~ between them. It is my desire that they should not be sold out of the family

I devise that the ballance of my property shall be sold to pay debts & if any is left after paying my debts I give & Bequeath it to the children of Saml. & Mary Roach of Fayett Co Tenn, to be divided equally among them, except Abram Roach who is not to have any portion of the same.

I hereby appoint my brother Abram R Herron & Andrew H Herron the executors of this my last Will & Testament & wish them to sell what may be necessary to pay my debts, either at private or public sale as they may think proper.

I hereby again declare & publish the above as my last Will & Testament. In testimony whereof I hereunto set my Name & Seal This February the 28th 1845

I A Herron (Seal)

Signed & acknowledged in the presence of it first being read to him in our presence

L H H Rice James Thomas A Watkins R C Malone

(P-292) State of Tennessee)
March Sessions 1845
Shelby County)

A paper writing purporting to be the Last Will & Testament of Isaac A Herron dcd. was produced in open court and thereupon came into Court L H Rice a Subscribing Witness thereto who being first duly sworn deposeth & saith that he was acquainted with the Testator & that he acknowledged the same in his presence to be his last Will & Testament & that he was of sound mind & disposing Memory at the time of Acknowledging the same, which is ordered to be recorded.

Recorded April 1st 1835, John W. Fuller Clk

John W. Fuller Clk

(P-293) W I L L I A M M O O R E ' S W I L L

State of Tennessee Shelby County

Know all men by these presents that I William A Moore of the State & County aforesaid being of sound & disposing mind but feeble body do make & ordain this my last Will & Testament. Viz

1st I will that all my just debts be paid out of my Estate

2nd That my Estate real or personal ne kept together for the benefit of My beloved Wife Maria Moore & my three sons Monroe, John and Thomas Moore & that they be raised & educated out of the proceeds of said Estate,

3rd That My Estate be so Kept together for said purposes during the Natural life of my ~~said~~ Wife Maria & at her death to be divided equally between my four children Viz. Josephine S Bell, Monroe, John & Thomas Moore,

4th Provided my wife Maria Should Marry then and in that case, I will that when Monroe my oldest son becomes of age, that My Estate be divided equally between My Wife & four children abovenamed,

5th I will & appoint my beloved Wife Maria & my respected friend Thomas T Goldsby Executors of this My last Will & Testament,

In testimony whereof I hereunto Affix My Name, this 22nd January A D 1845

Witness Joseph Locke Ira S Perry William A Moore (Seal)

Richd. C Wyatt

State of Tennessee)
February Sessions 1845
Shelby County)

A paper purporting to be the last Will & Testament of Wm. A Moore decd, was produced in open Court & thereupon came into Court Joseph Locke & Richd. C Wyatt Subscribing Witnesses thereto, who being first duly sworn that they were acquainted with with the sd. Testator & that he acknowledged the same in their presence to be his last Will & Testament & that he was of sound Mind & disposing Memory at the time of Acknowledging the same (P-294) which is ordered to be recorded

Recorded April 1st 1845 John W Fuller Clk

John W Fuller Clk

M A R G A R E T A. M U R R Y ' S W I L L

State of Tennessee)
April 19th 1844
Shelby County)

In my last Will & Testament I bequeath unto my daughter Mary Adilia

(P-294 cont.) Murray all my goods & chattels & all the Moneys due & on hand after all My debts are paid My property consists in household furniture Sixty dollars in cash, a debt due from John B Feeney three hundred dollars more or less My dower arising from the proceeds of the sale of a house & lot formerly owned by Feeny & Murry all of which I bequeath to the aforesaid Mary Adelia Murray After my debts are paid. I appoint my Mother Agnes Hawthorn to be the Guardian of My Daughter Mary Adelia Murray

Margaret A Murray

Witness

J A Terry J M Hawthorn
P A Hawthorn

State of Tennessee)
March Sessions 1845
Shelby County)

A paper writing purporting to be the last Will & Testament of Margaret A Murray dcd. was produced in open Court J M Hawthorn & J A Terry Subscribing witnesses thereto, being first duly sworn depose & say that they were acquainted with the Testator & that she acknowledged the Same in their presence to be her last Will & Testament & that she was of sound mind & disposing Memory at the time of acknowledging the same which is ordered to be recorded.

Recorded April 1st 1845 J W Fuller Clk.

John W Fuller Clk

(P-295) JOHN REID'S WILL

State of Tennessee)

Haywood County)

Be it remembered that at a County Court began and held for said County at the Courthouse in the Town of Brownsville on the first Monday in October 1842, it being the 3rd day of said month Present the Worshipfuls LyneS Taliaferro William Sangster & Charles P Taliaferro Justices of the Queram Court, that on Tuesday the Second day of said Term the following entry appears on the Minutes of said Court, towit,

This day the Noncupative Will of John R Reid was produced in open Court & the making thereof was duly proved by the Oaths of Thomas Ingram & Roderick McIver who also depose that said Will was made in the last sickness of Said Testator & at his dwelling house where he had resided for more than ten days previous to his death & that said Testator specially called on said Witnesses to hear & bear Witness to his said declaration & will & it appearing to the Court that process had issued to the Widows and next of kin to come & contest the same if they or either of them should think proper, and no persons appearing to contest said Will It is therefore Ordered by the Court that Said Will be Recorded.

The following is a Copy of the abovementioned Will

We Roderick McIver & Thomas Ingram do state the following Noncupative

(P-295 cont.) Will of John Reid was made by him on the 28th day of August 1842 in our presence to which we were especially requested to bear Witness by the Testator himself in (P-296) the presence of each other, that it was made in his last sickness in his own habitation or dwelling house and the same was as follows toWit: It was his desire that his effects should be disposed of after his decease in the following manner.

First. It was his Will that the sum of two hundred dollars be given as a donation to the Presbyterian Union Church Near his residence, of which he was a member.

Second, He gave & bequeathed to his brother Ambrose R Reid a Negro Man whose name is not remembered by Witness Ingram, but is Allen as remembered by Witness McIver,

Fourth, He gave & bequeathed to his brother David Reid of Fayetteville North Carolina a Negro Man Named Ned

Fifth He gave & bequeathed to his Nephew John R Murchison son of Duncan Murchison of North Carolina a Negro Boy Named Bob.

Sixth He gave & bequeathed to his Wife May C Reid all the property in his possession acquired by him in Marriage with his said wife also three Negroes towit, Maria, Malinda, & Margaret, the name of the last mentioned slave not being remembered by Witness Ingram to wit, the said Boy Ruffin the said Witness Ingram has no recollection

Seventh, It was his will that his interest in the tract or parcel on which he then resided be sold & that the proceeds thereof be applied to the payment of a thousand dollars the ballance of the purchase money for sd. tract yet unpaid & that the residue of said proceeds be applied to the purchase of a small place for his wife

Eighth, He gave & bequeathed to his Wife Mary C. his two black mares & barouch & stock

Ninth, It was his will in the event his Wife Mary C should have a living child, he supposing her to be then encient that all his property of every kind should then belong to said Wife & the said child (P-297) notwithstanding his gifts & bequests aforesaid.

Tenth. It was his Will that Roderick McIver & Ambrose R Reid should act as his Executors in Executing the foregoing & he accordingly appointed them his Executors & gave them further power as remembered by Witness McIver of winding up & fully settling his Estate.

Made out & Signed by us this 31st day of August 1842

Thomas Ingram

R McIver

And at the same term following entry also Appears on the Minutes of said Court, to Wit. And Roderick McIver one of the Executors named in said Will, having signified to the Court that he had declined Acting Ambrose R Read who is Mentioned in said Will as the other Executor came into

(P-297 cont.) open Court & entered into bond in the sum of Eighteen thousand five hundred dollars with Roderick McIver & William Murchison as his securities & the said Ambrose R Reid Agrees to take upon himself the burden & execution of said Will & took the oath required by Law.

State of Tennessee)

Haywood County)

I Littleton Joyner Clerk of the County Court of said do hereby certify that the foregoing is a true & perfect copy of the Noncupative Will of John R Reid decd, & also of the entries on the Minutes of said court relative to the probate thereof & other Matters connected with the Same from the records of My office

Witness My hand at office this 18th day of October 1844.

L Joyner Clk

(P-298) State of Tennessee)
February Sessions 1845
Shelby County)

A Copy of the Last Will & Testament of John R. Reid dedd. was produced in open Court, & it appearing to the satisfaction of the Court that the same had been regularly proved in the County Court of Haywood County Tenn, the Same is Ordered to be Recorded

Recorded April 1st 1845 John W Fuller Clk

John W Fuller Clk S C C

(P-299) D A N I E L H A R K L E R O A D ' S W I L L

State of Tennessee Shelby County

I Daniel Harkleroad Jr. of the County & State aforesaid being of sound Mind & disposing Memory & knowing the uncertainty of life & the Certainty of death do Make this My last Will & Testament, hereby revoking & Making Void all former Wills by Me heretofore Made-

Item first. I bequeath My Soul to God who gave it & My body to the Earth to be decently buried according to the usual Christian burial rights of my County the Expenses of which I direct to be paid out of My Estate without delay, together with all my debts of any denomination whatever,

Item Second - I give to my beloved Wife Ann L Harkleroad the control of all my Estate both real & personal so long as she remains my Widow to be by her & my Executors hereinafter Named Managed & disposed of as they may deem best for the interest of my said Wife & My children hereby investing my said Wife Ann L Harkleroad & My Executor with full powers to sell & Convey any of My Land of Negroes which they May Deem Necessary. It is my intention to embrace my property in Arkansas where I formerly resided as well as that in Tennessee,

(P-299 cont.) Item Third, If My said Wife Ann L. Harkleroad should marry, it is then my Will & desire that she Secure out of My Estate One Third part thereof to be ascertained by my Executor hereinafter Named to be used & enjoyed by her during her Natural life then at her death to be equally divided between My children-

Item Fourth, It is my will & desire that the property allotted to My Wife provided she should (P-300) Marry be held in trust for her separate use by my Executor hereinafter Named-

Item Fifth, It is my will & desire & I hereby direct My Executors as my children become of age or Marry that they receive such portion of My Estate as my said Executors may think reasonable & right to be accounted for by said child or children upon final distribution on My Estate, it being My Intention to let each of My children receive an equal portion of my Estate,

Item Sixth, It is my will & desire that in the event of its being deemed necessary by the parties interested to institute a suit or suits to procure a fair and equible distribution of My Fathers Estate in Arkansas or Elsewhere, that my Executors contribute their Equal proportion of Money out of My Estate to have Justice done all the legal heirs of my said father for whom I labored long and hard to make the Estate he now possesses.

Item Seventh, I constitute my wife Ann L Harkleroad & My friend Drury L Bettis My legal Executrix & Executor to this My last Will and Testament & having full confidence in them it is my request & desire that the Court will not rule them to security.

In testimony whereof I have hereto set My hand & affixed my Seal this the twenty first day of March in the Year of our Lord One thousand Eight hundred & forty five

Witnesses Daniel Harkleroad (Seal)

C.D. McLean Saml. H Thomas

Henry Lake

State of Tennessee)

April Sessions 1845

Shelby County)

A paper Writing purporting (P-301) to be the last Will & Testament of Daniel Harkleroad Jr. was produced in open Court and thereupon came into Court Henry Lake and Samuel H Thomas Subscribing Witnesses thereto who being first duly sworn depose & say that they are acquainted with the Testator & that he acknowledged the Same in their presence to be his last Will & Testament and that he was of sound Mind & disposing Memory at the time of ~~disposing~~ signing the same which Will is Ordered to be Recorded.

Recorded April 11th 1845 John W Fuller Clk

John W Fuller Clk

(P-302) EDWARD COX'S WILL

Item 1st I will that all my just debts be paid.

Item 2nd To my brother Mat J Cox I will & bequeath Jesse & his wife Jane - Stafford & Eliza-

Item 3rd To Will Henry Cox, I will & bequeath Watt _______ Walton & Milley_

Item fourth, To Bartley Alberinus Cox I will & bequeath Big Lewis, his wife Jenny, Little Louis & Charles Sarah & Mary and Daniel & Charley.

Item fifth To Robert R Cox I will & Bequeath Crump & his wife Betty, Virgie Mary & the infant of Betty & Aaron

Item Sixth. To Edward Payson Lumpkin son of my friend Col. Joseph H Lumpkin I will and bequeath My boy Frank who is unwilling to live with any of the family & who is desirous of returning to Lexington & also my favorite Mare Kitty and Gioso Stock,

Item Seventh, Joe Henry and family I will & bequeath to Will Henry Cox - provided he will account for their Value, to the rest of the Brothers,

Item Eighth, To my said Brothers I bequeath my plantation and other property not included in this Will- I hereby revoke all other Wills by Me Made and Nominate & appoint My friends William Dunn and Joseph H Lumpkin Executors of this My Last will and Testament

Witness my hand and Seal this 22nd day of May 1843-

Edwd Cox (Seal)

The foregoing Will Signed Seal & published in the presence of us who have attested it in the presence of the Testator & of each other,

George F Platt Simpson H Cox Josiah C.T. Jordon

(P-303 Edwd. Cox's Will, Continued) Georgia)

Oglethorpe County)

Personally appeared in open Court George F Platt and Josiah C. T Jordon two of the subscribing Witnesses to the within will and after being duly sworn deposeth & saith that they saw Edmond Cox, Sign, Seal publish & declare this writing to be his last Will & Testament, and that at the time thereof he was of sound deposing mind & Memory & that he did it freely, without compulsion & that they also signed the same as Witnesses to the best of Your Knowledge, So help You God -

George F Platt Hosiah C T Jordan

Sworn to & subscribed in open Court this fourth day of March, 1844,

Test, Henry Britain Clk

(P-303 Edwd. Cox's Will, Continued) Georgia) Court of Ordinary March
Oglethorpe County) Term 1844

The within Last Will & Testament of Edmond Cox deceased having been exhibited in open Court & duly proven upon the oaths of George F Platt and Josiah C T Jordon two of the subscribing Witnesses to the same, It is Ordered that the same be admitted to Record.

Recorded the 9th day of March 1844 Henry Britain C.C.O.

State of Georgia)

Oglethorpe County)

I Henry Burton Clerk of the Court of Ordinary in & for said County (P-304) and State, do hereby certify that the foregoing copy of Will is a true Copy of the last Will & Testament of Edward Cox deceased as Exhibited in open Court & duly proven & carried to probate & also a true copy from the records of My office.

Given under my hand & Seal of Office at office the 9th day of March 1844.

Henry Britain C.C.O.

State of Georgia)

Oglethorpe County)

I Henry Jordan one of the Judges of the Inferior Court of said County while sitting for ordinary purposes do hereby certify that Henry Burton whose name appears to the above & foregoing certificate was at the date of said Certificate and Still is Clerk of the said Court or Ordinary And that full faith & credit should be given to his Attestation as such & that full faith & credit should be given to the Official Acts of the said _ as Clerk aforesaid.

Henry Jordan J.S.C.

State of Tennessee)
April Sessions A D 1845
Shelby County)

A Copy of the last Will & Testament of Edward Cox was produced in open Court & it appearing to the satisfaction of the Court that the same had been regularly proven in Oglethorpe County in the State of Georgia & it is ordered to be recorded,

Recorded April 11th 1845 John W Fuller Clk

John W Fuller Clk

(P-305) W I N F R E D S P I C E R S W I L L

I, Winfred Spicer residing in Yallabousha County and State of Mississippi, being aged & infirm but of sound and disposing Mind & Memory and

(P-305 cont.) calling to mind the uncertainty of this life, do now make and publish this my last Will & Testament, - - in Manner & form following, That is to say, -

1st, I give and bequeath to my GrandSon Robert M. Spicer, the following Negro Slaves, Viz; Grace, Delpha, George, Peter, John, Minerva, Maria, Lewis, Washington, Jackson, Matilda, Fanny, Henry & Jim, and their increase-

And also, my old Woman Dolly & one feather bed, Bedstead & furniture, My large trunk all My Kitchen furniture & two cows & calves & all the rest & residue of My property, To have and to hold to my said Grandson for and during his Natural life, Expresly however in trust for the uses & purposes following towit

Whereas my said old Woman Dolly has served me long & faithfully, and I am in virtue bound, and feel particularly anxious to provide for her comfort, I have not given her to my Grand Son for any service she may render him, but for the purpose that he May protect & provide for her & to asssist in doing so, I give him the said Negro Fany, expresly for the purpose of being kept with the Old Woman Dolly as a Nurse & constant attendant during her lifetime & to administer to her various wants & in case Fanny should die before Dolly, it is in that case My will & desire that my said Grandson shall set apart some particular one of the other Negroes above named (P-306) or some other servant to serve Dolly instead of Fanny and one as capable & qualified as Fany is at this time ~~as Fany is at this time~~ and I also will and devise that Dolly shall have wholy the possession & use during her lifetime of the above named feather bed Bed Stead and furniture large trunk Kitchen furniture and two cows & calves, all of which property above set apart to the use of Dolly during her lifetime. I will & devise that the Same after the Death of Dolly be disposed of and appropriated to the same uses as the other property herein bequeathed.

I will and desire that all the property herein bequeathed except so far as, as provision is made as above for Dolly shall be kept in the possession of My said GrandSon during his Natural life & the increase & profits of the same be laid out & expended in the maintenance and Education of his children Namely John E Spicer Eliza C Spicer Robert A Spicer, Saml. S. Spicer Nancy C Spicer, James C. Spicer & such other children as my said Grandson may have born hereafter & also to purchase other property with sd. Profits and increase for said children if said profits & increase warrant it, But whereas it is reasonable & just that my said GrandSon should have some compensation for Keeping & holding said property and disposing of the proceeds and increase of the same for the purposes above named And it is difficult to define what compensation he Should have for Executing the trust vested in him whereas I desire to keep the interest of my GrandSon and his children Unded as there is a Natural beauty and utility in such blending of interest, whereas I have every confidence in the Justice of My GrandSon and in his love & providence for his children,, And whereas I am disposed to trust to the most (P-307) Kindly impulses of Nature and to have them free & unshackled, I therefore designedly leave unspecified, what Compensation my said GrandSon shall have out of the profits and increase of said Property for his trouble and care in Executing this trust. And I will and desire that My said GrandSon shall Not be held to Account to said Children for said profits and increase but that He shall account account only to his Sense of Justice and parental feelings-

(P-307 cont.) 2nd I will and bequeath all the property above described after the death of My Said Grandson to his Said children to have and to hold to them their heirs and assigns forever,

Lastly I nominate and appoint My GrandSon Robert M Spicer and my friend Executors of this My last Will & Testament and hereby revoke all other Will Wills & Testaments by me heretofore Made

In testimony whereof I the said Winfred Spicer have hereto set my hand and Seal the Nineteenth day of July in the Year of our Lord One thousand Eight hundred and thirty Nine-

Signed Sealed & published as her Last Will & Testament in Presence of

Samuel M Hankins
William M Hankins
Jno. E Baker

Winny Spicer (Seal)

State of Mississippi)
Probate Court June Term A D 1841
Carrol County)

Then was this Will proven by the Oath of William H Hankins & Ordered to be Entered of Record-

M.D. Kimbrough

Judge of Probate

(P-308) The State of Mississippi)

Carroll County)

I Samuel Hart Clerk of the Probate Court of Said County do hereby certify that the foregoing Transcript is a true Copy of the Last Will & Testament of Winfred Spicer as appears from the record of Wills of Carroll County in Book A, Pages 21,22 & 23-

Given under my hand and Seal of Office at Carrollton the 13th day of June A D 1841

Sam Hart Clk

By L B Hart D C

State of Tennessee)
April Sessions A D 1845
Shelby County Court)

A copy of the last Will & Testament of Winfred Spicer was produced in open Court it appearing to the satisfaction of the Court that the Same has been fully & Regularly proven in Carroll County in the State of Mississippi It is ordered that the Same be Recorded.

John W Fuller Clk

(P-308 cont.) Recorded April 12th 1845

John W Fuller Clk.

L C TREZEVANT'S WILL

(P-309) Shelby County Tennessee Nov, 23, 1843 -

I L C Trezevant M.D. formerly of the City of Charleston & State of So Ca, & for Many Years a resident of the State of Virginia but Now living in the County & State aforesaid being of Sound Mind & body, do make & hereby Constitute & appoint this as my last Will & Testament toWit,

Item 1st I Bequeath to my beloved wife Elizabeth the whole of my Estate after paying my first debts to her use & entire control during the time she remains a widow,

Item 2nd Should my wife survive our children, yet being my widow & dying so, I request that she will leave what Estate she may have to the dearest & most deserving four unmarried female relations who may be in needy circumstances If none such should be within her reach, then divide it equally among the Next Meritious (Meritorious) of them

Item 3rd In the event of My wifes Marrying again & any of my children being alive I desire that she may receive her lawful portion of My Estate & that the remainder be placed in the hands of the Guardian of My Children to be by him Managed to the best advantage for them,

(P-310) Item 4th, I request my friend John P. Trezevant receive the appointment as Guardian to my children & should they survive their Mother that he become a Father to them & his wife a Mother.

Item 5th I appoint my inestable Wife my Executrix and desire that no Security be asked of her as such.

Item 6th. It is my particular desire that my friend L Crouch Trezevant shall advise with & counsel My Dear Elizabeth in the management of her Affairs-

Item 7th In the Several Appointments I have made in this instrument I connect the Earnest request that my friends will Manage my affairs and control & direct my children essentially according to the system I have always deemed most conductive to their present well being & future happiness-

And now may God have mercy on them all & take them & their fond Mother in his holy Keeping & so enlighten the Minds of our children as to enable them to become ornaments of Society & bright examples of the goodness, Greatness & Glory of his adored Majesty.

1844 March 26th

L C Trezevant M.D.

I have this day added to Item 3rd of this Will, & between 1st & 2nd line the words "& any of my children being alive," I also desire that the following shall be considered as a codicill to my Will viz. that if my Wife Elizabeth survives our children,

(P-311) State of Tennessee)
May Sessions 1845
Shelby County)

A paper writing purporting to be the last Will & Testament of L.C. Trezevant M.D. was produced in open Court & thereupon came into Court L.C. Trezevant and James R Wray who being first duly sworn depose & say that they are acquainted with the handwriting of the Testator & that they believe the Signature to ~~to~~ said paper writing ~~to/to~~ is in the proper handwriting of the said Lewis C Trezevant M.D ___

It is therefore Ordered that said Will be recorded,

Recorded May 23 1845

Test. John W Fuller Clk

(Editor's Note: Page 312 of O MS is blank)

(P-313) GEORGE RIVES WILL

I George Rives do make and publish this as my last Will & Testament hereby revoking and Making void all other Wills by me at any time made,

First, I direct that my funeral expences and all my d ebts be paid as soon after my death as possible out of monies due me for Negro hire and other sources or out of any Money Monies that may first come into the hands of my Executor.

Secondly. I bequeath to my Niece Ann E Rives daughter of William Rives to Negro fellows (Towit) One Negro Man Named Congo Aged about forty and other Negro Man Named Bob, aged about twenty one years. It is further my will & desire that if the said Anne E Rives die without issue before she shall have arrived at the age of twenty one years, then the said Negroes Congo, and Bob shall decend to her eldest brother George H Rives. I also bequeath to my niece the Said Ann E Rives all my Miscellaneous and Classical Books.

Thirdly, I bequeath to my Nephew George H Rives son of William Rives the following Named Negroes (Towit) Sally a woman about forty two years old, together with her two youngest children both female now living. It is further my will and desire that if the said George H Rives should die before he shall have arrived at the age of Twenty one years without issue, then the said Negroes Sally & her two youngest children now born, shall decend to my Niece Ann E Rives provided she be then living, but should the said Anne E Rives be not then living then the said Negroes Sally and her two (P-314) youngest children Now living together, with the Negro Men Congo and Bob, chiwch will have decended to him the said George H Rives by the death of his Sister Ann E Rives shall decend to My Niece Adelaid R Rives. I do bequeath to My Nephew George H Rives one fine gold watch & chain,

Fourthly, I bequeath to my Niece, Adalade R Rives daughter of Christofer Rives One Negro Girl daughter to the said Sally named Patty about six years of age, and provid she shall die without issue before

(P-314 cont.) she shall have arrived at the age of twenty one years, then the said Negro Girl Named Patty together with the above Mentioned Negroes (towit) Sally and her two youngest children now born and Congo, and Bob, should they have decended to her by the death of the said Ann E and George H Rives shall decend to her brother Nathaniel D Rives-

Fifthly. I bequeath to my Niece Dorinda Rutherford daughter of my Sister May Rutherford One Negro girl daughter of the said Sally aged about Eighteen years of age Named Hanna and if she die without issue before she shall have arrived at the age of twenty one years, then the said Negro girl Named Hanna shall decend to her Next Sister Mary Rutherford.

Sixthly, I bequeath to my Mother Mary Rives my Riding Horse saddle bridle of the value of one hundred dollars, and also one other sorrel horse of the value of thirty dollars also one Black leather Trunk & one other light colored hair trunk.

Seventhly, I bequeath to my friend William T Avery all my Law Books, also one suit of cloaths consisting of the following described articles to be selected by himself out of my Wardrobe, ToWit, (P-315) One Black Cloth Coat, one Black Cloath Cloak, One pair Black French Doe Skin cashmere pants, one Frilled Silk Vest, One Black Silk figured Necherchief, One pair fine Calf Skin Boots, One fine Silk Handkerchief, One Shirt and drawers, also one Leather travelling trunk.

Eighthly, I bequeath to my friend John L, Williams one Suit of Cloths composed of the following Articles (Viz) One cloth coat, one pair Black French Doe Skin cashmere pants, One Black Satin Vest, one fine Bever hat, One Black Cloth Overcoat One fine Silk Handkerchief, one fine Black Silk Scarf, One Shirt & pair of drawers, And the remainder of My wardrobe I bequeath to my friends John S Williams and William T Avery to be divided between them as they May deem proper, with the exception of the following described suit of Cloaths (towit) One black cloth coat, one pair blush casimere pants, one black silk and flax Vest, one pair Waterproof Boots, one 1 leghorn hat, One black Silk Scarf One pair drawers, one shirt, and one pair suspenders which I desire to be given to a Negro boy belonging to my Mother Named Dick, excepting also two other pair of casimere pants which I desire to be given to My Negro Boy Named Bob -

Ninthly - I bequeath to my Nephew Nathaniel D Rives Son of my Brother Christopher Rives One fine Rifle Gun-

It is further my will and desire that my Executor so soon as convenient after my death dispose of the following mentioned property the proceeds of which to be handed over to the (P-316) Lodge of the Independent Order of Odd Fellows Towit, One Double Barrel Shot Gun, one dray and my half of one Office Store

Lastly I do hereby appoint & Nominate Thomas W Wilkerson my Executor

In Witness whereof I do to this my Will, set my hand and Seal this the 14th day of March 1845.

George Rives (Seal)

Signed Sealed and published in our presence and we have Subscribed

(P-316 cont.) our Names hereto in presence of the Testator this 14th day of March 1845

James Wichersham

H B Joiner

State of Tennessee)
May Term 1845
Shelby County)

A paper writing purporting to be the last will & Testament of George Rives was produced in open Court & thereupon came into open Court H D Joiner one of the Subscribing Witnesses thereto who being first duly sworn deposeth and saith that he was acquainted with the said Testator & that he acknowledged the Same in his presence to be his last Will & Testament & that he was of sound mind & disposing Memory at the time of the signing the same. Said Will is Ordered to be filed for further probate-

And at the June Term 1845 of the County Court the following Probate appears of Record, Towit,

A paper writing purporting to be the last Will & Testament of George Rives decd. which had been proven by the oath of H.B. Joiner one of the Subscribing Witnesses ~~thereto~~ at a former term of this Court, was reproduced to the Court - And thereupon came (P-317) into Court James Wickersham the other Subscribing Witness thereto who being first duly sworn Deposeth & saith that he was acquainted with the said Testator in his lifetime and that he Acknowledged the Same in his presence to be his last Will and Testament and that he was of sound Mind and disposing Memory at the time of Acknowledging the Same-

Recorded June the 10th 1845 John W Fuller Clk

John W Fuller Clk

(P-318) A N D R E W R E M B E R T S W I L L

While in perfect mind & Body I deem it expedient to write this my last will and Testament expressive of my mental feelings both Religeous and Political, as well as a distribution of my Estate, lest in future time I may be misrepresented. And May Almighty God receive my immortal spirit through the atoneing influences of Jesus Christ Amen.

1st My Religious faith Poetized -

The sun in his glory had sat in the West
When the Sweetness of sleep had given full rest,
I arose from my bed and delightfully found,
The Moon in her Splendor was passing her round,
The Stars two were singing in Silent delight,
The Storms were all hushed to soften the night,
It was then I reflected, on days that gone,
And I found myself living almost alone,

(P-318 cont.) For friends I so loved early in life,
Had left me submitting, to Earth & her Strife,
The campmeeting sounds; that gave Glory to God,
We abanded & left, exposed to the rod,
Oh! the relenting & troubles of that hour,
When Heaven withdraws her Mercy & power,
When the world shall dissolve & lost from the sphere
Home so compassionate to drop us a tear,
Oh! our wandering, hours then we will deplore
When Gabriels last trumpet shall reach every shore
The Momentary Shouts of passion alone
Will find us a Wreck & entirely forloan,
Then Sperit of God, awaken in us love,
Rose our affections & joys far above,
Then Earth May be Melted & all pass away
It only gives joys in eternitys day
(P-319) Unusual for a campmeeting to fail at Harmony
All hail to the Father, the Sperit & Son
In Trinity three - in Unity one,
Who will relight our lamps at Earths glazing fire
Comsumating all, we every could desire.

2nd. MY POLITICAL OPINION -

I am a Whig after the manner of our fathers of 76, Believing in a Constitutional guide as the only true Garantee, of our Republicanism I am therefore opposed to Modern democracy because they make the Executive superior to the legislative which should be only equal as contemplated by the framers of the Constitution but as now practiced unlimited in its exercise, Cancelling all the power of Congress, without regard to Constitutional Majority - This if Manifested by President Jackson taking possession of the Treasury,

The Judiciary a third and equal power is also mearged in the Executive by the President Acting contrary to their solemn decisions three time pronounced with the great Marshall at the head, This is instanced in the United States Bank - Again because he assumes the whol Appointing power puts in Office who he pleases, disregarding the restraints of law Instanced in Van Burens Mission to England. Again because the President has laid the foundation for a Monarchy if Not already established in having elected a Successor M. Van Buren & though he fell so far of Public Expectation as almost to be universally denounced Yet his herditary passion is so strong that he Makes a Second Nominee of one of his obsequi (P-320) ous fellows who Never had the energy or independence of Mind to conceive a patrictic Act, Much less to practice one. This is James K Polk. - I oppose these self styled democrats again because they appoint to high and Lucrative Offices Men Notorious in Violating their allegiance to their Country. This is instanced in Swartout Aaron Burr principal associate, when charged with treason perhaps some high in Office thought best to fill his Mouth with loaves and f fishes least something else might exercise his tongue. I oppose them again because they justify and defend all the public defaulters who have expended more and wasted more of the public fund in their short reign than we lost the preceeding fifty years - These with a long and almost innumerable tain of Abuses which are all endorsed by by Democrats Confirms Me in Whigary because my republican principals are entirely the opposite.

- - - - - - - - - -

(P-320 cont.) 3rd MY EARTHLY GOODS -

From the great affection showed me by my son Samuel Stokes in addition to what I have already given, I give unto him, his heirs & assigns all of my estate both real & personal with the following provisions, He Samuel Stokes is to give in addition to what I have already given my Daughter Harriet Morgan One Thousand dollars twelve Months after My death also Claiborn & Menus He is to ~~to~~ all owe ~~of~~ Robert Howard fifty dollars annually during his life, and as Janet was designed to be free by a former Master & her claims are (P-321) strengthened by her exemplary conduct & in good faith with her early impressions I hereby Manumit her & all her children giving them severally, three hundred dollars apiece under the Management of the Mother until of age with full privileges of removing as soon after my death as she pleases to any State or County - This Mary shall be paid One half in hand and the Other half twelve months after my death But should not this my last Will & Testament be fully carried out one half of my Estate shall be used for a County Academy under the supervision of John Pope, G.L. Holmes William Moore, Tenel T Goldsby, & Dr R Wyatt & the other half equally divided between my two children - With confidence I expect this my last Will & Testament to be faithfully & honorably carried out as we expect fidelity in Almighty God saving us Eternally. My Executor Samuel Stoke shall not give security in the performance of this Will because I have full Confidence Amen & Amen and May we all be Saved -

In Witness I hereunto Subscribe my hand & Seal this the 12th Octo 1844

Claiborn & Meny interlined Andrew Rembert (Seal

Test William Moore Miles W Goldsby
Benj. Dunkin W A Shelby Jno. Pope

(P-322) State of Tennessee)
June Term 1845
Shelby County)

A paper writing purporting to be the last Will and Testament of Andrew Rembert was produced in open Court, and thereupon came into Court Miles W Goldsby and Benjamin Duncan, subscribing witnesses thereto, who being first duly sworn depose and say that they were acquainted with the said Testator during his lifetime and that he acknowledged the same in their presence to be his last Will and Testament, and that he was of sound mind and disposing memory at the time of acknowledging the same.

Ordered that said Will be recorded. And thereupon came into Court Samuel S Rembert the Executor therein named and qualified according to law as executor of said Will, he not being required to give bond and security in said Will. Ordered that he have letters accordingly.

Recorded June 10th 1845 John W. Fuller Clk

John W Fuller Clk.

(P-323) Raleigh Tennessee April 28th 1842

Mr. Jesse M. Tate or whomever My Executors May be -

Sir

You are hereby authorized and requested to allow and permit to remain (with Mrs. Mary M. Smith) My Motherinlaw who is the grandmother of my children during her natural life to revert back to my estate at her decease, the use of my black boy Benjamin aged about fourteen Years, One horse and a large Poplar chest, which said chest I hereby give her in fee simple, all of which she shall keep and be entitled to whatever profits shall arise from their use during her lifetime as above Mentioned, but the boy shall in no wise be sold or pledged in any shape or form for any debt which she may contract, but shall simple serve the said Mary M. Smith as a Means of Maintenance and shall at he decease return untrammelled back to my Estate, and this instrument shall hereby exempt my Administrator or Executor from liability for the property above conveyed in any return or settlement he may make with the clerk or Commissioners of the County Court of the County in which the said Executor may reside, but I do also hereby forbid the removal of the Boy abovementioned from the immediate reach & vicinity of the Executor of My Estate. In addition to the above I have already provided an annuity of One hundred dollars to be Annually & regularly to her during her lifetime, in a Will already executed and in the hands of A (P-324) Dowell who is my Executor. The above life Estate to the said Mary M Smith is made in consideration of her remaining with Me during my lifetime, but should she not fulfil her obligations to Me, but should leave me, and not live with Me as I expect, then and in that event this shall be Null and void and shall not be allowed by my Executor.

Given under my hand and seal the date above written also the said Mary M Smith shall be provided with Meat & Meal for herself One Year after me decease

his
Leonard X Bosher
mark

Witness A West A Dowell
Richard Mason

State of Tennessee)
July Term A D 1845
Shelby County Court)

A paper writing purporting to be a codicil to the last Will and Testament of Leonard Bosher deceased was produced in open court and thereupon came into court A Dowell a subscribing witness thereto who being first duly sworn deposeth and saith that he was acquainted with the said Testator during his lifetime and that he acknowledged the same in his ~~their~~ presence to be a codicil to his last Will and Testament and that he was of sound mind and disposing memory at the time of acknowledging the same Ordered that the same be recorded

Recorded July 1845

John W Fuller Clk

(P-325) J O H N L B R O W N ' S W I L L

In the Name of God, Amen, I John L Brown being weak of Body but of sound and disposing mind and Memory do make this as my last will and Testament,

In the first place, I give my Sole to God, who gave it,

Secondly, I give to My ten half brothers & sisters who reside in Kentucky, Caldwell County ten cents each, to my father ten cents. I give and bequeath to my sister Malinda M Brown of Caldwell County, Kentucky my house and Lot in South Memphis where I now reside Lying on St Patrick Pontotoc Streets. I desire to be decently & plainly intered I owe Al~~exander~~anson Trigg One hundred dollars, To Alexander Trigg Twelve dollars. To Thomas Coghill Twenty dollars for money found by a Negro. I payed on that Twenty dollars to the Negro who found the money a pair of Boots at $4. to Editor for advertising Two dollars, To Alanson Trigg Ten dollars on Christmas Morning after it was found, deducting the same from the Twenty dollars found would leave me a debtor four dollars, I will owe my Physician for attending Me, I know of No other debts against Me. I desire that my lot be rented out until all my debts be paid. I trust none of my creditors will sacrifice my house & Lot but receive the rents until all are payed I know Triggs will not sacrifice My house & Lot from my dear Sister.

Lastly I appoint my friend and relation James Blasingame my Executor to Carry this My Will into Execution and should said Blasingame be unable from any cause to attend to the (P-326) same my desire is that he choose the Executor in his room and Stead. Alanson Trigg paid the two dollars for advertising the found money-

In Witness whereof I have hereto Set My hand & seal this 29th day of May 1845

his
John L X Brown (Seal)
mark

Test James C Cravens
Archibald White

State of Tennessee)
July Term 1845
Shelby County)

A paper writing purporting to be the last Will & Testament of John L Brown decd. was produced in open court & thereupon came into Court James C Cravens & Archibald White, Subscribing Witnesses thereto who being first duly sworn depose and say that they were acquainted with the said Testator in his lifetime & that he Acknowledged the same in their presence to be his last Will & testament & that he was of Sound Mind and disposing memory at the time of Acknowledging the Same.

John W Fuller Clk

Recorded July 12th 1843

John W Fuller Clk

(P-327) J A N E G A B B O T T ' S W I L L

I Jane G Abbott do make and publish this My Last Will & Testament, hereby revoking and making void all other Wills by Me at any time made.

First I direct that my funeral expences and all my just debts be paid as Soon after my death as possible out of what Moneys that I may die possessed of or may first come into the hands of My Executor.

Secondly I give and bequeath to My brother Wm. Winfrey's children five hundred dollars to be equally divided between them.

Thirdly - I give and bequeath all of the rest of My Estate to be Equally divided between the children of my three brothers Namely Henry Winfrey, John F Winfrey and William Winfrey.

Lastly I do hereby Nominate and appoint My brother William Winfrey My Executor.

In Witness whereof I do to this My Will Set my hand and Seal This the 23rd day of December 1844

her
Jane G X Abbott (Seal)
mark

Test
F S Jackson Robt. T Jackson
Lewis W Rainey his
Joe X Baugh
mark

State of Tennessee)
June Term 1845
Shelby County)

A paper writing purporting to be the last will and Testament of Jane G Abbott was produced in open Court and thereupon came into open Court Lewis M Rainey one of the Subscribing (P-328) witnesses thereto who being first duly sworn ~~depose~~ deposeth & saith that he was Acquainted with the said Testatrix in her lifetime And that she acknowledged the same in his presence to be her last Will and testament and that She was of sound Mind and disposing Memory at the time of Acknowledging the Same.

Ordered that said Will be Recorded.

Recorded July 13th 1845 John W Fuller Clk

John W. Fuller Clk

(P-329) F R E D E R I C K C H R I S T I A N ' S W I L L

I Frederick Christian of the County of Shelby, And State of Tennessee, Being of sound and perfect Mind and Memory do make and publish this my last will and Testement in manner and form following -

(P-329 Cont.) First I give and bequeath unto My two Beloved Children, Robert Edward Christian and Sally, Ann Francis Christian all My Estate real and personal, to be equally divided between them, bouth, their heirs and assigns

Secondly and Lastly I hereby Appoint My Brother Wyatt Christian Sole Executor of this my last Will and Testament, hereby revoking all former Eills by me Made With full power to sell any part of My Estate he may think proper for the use and benefit of My two children, or to purchase any property for the use & benefit of them, he may think proper with any Moneys which May come into his hands belonging to My Estate.

In Witness thereof I have hereunto Set My hand and affixed My Seal this the fifth day of August One thousand Eight hundred and thirty eight

Frederick Christian (Seal

Signed, Sealed, Published, & declared (P-330) by the above Frederick Christian to be his last Will and Testament in the presence of us, who have hereunto Subscribed our Names as Witnesses in the presence of the Testator,

his
Jas. G Mitchell Abraham X Booth
mark
Joshua C Lundy S.D. Irwin W P Matthews

State of Tennessee)
August Term 1845
Shelby County)

A paper writing purporting to be the last Will and Testament of Frederick Christian deceased was produced in open Court, And thereupon Came into ~~open~~ Court Wm P. Matthews, Silas D Irwin, and Boler Cooke who being first duly Sworn, depose and say that Abraham Booth One of the Subscribing Witnesses to Said Will has Since the time of Signing said Will departed this life, And that the Mark attached to his Name as a Witness is in the form in which he usually made his mark they also state that Jas G Mitchell and Joshua C Lunday the other Subscribing Witnesses to said Will are both at this time out of this State & that they are Acquainted with the handwriting of said J G Mitchell and J C Lunday and that they believe their Signatures as witnesses to said Will are in their own proper handwriting. It is ordered that said Will be recorded.

Recorded August 11th 1845

John W Fuller Clk

(P-331) J A M E S D A U G H E R T Y ' S W I L L

In the name of God Amen.

I James Daugherty of the County of Shelby and State of Tennessee being of sound mind and disposing memory and in view of the uncertainty of life do hereby make this my last Will & Testament and hereby revoking and making void all other wills by me at any time heretofore made in manner and form as fol-

(P-331 cont.) lows (viz)

Item 1st I resign my Soul to God who gave it and my body to its Mother dust and my body to be buried in a Christian like manner according to the discretion of my Executor hereinafter named.

Item 2nd It is my will and desire that my funeral Expences and all other Just debts that I may owe at my decease be paid out of the first Moneys that may come into the hands of my Executor hereinafter named out of any portion of my Estate

Item 3rd I do hereby direct and empower my Executor hereinafter named to sell all my Estate Either Personal Real or mixed Either publicly or privately as he may think best for the Interest of my Estate and make good title to the same

Item 4th It is my will & desire that after my decease my Executor hereinafter named Procure for my grave and for the grave of my deceased wife Teresa J Dougherty TombStones to be placed at the head and foot of Each with our births age and date of our deaths and other suitable suitable Inscription at the discretion of my Executor and that our graves be Railed in in the usual decent manner.

(P-332) Item 5th It is my will and desire that after all my Just debts ~~are paid~~ and all the Expenses in the management of my Estate by my Executor are paid that the ballance be Equally divided between my Brother and Sisters by my Executor hereinafter named and paid over to them

Item 6th I do hereby nominate constitute and appoint my friend S M Allen of the town of Raleigh County of Shelby and State of Tennessee My Executor to this my last Will & testament

In testimony whereof I have hereunto set my hand and Seal this 28th day of September in the year of our lord one thousand Eight hundred & forty five

Witnesses Present James Dougherty (Seal)

John W Fuller W P Reaves

State of Tennessee)
October Term A D 1845
Shelby County Court)

A paper writing purporting to be the last Will and Testament of James Dougherty decd. was produced in open court and thereupon came into court John W Fuller and William P Reaves subscribing witnesses thereto who being first duly sworn depose and say that they were acquainted with the said Testator in his lifetime and that he acknowledged the same in their presence to be his last Will & Testament and that he was of sound mind and ~~d~~ memory at the time of acknowledging the same.

It is ordered that said Will be recorded. Recorded November 25th 1845

John W Fuller Clk

(P-333) ALEXANDER ALEN'S WILL

I Alexander Allen being in infirm health but of sound mind do make this my last will and Testament (viz)

It is my will and desire that William Stewart (my Brotherinlaw) act as my Executor and that he shall not be required to file Security

It is my will that he shall sell my lands in Shelby County my crop and so much of my stock and furniture as he may think best at such time and on such a credit as he may deem best for the Interest of my Children and that he pay all my Just debts and after my children are educated that my negroes and money be equally divided between my children as they become of age

It is my will that my Executor remove all my children from Tennessee to the Nation in Arkansas Territory and that he keep them at school and educate them as well as their means will allow

In testimony whereof I have hereunto set my hand and Seal this 20th day of August 1845

Alexander Allen (Seal)

Witness his
Lewis X Brown
mark
Lewis Shanks

State of Tennessee)
November Term A D 1845
Shelby County Court)

A paper writing purporting to be the last Will & Testament of Alexander Allen decd, was produced to the court and thereupon came into court Lewis Brown a subscribing witness thereto who being first sworn deposeth and saith that he was acquainted with the said Testator in his lifetime and that he acknowledged the same in his presence to be his last will & Testament and that he was of sound mind and disposing memory at the time of acknowledging the same

Recorded November 25th 1845

John W Fuller Clk

(P-334) JAMES HERRON'S WILL

Owing to the uncertainty of life and being in bad health but of sound and disposing mind and memory I James M Herron do make and publish this my last Will and Testament

1st I give and bequeath unto my brother Andrew H Herron the undivided interest in the property bequeath to me by Isaac A Herron dcd.

(P-334 cont.) 2nd I given and bequeath to my brother Abram R Herron my two Negro women Cely and Tosanna and their increase

3rd I give and bequeath unto my brother Abram R Herron the sum of One hundred dollars

4th I give and bequeath all the balance of my property after my debts are paid out of the same to my four nieces Mary Sarah Eugenia and Elizabeth Herron daughters of Thomas R Herron decd. to be divided Equally among them share and share a like and in case either*of them should die without issue their respective shares are to be divided Equally between my brothers Abram R Herron and Andrew H Herron In case either of my said Nieces abovementioned should intermarry the property which I have bequeathed to them is not to be subject to the disposition of their husbands or in any way liable to the payment of the debts of their respective husbands-

I hereby appoint my brothers Aram R and Andrew H Herron Executors of this my last Will & Testament and do now wish them to be required to give bond and security as such Executors I furthermore authorize my said Executors to sell or dispose of any of the property they may deem necessary for the payment of my debts at private sale and on such Terms as they think proper

In testimony whereof I have hereunto set my hand

J M. Herron

Signed in the presence of us this 20th day (P-335) of May 1845 being first read in the presence of J M Herron Samuel Smith Jr John B Lancaster G E Goodwin

State of Tennessee)
November Term A D 1845
Shelby County Court)

A paper writing purporting to be the last Will & testament of James M Herran decd. was produced in open court and thereupon came into court John B Lancaster a subscribing witness thereto who being first duly sworn deposeth and saith that he was acquainted with the said Testator in his lifetime and that he acknowledged the same in his presence to be his last Will & Testament and that he was of sound mind and deposing at the time of acknowledging the same

Ordered that said Will be recorded. Recorded November 25th 1845

John W Fuller Clerk

(P-336) J E S S E ALEXANDERS WILL

State of Tennessee Shelby County

In the name of God amen, I Jesse Alexander considering the uncertainty of this natural life, and being of sound and disposing mind do make and publish this my last will and testament in manner and form following, that is to say

*or all

(P-336 cont.) Item 1st It is my will and desire that my executor shall first pay all my just debts, and also, that they have erected at my grave a pair of plain Tomb Stones

Item 2nd I give and bequeath unto my brother-in-law John B, Beasley. and my friend Charles A Leath as trustees all of my estate both real & personal, money notes and accounts, this bequeath is nevertheless in trust and for the following use & purpose and no other whatsoever that is to say. It is my will and desire that the said B. Beasley and Charles A Leath hold my said estate both real and personal, money, notes & accounts as trustees and that they suffer and permit my brother James M Alexander during his natural life to have a reasonable & comfortable support out of the same and the said John B. Beasley and Charles A Leath as trustees are hereby directed and requested to pay and furnish the said James W Alexander with all such money and other means as shall be necessary for his support as aforesaid and after his the said James W Alexanders death I give and bequeath all such remainder of my estate both real and personal, money, notes & accounts as shall then be remaining in the hands of the sd. John B Beasley & Charles A Leath as trustees or their representatives unto such child or children of my sister Mary Beasley and of his the said James W Alexander as shall be living at the death of the sd. James W Alexander to be equally divided and to be theirs forever.

Lastly. I nominate, constitute and appoint my brotherinlaw (P-337) John W Beasley and my friend Charles A Leath executors to this my last Will & testament hereby revoking all other will

In testimony whereof I hath hereunto set my hand and affixed my seal this 9th day of Oct. in the year one thousand eight hundred and forty five

Jesse Alexander (Seal)

State of Tennessee)

Shelby County)

Be in known that by the last Will and testament of Jesse Alexander dated and signed the 9th of October 1845 that Charles A Leath & John B Beasley appear to have been left executors & trustees thereto now this is to make known to the court of Probate that we the executors therein named refuse to qualify as such and request the court to grant letter of administration to Henry Alexander Esqr with the Will annexed and that in so doing it will meet our united approbation

given under our under and seals at Memphis the 27th Feby 1846

C A Leath (Seal)

John B Beasley (Seal)

A paper writing purporting to be the last will and testament of Jesse Alexander was produced to the court and thereupon came into court Wm. P Reaves & L P Hardaway & N. W Copeland who being first duly sworn depose & say that they are acquainted with the handwriting of the

(P-337 cont.) of the said Jesse Alexander decd. and that they believe the signature to the said Will is in his own proper handwriting it is therefore considered by the court that the same has been sufficiently proven and that it be recorded.

Recorded July 19th 1846

John W Fuller Clerk

(P-338) POLLY BENNETT'S WILL

State of Tennessee Shelby County

I Polly Bennett of said state and County do make and ordain this my last will and testament.

Item 1st My will is that all my just debts be paid out of any money or the sale of such property as my Executor may think proper.

Item 2nd My will is that Addaline be kept with my little daughters, and for their benefit untill the youngest one become of age or marry

Item 3 My will is that the balance of my property be sold to wit, my land & negro boy Lewis together with all my household and kitchen furniture plantation tools & utensils of all kinds &C &C

Item 4th My will is that when my youngest child becomes of age, that my Estate may be equally divided among my children Terecy C Bennett, Sarah R Bennett, Timothy R Bennett, Joseph P Bennett Maryan E Bennett, Frederick H Bennett, or the heirs of their bodies

Item 5th My wish and will is that William Battle be my executor to this my last will & testament as witness my hand Seal this 16th March 1846

her
Polly X Bennett Seal
mark

Signed, Sealed & delivered in the presence of

his
Attest R B Hargis Howard X Miller
mark

A paper writing purporting to be the last will and testament of Polly Bennett deceased was produced in open court and thereupon came into court, P.B. Hargis & Howard Miller subscribing witnesses thereto who being duly & depose & say the said Polly Bennett acknowledged the same & in their presence to be her last will & testament, and that she was of sound mind and disposing memory (P-339) at the time of acknowledging the same

ordered that the sd will be recorded Recorded July 17th 1846

John W Fuller Clerk

(P-339 cont.) P L E A S A N T G R I F F I N ' S W I L L

Memphis January 1846

Know all men by these presence being in sane mind do this day make my last will and testament I hereby appoint Breton Taylor ~~my~~ as the executor of the same and give to my beloved daughter Ann Eliza Griffin the land and half of my other effects and to my belobed George W Griffin the other half

given under my hand and seal this day and date above named.

his
Pleasant X Griffin
mark

Attest. James McQuire and
E M Prescott

A paper writing purporting to be the last will and testament of Pleasant Griffin decd. was produced to the court and thereupon came into James McGuire & E M Prescott, Subscribing Witnesses thereto who being first duly sworn depose and say that the were acquainted with the Testator during his lifetime and that he acknowledged the same in their presence to be his last will & testament and that he was of sound mind & disposing memory at the time of acknowledging the same

ordered that said will be recorded Recorded July 17th 184

John W Fuller Clk

(P-340) W I L L I A M P S T E W A R T ' S W I L L

In the name of God amen I William P Stewart being in sound and memory do make this my last will and testament revoking all former wills of whatsoever tenure or date.

First of all I will to God my soul, who gave it and my body to the dust from whence it came.

I wish my just debts to be paid out of the proceeds of my horses, mules, waggones, cattle and two small plantations I want my wife to have her own property. I want my daughter Susan J Stewart, to have little negro Girl named Vima and let them remain with my wife

I leave Franklin Colbert my exectutor

W P Stewart

Lewis L Brown Jno C Hardaway

A paper purporting to be the last will & testament of W P Stewart was produced in open court and thereupon came into court Lewis L Brown & John C Hardaway subscribing witnesses thereto who first being duly sworn depose & say that they were acquainted with the said testator in his lifetime and that he acknowledged the same in their presence to be his last will & testament and that he was of sound & disposing memory at the time of ac-

(P-340 cont.) knowledging the same

ordered that sd. will be recorded Recorded July 17th 1846

John W Fuller Clerk

(P-341) L Y D I A K I M B R O U G H ' S W I L L

I Lydia Kimbrough of the county of Shelby and State of Tennessee do make & publish this my last Will & Testament hereby revoking & making void all former will by me heretofore made at any time

First To George C Graham Lydiam Graham Albert Graham & Mary S Graham & Joseph Graham children of my daughter Sarah Graham I give & bequeath to each of them separately five dollars in cash (5)

Second - To Nancy Homes Kimbrough & Louisa Wiley Kimbrough children of my son Wiley Kimbrough I give & bequeath two hundred ($200) each in the following manner that is out of the money I may be possessed of when I die Buckley Kimbrough is to receive the two hundred dollars attached to Nancy Homes Kimbrough & James Kimbrough is to receive the two hundred dollars attached to Louisa Wiley Kimbrough and keep it at interest untill they or either of them are married or become of age then and not until then to pay to them or their heirs the two hundred dollar with interest from my death. Should either of the above named Nancy or Louisa die before they marry or become of age then and in that event the money & interest that is given them is to revert back to my estate & be equally divided amongst my children except the heirs of Sarah Graham

Third - - To my daughter E A Merson I will and bequeath the negro man about twenty years of age as her full share of my estate.

Fourth I will and bequeath to Buckley & Albert Kimbrough my sons all those tracts of land which I own on the state line road about five miles from Memphis, Buckley having the south & Albert the north ~~side~~ half of said tracts of land & to my son James Kimbrough all the right title interest I have to those tracts of land near Germantown on which he now lives.

Fifth I will & bequeath to Buckeley Kimbrough my negro woman Harriet & to James Kimbrough my negro woman (P-342) Mariah the balance of the negroes I will to be equally divided between Buckley, Albert & James Kimbrough except the old negro Donel and his wife Minden & Littice which negroes I will request be taken care of and supported by the above named children Buckley Albert & James & not divided as property.

Sixth. I will and bequeath to James Kimbrough all my stock house hold and kitchen furniture with a request to make such division between himself and Albert as he may deem proper, all other property & effects that I may be possessed of equally divided between the sd James Albert & Buckley Kimbrough.

I do hereby make and appoint Buckley, Albert & James Kimbrough Executors of this my last Will & testament no security is to be required

(P-342 cont.) of them for the faithful performance of their duties in relation to this Will

In Witness whereof I Lydia Kimbrough have this day hereunto affixed my hand & Seal 13 April 1846

her
Lydia X Kimbrough
mark

Test John D White
W B. Walden

State of Tennessee)
June term A D. 1846
Shelby County Court)

A paper writing purporting to be the last will and testament of Lydia Kimbrough deceased was produced in open court and thereupon came into court, John D White & Wm. B. Walden subscribing witnesses thereto who being first duly depose and say that they were acquainted with the said testator ~~it~~ & that she acknowledged the same in the presence to be her last will and testament, and that she was of sound mind and disposing memory at the time of acknowledging the same

ordered that the sd will be recorded Recorded July 17th 1846

John W Fuller Clk

(P-343) E. J SHIELD'S WILL

I hereby make ordain and publish this my last will and testament revoking and annulling all others

Item I give and bequeath & devise (after the payment of my just debts) all my estate whether personal or real or mixed to my beloved wife Mary L Shields to be hers absolutely in fee simple and at her sole and individual disposal forever.

In testimony whereof I have hereunto set my hand & seal this 25th day of Feby A.D: 1846

E.J. Shields (Seal)

The words, to my beloved wife Mary L Shields were interlined before signature & delivery

Test M H Kerr
James Rose Jr.

State of Tennessee)
June term A D 1846
Shelby County Court)

This day a paper writing purporting to be the last and testament of E. J Sheilds was produced in open Court. And thereupon came into Court James Rose Jr. one of the subscribing witnesses thereto who being

(P-343 cont.) first duly sworn deposeth that he was acquainted with the said testator and that he was of sound mind and memory at the time he acknowledged the same in his presence to be his last will & testament.

It is considered by the court that sd. Will is sufficiently proven and that the same be recorded

Recorded July 17th 1846

John W Fuller Clk.

(P-344) MIRRAM L SANDER'S WILL

In the name of God Amen. I Mirram L Sanders being of sound mind and competent ~~estate~~ to dispose of all my personal & real estate do hereby declare the following to be my last will & testament

1st It is my wish that my body should be burried in a plain & decent manner

2nd Neither my son in law nor any other relative shall administer on my estate or be the guardian of my children or in any way manage the business of the estate-

3 I appoint Charles Lofland, Cesario M Bias & F.P. Stanton of the town of Memphis State of Tennessee the executors of this my last will & testament and authorize two or more of them to act as hereinafter directed in all matters connected with the management of my estate

4th I wish and authorize them to sell as soon as in their judgment it will be for the interest of my estate the houses and two lots in the town of Memphis known as the Mississippi house and at present occupied by T. Comroy this I wish done to pay the debts of the estate and what durplus may remain after paying the debts as above directed I wish the money to be vested in negro servants 3 servants to be hired to good and kind masters for the purpose of raising & educating my sons and for the support of my daughter Margaret. I wish my son Joel to be immediately sent to Jackson College in the town of Columbia and placed under the care of Wm. P. Martin to board with his other two brothers, where I wish him to remain until the course of instruction pursued in that college is completed I desire the same course to be pursued with my two older sons Napoleon & Zenophan My negrom man Doctor a good and faithful servant I wish hired out for ten years to assist in the support and education of my children after which time I wish my oldest son Napoleon to take possession of him and treat him kindly the balance of his days I have also a servant woman named Patsey whom I wish carried to Memphis and hired to some (P-345) kind person to assist in raising, educating and supporting my four childrem, Margaret, Napoleon, Xenophan & Joel after hiring Patsey two years the proceeds of her hire to be applied ~~to~~ as above directed then she and her increase if any to be given to my daughter Margaret & her children forever. In the event my daughter should die without children living then Patsey & her increase to be given jointly to my three son Napoleon-Xenophan & Joel, I wish my debts to be paid as soon as possible and for this purpose I desire that the dwelling house & Lot in the town of Memphis on which I now reside to be rented at

(P-345 cont.) a fair price to a careful tenant after the debts of my estate are paid I desire my executor after my youngest son Joel becomes of age to sell the above property and invest the proceeds in negroes these negroes to be equally divided among my Margaret, Napoleon, Zenophan & Joel & their children forever I wish my daughter Sarah to have one hundred dollars after my debts are paid as her portion of my estate- I desire my household & kitchen furniture to be sold of every description except the articles hereafter mentioned the silver I wish divided among my children as known to my daughter Margaret The piano I give to my daughter Margaret.

In the event of my children Margaret Napoleon Zenophan & Joel should die without children living then it is my desire that any portion of my estate which they or either of them may die possessed of shall be equally divided with the surviving children as my daughter Sarah is provided for by her marriage and the education which I have given her I consider equivalent to the respective amounts I have bequeathed to my four children abovenamed.

March 27th 1846

M. L Sanders (Seal)

Signed & acknowledged in presence of witness & of Testator

R.C. McMorlan John A McEwen & R.H. McEwen

(P-346) State of Tennessee)
July term A.D. 1846
Shelby County Court)

A paper writing purporting to be the last will and testament of Miriam L Sanders dec'd was produced to the court and thereupon came into court John A McEwen a subscribing witness who being first duly sworn deposeth and saith that he was acquainted with the said testator in her lifetime and that she acknowledged the same in his presence to be her last will and testament and that she was of sound mind and disposing memory at the time of acknowledging the

Ordered that said will be recorded Recorded July 19th 1846

John W Fuller Clerk

THOMAS WASHBURN' WILL

In the name of God Amen I Thomas Washburn now of the County of Shelby & State of Tennessee being of sound mind and memory do this 4th day of december Eighteen hundred and forty three make this my last will and testament knowing that it is so ordained that all men must die sooner or later I for the natural love & affection that I have for my beloved wife Anne Washburn I loan her a certain negro boy by the name of Dick aged about thirteen years old also all my perishable property with what money, note of hand & other claims which is due or may become due after my death I also

(P-346 cont.) loan to my beloved daughter Elizabeth Washburn a certain negro girl by the name of Sarah Ann during her lifetime but should she marry and have any living children I give said girl Sarah Ann to her child or children Should she fail to have children or a child then I give said girl Sarah Ann to my son John Washburn & My daughter Pricilla Cain with all the negro girl's increase to be equally divided between (P-347) them and their increase and further more as for my daughter Susan Rodgers I have already heretofore given her all her part of my property that I intend for her. I desire also and will it that my daughter Heir equally with John & Pricilla Cain in the negro girl & her increase and after her death of my beloved wife Anne my will is that my son John Elizabeth & Pricilla Cain Heir the negro boy Dick with perishable property she may I wish and desire my son John Washburn and my friend Robt. B Daniel to be executors to this my last will & testament

In ~~testimony~~ witness whereof I hereunto set my hand & affix my seal this the day & year first above written.

Thomas Washburn (Seal)

Witness
Neely M Smith
James N Edwards

A paper writing purporting to be the last will and testament of Thomas Washburn was produced to the court and thereupon came into court James N Edwards a subscribing witness thereto who being first duly sworn deposeth & saith that he was acquainted with the said testator during his lifetime and that he acknowledged the same in his presence to be his last will and testament and that he was of sound mind and disposing memory at the time of acknowledging the Same

ordered that Said will be recorded Recorded July 20th 1846

John W Fuller Clerk

E L I S H A C L A R K E ' S W I L L

I Elisha Clarke of Shelby County and State of Tennessee do make hereby this my last will and testament in manner & form following '(towit)"

It is my will and decree after all my just debts are paid that all and singular my estate bost real and personal shall belong to my beloved (P-348) wife wife Nancy during her natural life with the exception of a certain negro slave girl named harriet

It is my decree that at the death of wife Nancy that all and singular my estate that she may leave at her death shall go to and belong to my dear niece Lucy Jane Alsup and her bodily heirs forever with the above exception of the negro girl Harriet which negro girl slave for life I desire shall go to Joseph Clarke Alsup the son of my niece Lucy Jane Alsup. It is my desire that my Nephew in law Oswell M Alsup be my executor to this my last will and testament

given under my hand and seal this the third day of December in the ((p-348 cont.) in the year of our lord one thousand eight hundred and forty five

Elisha Clarke (Seal)

Attest Reuben Massey
James Roach
Joshua Ecklin

State of Tennessee)
July term 1846
Shelby County Court)

A paper writing purporting to be the last will and testament of Elisha Clarke dec'd was produced and thereupon came into court J M Roach & Joshua Ecklin Subscribing witnesses thereto who first being duly sworn depose and say that they were acquainted with the said testator in his life time and that he acknowledged the same in their presence to be his last will and testament and that he was of sound mind and disposing memory at the time of acknowledging the same

ordered that said will be recorded Recorded July 20th 1846

John W Fuller Clk

(P-349) A L E X A N D E R G J O N E S ' S W I L L

I Alexander G Jones being weak in body but of sound mind and knowing the uncertainty of life and the certainty of death do hereby make my last will and testament

1st I give my soul to god who made -

2nd It is my will that my dear wife Mary E Jones shall keep all my property both real amd personal during her widowhood and manage and control the whole as she thinks best

Thirdly It is my will that my dear wife Mary E Jones aforesaid shall have the power to give to any of our children whatever portion of aforesaid property she may think proper so as not to give more than what will amount to an equal division for each.

As Witness My name A G Jones (Seal) Feby 22 1846

B H Eddins L D Mullins

State of Tennessee)
July term A D 1846
Shelby County Court)

A paper purporting to be the last will and testament of Alexander G Jones was produced to the court and thereupon came into court B H Eddins and L D Mullins who being first duly sworn depose and say, that they were

(P-349 cont.) acquainted with the said testator in his lifetime and that he acknowledged the same to be his last will and testament in their presence and that he was of sound mind and disposing memory at the time of acknowledging the same

ordered that sd. will be recorded Recorded July 20th 1846

John W Fuller Clk.

(P-350) DURANT HATCH'S WILL

State of Tennessee Fayette County

Whereas my father general Durant Hatch late of Craven county North Carolina now deceased did by deed and will duly recorded in the proper offices of said ~~/////~~ Craven and Fayette county convey certain property both real and personal to me in trust for the benefit of my wife and children and vested in me power to sell and dispose of the same and to vest the proceeds in other property and to give the same by deed or will to my wife and children and to divide an apportion the same among my wife and children in such manner and in such propotion as I may judge to be expedient and proper And whereas all the property, and estate of every nature and kind whatsoever in my possession belongs to my sd wife & children as the original or acquired trust property Now therefore I Durant Hatch formerly of Jones County North Carolina now of Fayette County Tennessee do this 31' day of July, A D 1840 make this my last will and testament. And by virtue of the said deed and will of my father give and bequeath the said trust property as follows, - viz:

1st. I give to my wife Mary R Hatch her heirs and assigns forever negroes Dave and his wife Sally - also my carriage and harness and two horses to be selected by her out of all my stock - two cows and calves - one yoke of oxen and a wagon to be selected by her. - All implements and gear on the plantation where I live - All my household and Kitchen furniture all the crop growing and provisions & provender being on the plantation on which I live at the time of my death-

Whereas Henry G Smith the husband of my daughter Caroline and George M Smith the Husband of my daughter Betsy are my securities and accommodation indorsers in my notes, obligations and contracts - Some or all of which notes (P-351) obligations & contracts may be unpaid or undischarged at the time of my death and said Henry G Smith & George M Smith may be liable thereon Now to the intent that the sd Henry G Smith nor the said George M Smith may not loss by reason of such liabilities and to indemnify them against such as may be standing against either of both of them at the time of my death I give and bequeath

2nd Unto my daughter Caroline the wife of said Henry G(Smith) in addition to any other bequest or devises in her favor contained in this my last will and testament as much of said trust property as will be equal in value to the amount of loss which her said husband Henry might or could suffer by reason of his liability as aforesaid - and

3rd Unto my daughter Betsy the wife of said George M (Smith) in ad-

(P-351 cont.) dition to any other bequest or devises in her favour contained in this my last will and testament as much of said trust property as will be equal in value to the amount of loss which he said husband George Might or could suffer by reason of his liabilities as aforesaid should said trust property given in the preceeding 2' & 3' Clauses be insufficient to indemnify both the said Genry G and George M. according to the meaning hereof it is my intention and declaration that neither of the said Second and third clauses shall have precedence over the other but that the said Caroline and Betsy shall share and take in propotion to the respective losses of their said husband I intend and declare that in giving effect the foregoing second and third clauses - all the negroes and other personal property not given to my wife Mary in the first clause shall be first applied, and if it be sufficient then I given and devise

4th Unto my wife Mary the plantation and place on which I now reside containing about One hundred and twenty one acres to her, her heirs & assigns forever.

5th I give the remainder and residue of said property and estate - after the aforesaid legacies and indemnities to my wife Mary and children Caroline & Betsy Mary, Sidney, Robert Henry Susan & Paul West to be equally divided among them share & share alike

6th I constitute and appoint my wife Mary sole guardian of My children Mary Sidney (P-352) Robert Henry Susan & Paul West

7th I constitute and appoint Henry G Smith husband of my daughter Caroline sole executor of this my last will and testament - And I hereby revoke and annull all and every other wills and testaments by me heretofore made

In witness whereof I have hereunto set my hand and seal this 30th day of July A.D. 1840

Durant Hatch (Seal)

Signed & Sealed in presence of Jesse Alexander Samuel O Ballard

State of Tennessee)
Feby term A D 1846
Shelby County Court)

Henry G Smith produced to the court a paper writing purporting to be the last will and testament of Durent Hatch deceased and thereupon came into court R.C. Brinkley, who being first duly sworn deposeth that he is acquainted with the handwriting of the sd Durant Hatch and James Alexander one of the subscribing witnesses thereto and that said Alexander has departed this life and that he believes the signature to said Will to be in sd Alexanders own proper hand writing and that he believes the signature to said will to be in said Hatch's own hand writing

Ordered by the Court that said Will is sufficiently proved and that it be recorded

Recorded 2nd July 1846 John W Fuller Clk

(P-353) JAMES S MICKLEBERRY'S WILL

I James S Mickleberry being of sound and perfect mind and memory do make and publish this my last Will and testament in manner and form following

first. I wish all my perishable property sold soon after my deee cease (only such things as hereinafter named) for the purpose of paying my debts. I also wish all my negroes hired out and my land rented out until all my Just debts are paid except a negro Woman named Hanah the said negro woman (Hanah) to be for the express use of my wife until all my debts are paid

Secondly I give and bequeath unto my beloved Wife Mary a negro man named Westin also a negro woman named Hanah also a negro girl named Susanah the above named negroes to be hers during her natural life and at my wifes death the above named negroes with their increase to go to my Two children (to wit) Elizabeth A Mickleberry and Rebecca J. S Mickleberry I also give to my beloved wife two beds and furniture one Bureau one dressing table one horse to be worth fifty dollars and one cow and calf the six last named articles for her use to dispose of as she may think proper. I also wish for my wife Mary, to have one third of the tract of land I now live on during her life whether a deed is procured before or after my decease

thirdly. I give the balance of my property to my two daughters Elizabeth A Mickleberry and Rebecca J S Mickleberry (to wit) one negro boy named Musk one negro girl named Fanny one boy named Tennessee and one girl named Missouri I wish no division made in the property that I gave to my children until the oldest becomes of age or Marries then I wish an equal division of the property made between the two. I hereby appoint John A Mickleberry and Turner Persons sole executors of this my last will and testament hereby revoking all former wills by me made

in witness whereof I have hereunto set my hand and affixed my seal this the 28th day of October 1845

J S Mickleberry (Seal)

Signed Sealed Published and declared by the above J S Mickleberry to be his last will and testament in the presence of us who have hereunto subscribed our names as witnesses in the presence of the testator

A Snead, Frances L Roulhac Edwin McLemore Wm. Rose

State of Tennessee (
July term A D 1846
Shelby County Court)

A paper writing purporting to be the last will and testament of James Mickleberry was produced to the court and thereupon came into court Edwin McLemore a subscribing witness thereto who being first duly sworn depose and say that he was acquainted with the said testator in his lifetime and that he acknowledged the same in his presence to be his last will and

(P-354 cont.) testament and that he was of sound mind and disposing memory a at the time of acknowledging the same

ordered that sd Will be recorded Recorded 20th July 1846

John W Fuller Clerk

MARY JANE KEON' WILL

My dearly beloved Aunt. If I had millions to leave to you and my dear cousin Thomas - They would prove but weak testimony of my gratitude - for all the kindness you both have bestowed upon me but I have nothing but six shares in the Merchants bank at Newburn & Dorothy & her two children which I give to my ever dear Aunt - (wish the exception of her eldest Elle whom I give to my dear little Susan Ellen forever & ever) during her life & than to my dear cousin edward or to do as they please with during their lives. God bless you my dear (P-355) Aunt and all so near & dear (Editor's Note: part of page gone)

Mary Jane Keon

June 8th 1845

Mr Edward E Graham of Newburn has the certificate of the shares in the bank as they were among Mrs. Hamilton C Grahams papers M.J.K. Mr. H.C. Graham's letter containing the power of attorney for drawing the dividends from the bank is with this paper.

State of Tennessee)
Feby term, A. D 1846
Shelby County)

On Motion of Thomas Keon a paper writing was presented to the court as the last will and testament of Mary Jane Keon decd, and thereupon came before the court Thomas H Keon and Mary Lanston who being first duly sworn depose that said paper writing is all in the handwriting of sd Mary Jane with whose hand writing they are acquainted and that the same was found since the death of the said Mary Jane among her private papers it is therefor considered by the court that sd Will is sufficiently proven and that the same be recorded Recorded July 20 th 1846

John W Fuller Clerk

WYATT CHRISTIAN'S WILL

In the name of God amen! I Wyatt Christian of the county of Shelby and city of Memphis and State of Tennessee being now ill of health and mindful of my later end, but being of sound mind and of disposing memory (thanks be to God) do now declare and ordain this to be my last will and testament revoking all others

Item 1st It is my will and desire that the Estate which I have conjointly with my late Brother Frederick Christian in Shelby County (P-356) shall continue undivided with his as it now is until the marriage, or death or the arrival at the age of twenty one of my niece Sally Ann Francis

(P-356 cont.) Christian during which connection the said property shall be used for the joint interest and benefit of my wife and Children and my said niece Sally Ann Francis

Item 2 In the event of the marriage of death of the said Sally Ann Francis or in the event of her arriving at the age of twenty one years then it is my will and desire that all of my estate of whatever nature and description shall after the payment and discharge of all my just debts go to my wife Mary Bailey Christian, to be used and disposed of by her during her life time for the joint benefit of her and my children

Item 3rd If my wife desires during her life to advance the interest of my daughter Mary Carver (now Mrs. Weld) by giving her a negro or any other property, it is my will and desire that she should do so. And it is further my will and desire that my wife shall have the same privilege of advancing to any of my other children whenever she may think their circumstances or wants in life may demand it

Item 3rd It is further my will and desire that at the death of my wife all my estate of every description whether personal or real shall be equally divided among my three children Mary Carver Sally Francis and Carolina Wyatt taking into account however whatever advance or interest that may be made to either of them by (P-357) their mother during her life time

Item 4 I hereby appoint my friend William Mathews and James T. Leath the executors of this my last will and testament

And as I have full confidence in their fidelity I hereby discharge and release them from giving bond and security

In Witness Whereof I hereunto affix my hand and seal on this the 15 day of September A.D. 1846 And in the presence of the subscribing witnesses Wm

Wyatt Christian (Seal

Wm. Park
H L Guion
J W Doyl

State of Tennessee)
October Term A D 1846
Shelby County Court)

A paper writing purporting to be the last will and testament of Wyatt Christian Deceased was produced in open Court and thereupon came into Court H.L. Guion J W Doyle and Wm. Park subscribing witnesses thereto who after being duly sworn depose and say that the said testator acknowledged the same in their presence to be his last will and testament and that he was of sound mind and disposing memory at the time of acknowledging the same which is ordered to be recorded

Recorded March 12 1847

John W Fuller Clerk

(P-357 cont.) JAMES P HARDAWAY'S WILL

Know all ye whom it may concern that I James P Hardaway of the City of Memphis being low in health but of sound (P-358) mind and disposing memory and apprehending the uncertainty of life have deemed it proper to make the following expression of my will and the disposition which I desire should be made of my property in case of my death

Item 1st I do hereby give and bequeath to my beloved sister Anne Lots No 246 (two hundred and forty ~~four~~ six) and No 247 (two hundred and forty seven) in the City of Memphis being the same on which she now resides.

Item 2nd Of the rest and residue of my property it is my desire that as much may be sold as shall be necessary to settle and discharge all my just debts.

Item 3rd All the rest and residue of my estate both real personal and mixed I do hereby give and bequeath share and share alike to my three brothers Lemuel John and Charles and the legal heirs of my brother Joseph giving to the said heirs collectively in the same proportion as each of my said three brothers and no more

In Testimony of which I have hereto set my hand and seal at Memphis July 19, 1846

Done in the presence of Jas P Hardaway (Seal
M B Winchester
Tho W Hunt Sam R Brown (P G. Gaines (acknowledged

State of Tennessee)
August Term A.D. 1846
Shelby County Court)

A paper writing purporting to be the last will and testament of James P Hardaway (P-359) Dec'd. was produced in open Court and thereupon Came into Court M.B. Winchester and P G. Gaines subscribing witnesses thereto who after being duly sworn deposeth and saith that the said testator acknowledged the same in their presence to be his last will and testament and that he was of sound mind and disposing memory at the time of acknowledging the same

ordered that said will be recorded Recorded March 12 1847

John W Fuller Clerk

WILLIAM SHEPHERD'S WILL

I William Shepherd of Newborn declared the following to be my last will and testament

I give to my beloved wife Mary her heirs and assigns forever the Lot

(P-359 cont.) and improvements in the town of Newborn which I lately purchased of Mrs Cook togethrer with all my houdehold furniture of every description my carriage and horses and ten negroes such as she may choose being an equal number of males and females; also ten thousand dollars of United State six per Cent stock being part of that now standing to my credit on the loan office Brooks at Philadelphia which said gift is in lieu of Dower and in consideration that the deeds conveying to me her lands in Pasquotank and Camden Counties to be recorded and made effectual

All the remainder of my estate real and personal I give to my Children to be divided among them equally share and (P-360) share alike subject to the following regulations. No final division of my estate to be made until my youngest child arrive at full age meantime I desire that the property be kept together and farmed out in such way as to produce the greatest income. With the consent of my wife I desire that the whole of my estate be kept in common and the profits used for the support of herself and out children. All the surpluss profits if any and all monies received for property sold to be invested in some profitable stock for the benefit of my estate.

All my children shall be educated and supported out of my estate the sons until they are twenty one year of age and the Daughters until they are married or until a final division takes place

When smy sons arrive at the age of twenty one years and my daughters be married and have arrived at the age of eighteen years my will is each of them receive from my Executors the sum of five thousand Dollars in Cash or other property or equal value. My Executors may sell at their discretion any or all of my lands on North River in Carteret County at Orchard Creek in Craven County or at Pasquotank and Camden Counties also any of my negroes whose bad conduct may render it advisable. I appoint my wife Mary my executrix to continue during her widowhood and no longer and my soninlaw Mr. Ebenezer Pettigrew my Executor. I also nominate and appoint my two sons John S Shepherd and William B Shepherd Executors of this my last will(P-361) to commence as they respectively arrive at the age of twenty one years

Newborn 4th April 1816

Wm Shepherd

James Camey John M Roberts

State of North Carolina)
June Term A D 1819
Craven County Court)

The foregoing last will and testament of William Shepherd was produced in Court and the execution thereof by said testator was proven in open Court and in due form of law by the oaths of James Camey and John W Roberts subscribing witnesses thereto at the same time John S Shepherd one of the executors named in said will appeared and qualified

Ordered that letters testamentary issue and that said will be Registered

Attest J.G. Stanley C.C

(P-361 cont.) State of North Carolina)
S S
Craven County)

I James G Stanley Clerk of the Court of pleas and Quarter session of Craven County aforesaid do certify that the foregoing is a true Copy of the original Will of William Shepherd decd filed among the records of said Court and registered in book of wills letter C folio 180 & 181

In Testimony whereof I hereunto set my hand and affix the seal of said Court at Newber this fifteenth day of July A D 1840

(S E A L) J G Stanley C C

(P-362) State of North Carolina)
S S
Craven County)

I William S Blackledge Chairman of the Court of pleas and Quarter Session of Craven County do hereby certify that James G Stanley is Clerk of said Court and his attestation to the foregoing copy of a record is in due form of law.

In Witness Whereof I hereunto set my hand at Newborn this 15th day of July A D 1846

William S Blackledge Chairman

State of North Carolina)
S S
Craven County)

I James G Stanley Clerk of the Court of pleas and Quarter Session of Craven County aforesaid do certify that William S Blackledge Esqr. is Chairman of said Court duly commissioned and qualified and the foregoing is his signature

In Testimony Whereof I hereunto set my hand and the seal of said Court at Newborn this 15 day of July A.D. 1846

J G Stanley C C

State of Tennessee)
December Term 1846
Shelby County Court)

A certified copy of the last will and testament of William Shepherd Decd was produced in open Court and it appearing to the satisfaction of the Court that the same had been regularly proven and recorded in the State of North Carolina Craven County

it is ordered by the Court that the said copy of Wm Shepherd's will be recorded Recorded March 12, 1847

John W Fuller Clerk

(P-363) I Benjamin Stanton of the County of Panola State of Mississippi being of sound mind and memory and being about to start on a journey to the North and considering the uncertainty of life and the dangers incident to traveling have thought it wise and provident to make and ordain this my last will and testament in words as follows to wit

First of all I wish my just debts to be paid as soon after my death as possible I wish all my property except my household furniture and Slaves to be sold and the proceeds converted into cash that is Notes Book accounts personal and Real Estate which I desire as follows

First I give and bequeath to my adopted son John C Stanton the one sixth part of the nett proceeds of all my estate excepting Slaves plate and household furniture on the following consideration to wit that his person and property shall remain under the care of Sarah M Stanton my wife and Arthur & James S Stanton and Daniel & John S Stanton whom I do by these presents appoint Guardians of his person and property until he shall reach the age of twenty one But should his natural mother and stepfather or others of his relations cause his person to be removed from the care and Guardianship of the Guardians aforesaid then this legacy of one sixth of my estate shall relapse to my Estate and be divided equally between my wife Sarah M Stanton and my son Thomas S Stanton

(P-364) Second I give and bequeath to my brother John S S Stanton two thousand Dollars on the following condition Viz that he continue and wind up and settle up the entire concern or that he remain and use his best endeavors to do so until the first of January 1846 and that he charge nothing for his services and further that he give up a note which he holds against me of between $800 and $900

Third the balance and residue of my Estate excepting slaves plate and household furniture I hereby give and bequeath to my wife Sarah S Stanton and my son Thomas S Stanton share and share alike Should my son Thomas die before he is of age and leaving no lawful heir in that event it is my will that his property should fall to my adopted son John C Stanton provided that his property and person continue in possession of his Guardians aforesaid until he is of lawful age. And should my adopted son John die before he is of lawful age ~~age~~ in that ~~case~~ his proportion of my Estate shall go to be inherited by my son Thomas S Stanton his heirs and assigns forever

Fourth I give & bequeath to my wife Sarah S Stanton my entire household furniture and plate My will is I give and bequeath to my wife my negroes Slaves William Mary and Matilda to be held by her until my son Thomas arrive at the age of twenty one years and then said negroes with all their increase to belong to my said son Thomas his heirs and assigns forever until my said son Thomas shall arrive at the age of twenty one my wife to have full control and earnings of said slaves

Fifth I give to my son Thomas my gold watch

Sixth I hereby appoint my wife Sarah S Stanton and my brother John S Stanton Executrix and executor to this my last will and testament and my will is that they proceed to settle up said Estate (P-365) and carry this will into execution without the usual form of giving security as I do not owe five hundred dollars except what I owe to my brother John aforesaid

(P-365 cont.) Sixth It is my will that should either of the persons named as Guardian to the person and property of my adopted son John C Stanton that the survivors continue to act as his Guardian

In witness whereof I have hereunto set my hand and seal at Belmont Panola County Miss this 9 July 1844

Benjamin Stanton (Seal)

Signed sealed & acknowledged to be the last will & testament in presence of us

Henry Laird James Laird John Bradford

State of Mississippi) In the Probate Court of Panola County
) At the October Term A.D. 1846
Panola County)

Be it remembered that at a term of the Probate Court of the County of Panola in the State ~~of Mississippi~~ aforesaid begun and held at the Court House in and for said County on the third Monday in October in the year A D 1846 Personally appeared in open Court Henry Laird one of the subscribing witnesses to a certain instrument of writing purporting to be the last will and testament of Benjamin Stanton deceased late of said County who having first been duly sworn deposed and said that the said Benjamin Stanton sign publish and declare said instrument as his last (P-366) will and testament on the 9 day of July 1844 the day of the date of said instrument in the presence of this deponent and James Laird and John Bradford the other subscribing witnesses to said instrument that the said testator was then of sound and disposing mind and memory and twenty one years and upwards of age that he said deponent and the said James Laird and John Bradford subscribed and attested said instrument as witnesses to the signature and publication thereof at the special instance and request and in the presence of the said testator and in the presence of each on the day and year of the date thereof

Sworn to and subscribed in open Court this the 19 day of October A D 1846

J C Armstrong Clk Henry Laird

The within will has been examined and approved by me this 19 day of October 1846

J T M Burbrudge

Judge of Probate

The foregoing will and probate thereto was recorded on the 2nd day of October A D 1846

J C Armstrong Clk

(P-366 cont.) State of Mississippi)

Panola County)

I James C Armstrong Clerk of the Probate Court of the County of Panola State aforesaid do hereby certify that this sheet of paper contains a true and perfect transcript of the original will and probate thereon of Benjamin Stanton Deceased as fully and completely as the same remains of record and on file in my office

(P-367) In Testimony Whereof I have hereunto set my hand and the seal of said Court at Panola the 16 day of November A.D. 1846

J C Armstrong Clk

(S E A L)

The State of Mississippi)

Panola County)

I John T. M Burbridge Judge of the probate Court (sole and presiding) of the county of Panola State aforesaid do hereby certify that James C Armstrong whose genuine signature appears to the foregoing certificate and attestation is and was at the date thereof Clerk of said Court duly elected qualified and commissioned that his said certificate and attestation are in due form of law and that all of his acts in the premises are and ought to be entitled to full faith and credit in judicature and thereout

Given under my hand and seal this 16 day of November A D 1846

J T. M Burbridge

(S E A L) Judge of Probate

The State of Mississippi

Panola County

I James C Armstrong Clerk of the probate Court of the Court of Panola State aforesaid do hereby certify that J T M Burbridge whose genuine signature appears to the foregoing certificate is and was at the date thereof Judge of said Court(sole and presiding) duly qualified and commissioned and that all of his acts in the premises are and ought to be entitled to full faith and credit in Judicature and thereout

In Testimony whereof I have (P-368) hereunto set my hand and the seal of said Court at Panola the 16th day of November A.D. 1846

(S E A L) J C Armstrong Clk

(P-368 cont.) State of Tennessee)
December Term 1846
Shelby County)

A certified copy of the last will and testament of Benjamin Stanton dcd. was produced in open Court and it appearing to the satisfaction of the Court that the same had been regularly proven an recorded in the State of Mississippi Panola County is ordered by the Court that said copy of the last will and testament of Benjamin Stanton be recorded

Recorded March 12 1847

John W Fuller Clerk

THOMAS ALLISON'S WILL

Memphis Sept 24 1846

Be it known to all whom these presents may concern that I Thomas Allison being in perfect health both in body and mind do declare this instrument of writing to be my last will and testament in manner and form following that is to say

I give and bequeath to my wife Jane Allison all my negro property viz my negro man Dick and his wife Nervy and child Henry Clay also my negro man Abe and his wife Nancy and child Gillis Likewise my negro boy Henry and old Cato with all my household and kitchen furniture to have and to hold during her natural lifetime My will is further here made (P-369) known that my wife Jane Allison at or before the time of her death so dispose of the above named property to such of my daughters as in her judgment may seem to stand most in need of it with these remarks I come to close

Witness my hand and seal the day month and year first above written

Thomas Allison (Seal)

Witness George F Allison
Harriet C Allison

State of Tennessee)
January Term 1847
Shelby County Court)

A paper writing purporting to be the last will and testament of Thomas Allison Decd. was produced in open Court and thereupon came into Court George F Allison Jr. Harriet C Allison who after being duly sworn deposeth and saith that the said testator acknowledged the same in their presence to be his last will and Testament and that he was of sound mind and disposing memory at the time of acknowledging the same

ordered that said will be recorded Recorded March 13, 1847

John W Fuller Clerk

(P-369 cont.) C H A R L E S W L E W I S ' W I L L

I Charles W Lewis of the State of Tennessee and County of Shelby do hereby make and publish this my last will and testament hereby revöking all others previously made

1st I direct all my just debts to be paid out of the proceeds of my property as soon as convenient

(P-370) 2nd I wish my dearly beloved mother Martha F Lewis to be amply supported out of the proceeds of the remainder

3rd I wish my dearly beloved wife Maria L Lewis to have and to hold during her natural life all my property real personal or mixed with the privilege of disposing of the boy Nelson now about four years old at her death as she pleases and I do hereby appoint my wife my sole executrix of this my last will desiring that she be required to give no security unless she should marry again and I desire that she be allowed to remove with the property to any part of the United States as she pleases and lastly I give at her death the residue with its increase to the Children of my three brothers William M Lewis Patrick H Lewis and John N Lewis to be equally divided between them

Whereunto I have set my hand and affixed my seal this 3rd day of March 1846

Chs W Lewis (Seal)

Witness Erasmus T Rose
Bennett Bagby

State of Tennessee)
November Term 1846
Shelby County Court)

A paper writing purporting to be the last will and testament of Charles W Lewis Deceased was produced in open Court and thereupon came into Court Erasmus T Rose and Bennett Bagby subscribing witnesses thereto who after being duly sworn deposeth and saith that the said testator acknowledged the same in their presence to be his last will and testament and that he was of sound (P-371) mind and disposing memory at the time of acknowledging the same

ordered that the said will be recorded Recorded March 13 1847

John W Fuller Clerk

B E N J A M I N B I G G S ' W I L L

In the name of God Amen. I Benjamin Biggs of the State of Tennessee and County of Tipton do this twenty sixth day of March one thousand eight hundred and forty three make and publish my last will and testament in manner and form following to wit

First It is my will and desire that all my just debts and funeral

(P-371 cont.) expenses be paid out of my perishable property

Secondly All my stock horses and cattle and hogs all to ~~be~~ sold and

thirdly I give to my daughter Mancaawn five dollars & to Ulan Chapman five dollars

fourth I give my wife Rachiel my land in Yellow Bushy County State of Mississippi known by the name of Menascon/~~$10n~~ place and to William Lafayett the son of my daughter Jacklinner Burlisson I give one hundred acres of land of the North end of the Bledsoe tract of land and to James Burlisson I give five dollars and the balance of my land in Tennessee to be equally divided between my three children now with me to wit Benjamin and James and Saaner and to my wife Rachiel I give one thousand dollars out of the money arrising from the sales of the stock and also I give to my wife Rachiel all my household and kitchen furniture and farming (P-372) utensils and then all the balance of monies and negroes to be equally divided between my wife and my three Children now with me to wit Benjamin James and Suaner and to my wife Rachiel I give a third of the lots in Memphis

Witness my hand and seal the day and date above written

Benjamin Biggs(SEAL)

Test
Hugh F Ross
Charles Sullivan
Isaac W Turnage

State of Tennessee)
November Term 1846
Shelby County Court)

A paper writing purporting to be the last will and testament of Benjamin Biggs Decd. was produced in open Court and thereupon came into Court Hugh F Ross Charles Sullivan and Isaac W Turnage who after being duly sworn deposeth and saith that the said testator acknowledged the same in their presence to be his last will and testament and that he was of sound mind and disposing memory at the time of acknowledging the same which is ordered to be recorded

Recorded March 13 1847

John W Fuller Clerk

M A R Y A N N B A T E S ' W I L L

In the name of God Amen. I Mary Ann Bates being low in health but of sound and disposing mind do make this my last will and testament revoking all other wills made by me

(P-372 cont.) First I bequeath and will to my daughter Sarah Harrison for her sole use and benefit (P-373) during her natural life and then to the children of her body forever my slave Harriet and her increase

2nd I will and bequeath to my two little Grand Sons to wit Charles Childress and William Childress my negro boy Pompey at the time the youngest becomes of age until then said boy is to remain in the possession of my son James Bates free of hire

3rd I will and bequeath to my son James Bates all the residue of my negroes to wit Jane Frank Joe Mary Syrene and I also give and bequeath to my son James the house and lot I now reside on and also seven hundred dollars in cabh and the residue of my personal property of every kind whatsoever My son James is to pay all my liabilities out of the means I have given him I leave to my son James Bates my sole executor of this my last will and testament

Given under my hand and seal this August the 5 1846

her
Mary Ann X Bates (Seal)
mark

In presence of
P Magiveney
P G Gaines

State of Tennessee)
September Term 1846
Shelby County Court)

A paper writing purporting to be the last will and testament of Mary Ann Bates decd was produced in open Court abd thereupon came into open Court P Magivney and P G Gaines subscribing witnesses thereto who after being duly sworn deposeth and saith that the said testatric acknowledged the same in their presence (P-374) to be her last will and testament and that she was of sound mind and disposing memory at the time of acknowledging the same.

ordered that said will be recorded Recorded March 15 1847

John W Fuller Clk

I S A A C S U G G S ' W I L L

Know all men by these presents that I Isaac Suggs of the County of Shelby and State of Tennessee being of sound mind and disposing memory do make this my last will and testament viz.

Item the first After my just debts shall have been paid togwther with my burial expenses I desire for the whole of my estate both personal and real to be legally and fully vested in the possession of my wife Margaret M Suggs Wm L Suggs and John C Suggs to be fully at their disposal

(P-374 cont.) and management, but particularly my landed estate which I hereby empower them to dispose of at any time and move out of the State if it is deemed by them to the interest of the family It is further my desire for them to keep the property together and jointly manage it to the best advantage until all of my children shall have obtained their majority when it shall be equally given to all my grown children except Wm. L Suggs viz J C Suggs Mary C and Harriet S Suggs a horse and saddle I desire if the estate can afford it for each of my now grown Children to have a horse &c of the value of seventy five dollars when they become of age

(P-375) In Testimony whereof I hereunto set my signature This 21 of August 1846

Isaac Suggs

Signed or acknowledged in the presence of
T M M Cornelius
Robert C Ledbetter

State of Tennessee)
December Term 1846
Shelby County Court)

A paper writing purporting to be the last will and testament of Isaac Suggs Decd was produced in open Court and thereupon came into Court T.M.M Cornelius and Robert C. Ledbetter subscribing witness thereto who after duly sworn depose and say that they wer acquainted with the said testator and that he acknowledging the same in their presence to be his last will and testament and that he was of sound mind and disposing memory at the time of acknowledging the same

ordered that said will be recorded Recorded March 15 1847

John W Fuller Clerk

S A M U E L G D U N N ' S W I L L

I Samuel G Dunn do make and publish this as my last will and testament hereby revoking and making void all other wills by me at any time made

First I direct that my burial expenses and all my just debts be paid as soon after my death as possible out of my money that I may die possessed of or may first come into the hands of my executors. It is my (P-376) desire that all my estate should be sold of every description my negroes to be sold in families and on such terms as my executors may think best

First I give and bequeath to my son William M Dunn Two Thousand Dollars to be raised out of my estate

Second the balance of my Estate I want equally divided betwixt

(P-376 cont.) my two sons William M Dunn and Samuel J Dunn

I do hereby ~~appoint~~ nominate and appoint William M Dunn and Thomas Holeman my executors

In Witness Whereof I do to this my will set my hand and seal this thirty first day of March one thousand eight hundred and forty two

Samuel G Dunn (Seal)

Witnesses present
Chas. Lofland
Th Pittman
Wm O Lofland

State of Tennessee)
September Term 1846
Shelby County Court)

A paper writing purporting to be the last will and testament of Samuel G Dunn Decd. was produced in open Court and thereupon came into Court Charles Lofland one of the subscribing witnesses thereto who after being duly sworn deposeth and saith that the said testator acknowledged the same in his presence to be his last will and testament and that he was of sound mind and disposing memory at the time of acknowledging the same and he further deposeth and saith that he is acquainted with the hand writing of William O Lofland and Tho Pitt (P-377) man whose names are signed to said will as witnesses and he believed said signatures to be in their own proper hand writing and William R Poston who after being duly sworn deposeth and saith that he is acquainted with the hand writing of said W O Lofland and Pittman and he believed that said signature to be in their own proper hand writing

ordered that said will be recorded Recorded March 15, 1847

John W Fuller Clk

H E N R Y W I S E ' S W I L L

South Memphis Nov. 9 1846

I Henry Wise of the county of Shelby and State of Tennessee being weak of body but of sound and disposing mind do make this my last will and testament hereby revoking all former wills and testaments heretofore be me made

Imprimis my will and desire is that my body be decently buried and after payment of my just debts and funeral expenses my next will and desire is that the sum of two thousand dollars be raised by my executor and that fifteen hundred dollars part thereof be paid to my mother and sister now supposed to be in Hanover Germany and my executor is desired to distribute the other five hundred dollars amongst the poor of this county according to his

(P-377 cont.) best judgment out of the money on hand

In the third place my will and desire is that my partner John Lane have (P-378) the house and lot on Beal Street now occupied by him together with the stock of goods on hand in said house and also my interest in the house and lot on Beal Street lately purchased of Causey to him and his heirs forever in fee simple

In the fourth place My will and desire is that John Vogt or White have my Boat at the River with its contents and also my two houses and lots on the Raleigh Road to him and his heirs forever in fee simple

In the fifth place My will and desire is that my friend John A Cook be and he is hereby appointed executors of this my last will and testament and he is to execute the same under the advisement of my counsel R H Patillo Esq who is to be liberally compensated for his services should it be necessary said John Lane and John White my said legatees are to contribute equally out of their said legacies to the paying of expenses and raising the two thousand dollars provided for above &c

My said executor is to be released from the payment of a bill of goods paid by me for him in New Orleans

Witness my hand and seal this 9 day of November A.D. 1846

H Wise (Seal)

Witness
R H Patillo
Cajeton Levesque
M C Gaither

State of Tennessee)
December Term 1846
Shelby County Court)

(P-379)A paper writing purporting to be the last will and testament of Henry Wise Deceased was produced in open Court and thereupon came into Court Cajeton Levesque and M C. Gaither subscribing witnesses thereto who after being duly sworn depose and say that the said Testator acknowledged the same in their presence to be his last will and testament and that he was of sound mind and disposing memory at the time of acknowledging the same which is ordered to be recorded

Recorded March 15 1847

John W Fuller Clerk

ROBERT S WORTHAMS WILL

I Robert S Wortham being sick but of sound mind do make this my last will and testament

First I request that all my just debts be paid and the balance of

(P-379 cont.) my whole estate I do bequeath unto my beloved wife to do and manage as she may think best

And I do appoint my beloved brotherinlaw James R Williams my executor

Given under my hand and seal this the 3rd day of September one thousand eight hundred and forty four

R S Wortham (Seal)

Signed & Sealed in the presence of

J B Montgomery
Willis G Eddins

State of Tennessee)

Shelby County)

Pleas at the Court House in the town of Raleigh in & for the County of Shelby and State of Tennessee on the first Monday being the 2nd day of June 1845 Honora(P-380) ble William C. Dunlap Judge of the 11th Judicial Circuit in and for the State ~~of the~~ of Tennessee presiding the following appears of record on 8th of said Term and 10th of said month

James R Williams Executor &c)

201 vs

Samuel H Peake)

This day came the parties by attorneys and thereupon came a jury of good and lawful men to wit William Robins Robert a. Motley Lavin Bland William Bond R Shivers William S Garner Terrell G Goldsby Nathan Gregory John M Shelby Alexander Munn Benj. L Branch and Robert H Adams who being elected tried and sworn well and truly to try the issue joined and a true verdict give according to the evidence and thereupon the argument of the counsel not being concluded the jury are permitted to disperse until the meeting of the Court on tomorrow morning.

James R Williams Executor of)
the last will & Testament of
Robert Wortham Deceased)

201 vs)

Samuel H Peake)

This day came the parties by attorneys and thereupon came into court the same jury who were on yesterday elected tried and sworn well and truly to try the issue joined and true verdict give according to the evidence upon their oaths do say that they find the will in controversy to be the last will and testament of Robert Wortham deceased. It is therefore considered by the Court that the plaintiff recover from the defendant the costs in this behalf expended and that the verdict (P-381) of the jury and judgment of the Court in this case be certified to the

(P-381 cont.) County Court

State of Tennessee)
Shelby County)

I Samuel R Brown Clerk of the Circuit Court of said County and State do hereby certify that the foregoing is a true and perfect transcript of the judgment in the suit wherein James R Williams Extr &c is plaintiff and Samuel H Peake defendant as the same appears of record in my office

Given under my hand at office February 1 1847

Sam R Brown Clerk
Recorded March 15 1847 By Robt L Smith Dep Clk

John W Fuller Clk

CHARLES BOLTON'S WILL

In the name of God Amen I Charles Bolton of the County of Shelby and State of Tennessee Now of sound mind and memory But weak in body and aware of the uncertainty of life feel the propriety and necessity of arranging my worldly affairs and concerns

(First) It is therefore my will and desire that after my decease my body be committed decently to the earth whence it came and my soul to God the giver

Secondly that all my just debts and funeral expenses be paid out of my crop

Thirdly I give and bequeath to my wife Lucy Bolton during her natural life all my household and kitchen furniture my land of one hundred and sixty and 2/3 Acres the farm (P-382) I now reside on also my farming utensils my Gray Horse and two mules all my cattle and hogs my waggon and oxen Also my two negro men Jerden and Aaron and Nancy' Aaron's wife and her children Tom and Patsy all of which property at the decease of my wife Lucy Bolton I wish equally divided between my children Louise Estill Sindarilla Bolton Jefferson Bolton and Lucretia Elliotte

Fourthly I wish it further understood that I heretofore made allowances to my children on their marriage as follows to wit. To my son Jefferson Bolton a negro girl Crit worth five hundred dollars also a girl Suffroud worth four hundred dollars and I have paid him in cash four hundred dollars making in all thirteen hundred dollars

To my son Washington Bolton bought with cash a negro man Elijah a woman and child Eleven Hundred dollars a boy Bell for four Hundred Dollars and a negro boy Willis five Hundred Dollars cash used one Hundred Dollars and paid for land for him one hundred and sixteen making in all Two Thousand Two Hundred and Sixteen Dollars. This being the amount I wish him to have or ever intend him to have I have also advanced to Milton Estill Two negro women Gilla and her child and Lucy valued at Nine Hundred Dollars and cash in lieu of a Negro man Seven Hundred Dollars and

c

(P382 cont.) cash used by him Three Hundred Dollars and cash used by him Three Hundred and four Dollars making in all Nineteen Hundred and four Dollars

I have also advanced to Sindarilla Bolton a Negro Woman Jenny and child worth five Hundred Dollars a girl Lettie Mary Four(P-383)Hundred Dollars a girl Francis Two Hundred Dollars making in all fourteen hundred and fifty dollars

I have also advanced to Lucretia Elliott a Negro Woman Sarah worth Four Hundred Dollars and her children Harriet worth Three Hundred Dollars Isaac worth Two Hundred and fifty Dollars Angeline Two Hundred Dollars and Nelson at one Hundred Dollars. Also the negro child John and let it be understood the said negro child John Motherless whom I give to my said Daughter Lucretia in his infancy if she could raise him which she has done he is therefore her property making in all twelve Hundred and fifty Dollars

And the balace of my negroes not named heretofore in this Indenture to wit Nan and her infant at Eight Hundred Dollars Jim at Three Hundred Dollars one woman Mary and her child Prolina at Nine Hundred Dollars one negro boy Dick at Three Hundred Dollars and all their future increase I will and bequeath to be equally divided between my daughters Louisa Estill Sindarilla Bolton Lucretia Elliot and my son Jefferson Bolton after my decease so that taking the above schedule of advance as a criterian they all become equal legatees of my estate above described

I also give and bequeath to my son Charles Bolton all the lands he now resides on in Smith County State of Tennessee within the lines I marked off for his portion be the same more or less I also give and bequeath to my son James Bolton all the lands he now(P-384) resides on adjoining Charles Bolton said County and State aforesaid within the lines marked off for his portion be the same more or less And as I gave all I ever intended except the following legacies to my sons Moses Bolton Charles Bolton Wilson Bolton James Bolton and Lent their brother and to my daughter Elizabeth Lucy and Frances I do now give and bequeath unto the heirs of Moses Bolton five dollars and to my son Charles Bolton five dollars and to my son Wilson five dollars and to my son James Five Dollars and to my son Lent five Dollars and to my daughter Elizabeth five dollars and to my daughter Lucy five Dollars and to my daughter Frances five Dollars to be paid to each and every one of them their heirs or assigns by my Executor out of the first cash payments of my Estate And for the purpose of carrying into effect in all its bearings agreeable to its true spirit this last will and testament of mine I appoint Isaac S Bolton my Executor to the same hereby revoking all former wills or parts of will heretofore made

Given under my hand and seal this 13th day of December 1841

Test Haywood Joyner Charles Boulton (Seal)
Saml Acock Francis K Dandridge
Robert Reynolds John P E Bolton W.H. Bolton

I Charles Bolton having heretofore made and published my last will and testament do make and declare this as a (P-385) codicil thereto

(P-385 cont.) First I do give and bequeath to Louisa Estill Jefferson Bolton Sindarilla Bolton and Lucretia Elliot one negro boy Smart aged about 16 years to be disposed of in the same way as Nan and her child was to have been in my will of the 13 of December 1841

Secondly I also give and bequeath unto Louisa Estill Jeff Bolton Sindarilla Bolton and Lucretia ~~Elliott~~ Two mules 1 Gray Colt and one sorrel horse to be distributed among the said parties Equally

Lastly it is my desire that this codicil be attached to and constitute a part of my will to all intents and purposes

Given under my hand and seal this 11 day of May 1843

Test Charles Boulton (Seal)
Geo G Holloway
Harmon Harral

State of Tennessee)
March Term 1847
Shelby County Court)

A paper writing purporting to be the last will and testament of Charles Bolton deceased was produced in open Court and thereupon came into Court Samuel Acock Francis K Dandridge and Robert Reynolds subscribing witnesses to said will after being duly sworn depose and say that the said testator acknowledged the same in their presence to be his last will and testament and that he was of sound mind and disposing memory at the time of acknowledging the same and said paper writing having a codicil attached to it purporting to be a codicil of said will and George (P-386) G Holloway one of the subscribing witnesses to said codicil also appearing in open Court and after being duly sworn deposeth and saith that the said testator acknowledged the same in his presence to be his codicil to his last will and testament and that he was of sound mind and disposing memory at the time of acknowledging the same and the said George G Holloway after being duly sworn further stated that Harmon Harral the other subscribing witness to said codicil subscribed his name as witness to said codicil in his presence and that he has since departed this life said will and codicil are considered by the Court to be fully proven which are ordered to be recorded Recorded March 16 1847

John W Fuller Clerk

(P-387) R H PATILLOS WILL

I Robert H Patillo, being of weak body but of sound and disposing mind do make this my last Will and Testament, hereby revoking all others heretofore by me made

First I give and bequeath the house and lot now occupied by me as a residence to my five unmarried sisters to Wit Mary A Martha C Hattiet J Maria L and Paulina C and in case of the death of either of ~~them~~ of my said sisters the said house and lot with the improvements shall go to the survivors or survivor of them

(P-387 cont.) Second I give and bequeath my acre and a half lot on North side of Union Street now occupied by Dr R H Patillo to Dr R H Patillo provided he pays some seven or eight hundred dollars being part of the purchase money of said lot and improvements and should the said Doct R H Patillo fail to make said payment then and in that case the said ~~lot~~ mentioned lot and improvements shall go to my sisters aforesaid upon the same condition as my first mentioned property with this proviso however, that the said Doct R H Patillo shall continue to occupy said last mentioned house and lot under the control and at the option of my said sisters It is my will and desire that my slave Eliza and her increase shall be sold and the proceeds applied in the purchase of another women which together with all my slaves I give and bequeath to my said sisters and the survivors or survivor to them during their natural lives and in the event of death of all my said sisters then in that case all my said slaves are to be emancipated

I give and bequeath all my household and kitchen furniture to my said five sisters

(P-388) I give ~~all my debts~~ and bequeath all the debts due me choses in action and the balances of my personal property to my sisters aforesaid and to the survivors or survivors of them

And I hereby ~~appoint~~ constitute and appoint Augustus Pierce Executor of this my last will and Testament and it is my will and desire that my said Executor shall not be required to give security for the performace of his executorship

Witnesses L Pope Jr.
A Hopston
John A Wilson

R H Patillo (Seal)

State of Tennessee)
May Term A D 1847
Shelby County Court)

A paper writing purporting to be the lastWill and Testament ~~was produced~~ of R H Patillo was produced in open court and thereupon came into court L Pope Jr & A Hopston subscribing witnesses thereto who being first duly sworn depose and say that the said Testator acknowledged the same in their presence to be his last will and Testament on the 8th of April 1847 and that he was of sound mind and disposing memory at the time of acknowledging the same

Ordered that said will be recorded Recorded May 6th 1847

John W Fuller Clk

SHELBY COUNTY

WILL RECORD 1-C
PROBATE COURT OF SHELBY COUNTY
JAN. 1830 to MAY 1847

INDEX

Note: Page numbers in this index refer to those of the original volume from which this copy was made. These numbers are carried in the body of the manuscript within parentheses.

I

J

Y

Milton Keynes UK
Ingram Content Group UK Ltd.
UKHW050017191124
451263UK00010B/111

9 780788 487774